Lexicon of Limerence

Obscure language for romantic infatuation

By
Etoile Marley

Lexicon of Limerence

Author: Etoile Marley

Copyright © 2025 Etoile Marley

The author asserts the moral right to be identified as the author of this work.

The right of Etoile Marley to be identified as author of this work has been asserted by the author in accordance with section 77 and 78 of the Copyright, Designs and Patents Act 1988.

First Published in 2025

ISBN 978-1-83538-739-9 (Paperback)
      978-1-83538-740-5 (Hardback)
      978-1-83538-741-2 (E-Book)

Cover Design: Irene-Anne Jordanides

Book Layout by:
    White Magic Studios
    www.whitemagicstudios.co.uk

Published by:
    Maple Publishers
    Fairbourne Drive, Atterbury,
    Milton Keynes,
    MK10 9RG, UK
    www.maplepublishers.com

A CIP catalogue record for this title is available from the British Library.

All rights reserved. No part of this book may be reproduced or translated in any form or by any means, electronic or mechanical, including photocopying, recording or by any information storage and retrieval system without written permission from the author.

While every effort has been made to ensure accuracy of the information in this book, the author does not assume any responsibility for errors or omissions, accuracy, usefulness, timeliness of content or for completeness. The author disclaims all responsibility and liability to any person for any action or inaction based upon information in this book.'

Lexicon (n.) a set of meaningful vocabulary
in a language, of a person or branch of knowledge.

Limerence (n.) romantic infatuation.

CONTENTS

i. Love symbols from around the globe 5
ii. Viking Rune symbols for love 6
iii. EXORDIUM 7
iv. A-Z 11-232
v. Portmanteaus 233
vi. Etoile's Neologisms 244
vii. Index 249
viii. References 293

Love symbols from around the globe

 Celtic love knot features two interlocking hearts in a continuous loop. Symbolising two people joined together in everlasting love.

 The Bowen knot, true lovers knot. Symbolising everlasting love, from Celtic traditions, consisting of a rope in a continuous looping pattern.

 Triskeles, celtic love knot. An ancient Celtic symbol representing the interconnectedness of body, mind and spirit.

 Osram ne Nsoramma, moon and star represents love, harmony and fidelity especially in marriage. An Adinkra symbol from the Akan people of Ghana, West Africa.

 Odo Nyera Fie Kwan: "love never loses it's way home". Also an Adinkra symbol from the Akan people.

 The Anahata, heart Chakra symbolises our ability to love, emotional balance and communicate with compassion. From Hindu, Shakta and Buddhist traditions of Asia and India.

 The eternal lovers, two birds connected by their beaks; from the Taino people in northeastern South America (Cuba, Jamaica, Puerto Rico).

 The Claddagh, depicted by two hands holding a heart and often with a crown atop. An Irish symbol representing love, friendship and loyalty.

 The Ankh, Egyptian symbol of life also recognised as the joining of man and woman.

Viking Rune symbols for love

 Ingwaz: fertility, true love, harmony

 Eternal love

 Woman for man

 Man for woman

 Woman for woman

 Man for man

EXORDIUM

Why did I write this book? Why words?

I learnt three languages (English, French and Spanish) growing up attending a French school in Canberra, the capital of Australia. Being trilingual developed my curiosity around how we use language and how it shapes feelings, events and descriptions differently according to the culture it belongs to.

When I was 20, I moved away to the north coast of Australia to dance full time whilst I simultaneously began writing my first songs. I soon realised that what fascinated me the most about songwriting was the craft of lyricism. I endeavoured to use more original language so as to not sound cliché in my lyrics, particularly when tackling the most coveted topics in songwriting such as love and heartbreak. This led me down a path of research and exploration, collecting dictionaries (this was pre smart phones or owning a laptop!) and books on obscure words.

Discovering new words was like uncovering lost treasure to me. I couldn't quite believe how many words were never used in everyday language, and it blew my mind that there were lexicons of words to describe the most specific actions or feelings. I wondered why they fell out of use? Why have we let our vernacular become so narrow in breadth? On the other hand, every day new words are being invented in the forms of portmanteaus and neologisms, repeatedly reshaping our language, much to my amusement and interest.

I first started sharing obscure words on my social media channels several years ago, simply because I was excited by my findings and I thought that others might find them interesting and entertaining too. I was blissfully unaware of anyone else doing so before I discovered the wonderful Susie Dent and other social media personalities with their own styles of defining obscure words on social media.

As my following started to grow, I realised that my little community particularly enjoyed my specific selections of words, helping me to grasp a sense of what my audience related to the most. Unsurprisingly, the greatest discussions were instigated whenever I shared words that revolved around love in all its forms!

Over the last three years I have curated an agglomeration of obscure, obsolete, rare and foreign words relating to love, lust, heartbreak, betrayal, infatuation, fetish, and jealousy to hopefully inspire an expansion of vocabulary in those that are curious about the ways in which we can describe these sentiments. Though some words may seem far-reaching by definition and relationship to the topic, (with a few not so obscure additions) applied in context to limerence gives reason to their placement in this collection.

My greatest wish is to be useful, so I hope the Lexicon of Limerence brings you joy, a laugh and perhaps a little inspiration to bring back long lost obscure words into modern day conversations. A suggestion for how you may like to use the book is to read the word first and then try to guess its meaning. This makes for a great dinner party game!

Profoundly without equivocation,

Love and Lust,
Etoile Marley

Lexicon of Limerence

"Be careful how you speak to yourself and others, words have power and can cast spells, that's why it's called spelling."
— Unknown

Legend

n. Noun

v. Verb

adj. Adjective

adv. Adverb

p. Phrase or saying

e. Etymological roots and other linguistic relationships. Languages in their ancient forms (Ancient Greek, Classical Latin, Old English, Old or Middle French etc.) are implied where I have simply written the country of origin to save on space. Sometimes I include the French, Spanish and Italian equivalents to demonstrate the similarities.

Neologism: A new word suggestion that has been in circulation for a relatively short time.

Pronunciation: I have made these suggestions in parenthesis according to what I hope may be the most tangible pronunciation for different native speakers.

A.

ABDITIVE (AB-deh-tiv)
adj. Capable of concealing. Disguised, secret, hidden.
"*His abditive love for her slowly turned to heartbreak as he witnessed her marrying another.*"
e. *Abditīvus, abdere, abditus* (Latin) hidden from sight.

ABSQUATULATE (ab-SKWAT-yoo-late)
v. To suddenly make a hasty departure. To flee, decamp, or send away. To leave quickly; to 'split'.
"*After drunken shenanigans, many find themselves absquatulating from whence they have found themselves upon waking.*"
e. A humorous adaptation and fusion of abscond, capitulate, perambulate.

ACCISMUS (ak-SIZ-muhs)
n. When your temperature is secretly rising on the inside, your pulse quickening, upon accidentally encountering a certain person, whilst you act as though your excitement is on the level of folding laundry. An ostensible masquerade of disinterest in the thing or person one desires most. Pretending not to be infatuated with your crush when somebody asks if you are into them. Feigning indifference.
"*His actions towards her were accismus even though he had been fawning over her photos for months.*"
e. *Akkismos* ἀκκισμός (Hellenistic Greek) - coyness, affectation.

ACOLAUST (AK-uh-laast)
n. A person unrestrained by chastity, one who indulges in sensual and sexual pleasures. Disregarding social norms of morality by having promiscuous habits.
adj. *Acolastic/Akolastic.* That lives without restraint, licentious, immoral, salacious.

"Some might consider that a phase of being an acolaust is essential to one's own sexual development and maturation."

e. A variation of akolast. *Acolastus* (Latin) is the title of a famous 16th century play based on religious stories of the prodigal son. *Akolastos* ἀκόλαστος (Greek) - undisciplined, libertine, licentious.

ADAMITICAL (ad-uh-MIT-uh-kuhl)

adj. To be without any garments or adornments whatsoever, displaying one's nakedness. In the buff, raw or scud as it were. Naked as the day you were born. Starkerz, nudey rudey, neked, disrobed, au naturel, without a stitch.

"After an afternoon of drinking and dancing on the beach, they stripped off until adamitical, and frolicked in the sea."

e. *Adamitic, Adamiticus* (Latin) - in reference to something that is characteristic of or resembling in nature to the biblical (naked) Adam.

ADAMATISM (ad-ah-mah-TIZ-um)

n. The practice of parading one's nakedness particularly to demonstrate a state of spiritual purity. To walk around naked. To be nudey-rudey, in the buff, starkers.

"Most would find it perverse to practice Adamatism anywhere but in the bedroom."

e. *Adamite* - a member of a religious group who imitated the biblical man Adam, by being in the nude.

ADAMSKOSTÜM (AD-ams-kos-toom)

n. The bare skin and form that mother nature blessed you with. To be in your Adamskostüm is to be in your 'birthday suit'. To be-eth butt naked-eth, in the nude, in the nuddy, in the buff.

"The fancy dress theme of the party was 'Adam & Eve', so some of the guests decided to go in their Adamskostüm."

e. German, *(lit)* translation 'Adam's costume', *(fig)* naked, birthday suit, as nature made one.

ADELPHOGAMY (a-del-FOG-ah-mee)

n. The practice of sharing a spouse between siblings such as two brothers sharing a wife or one man marrying three sisters. Also an incestuous marriage between a brother and sister.

"*Adelphogamy is generally considered morally wrong and outlawed in most societies but still practised in some indigenous tribes and religious cults.*"

e. *Adelfós* ἀδελφός (Greek) brother + *-gamy* - of marriage or a sense thereof.

ADOSCULATION (a-doss-kyoo-LAY-shun)

n. Mouth to mouth kissing. A literal or figurative impregnation without penetration. Something that leaves a long lasting impression as though impregnated. A verbal declaration of love.

"*Their adosculation on the couch at her party was quite the spectacle and left other guests wondering why they didn't just leave to get a room.*"

e. *Adosculari* (Latin) to keep on kissing. In biology, the fertilization of a plant via pollination, the mating of an animal via external contact with the genitals.

ADULATION (ad-yoo-LAY-shun)

n. Excessive, obsequious flattery or admiration expressed towards someone (particularly in public). Showering a person with compliments or praise to the point it is uncomfortable and awkward for themselves or those around. Praise that may be well intended but comes off a little insincere.

"*One who has an insecure ego will seek out forms of adulation.*"

e. *Adulation* (French) - servile flattery; *adūlātiōn* (Latin) - the act of fawning upon, obeisance.

ADRONITIS (ad-roh-NAHY-tis)

n. A feeling of exasperation felt after meeting a new and enchanting person with whom you wish to share deep secrets and conversation, only to be faced with the painstaking prospect of how long it takes to truly get to know a person.

"She felt an undeniable chemistry between the pair followed by a deep sense of adronitis."

e. From the *Dictionary of Obscure Sorrows* by John Koenig, a type of architecture from Ancient Roman times, an *andronitis* was a hallway connecting a sophisticated central atrium to the front of the house. A metaphor for the outer layers one has to peel back in order to get to the central being. Also *andrōn*, ἀνδρών (Greek) - man cave.

AESTHETE (ESS-theet)

n. A person who prides themself on having a superior appreciation, knowledge and admiration for that which is beautiful. Obsessively preoccupied with beauty.

"The aesthetes of social media channels make sweeping statements about what makes a woman or man aesthetically beautiful, stupidly disregarding that physical beauty is based on personal tastes not their opinions."

e. *Aisthitís* αἰσθητής (Greek) - person who perceives, a feeler. *Esthète* (French) - a person who impacts the culture (with their aesthetic) or a formal beauty.

AFFINE (ah-FINE)

n. A relation connected to you due to marriage. An in-law.

"They gathered with their siblings and affines to celebrate the birth of the newest grandchild."

e. *Affin* (French) relative by marriage, *affinis* (Latin) relatives, bordering, closely related, connected.

AGACERIE (ah-gass-ah-REE)

n. An act intended to tempt, attract and lure. A coquetish flirtation. A seductive allurement.

"All were in admiration of the burlesque performers' effortless agaceries and she slinked her way around the audience, teasing them with her curves."

e. *Agacer* (French) to irritate.

AGAMIST (AG-ah-mist)

n. One who is against the establishment of marriage; an unmarried person.

"Many are questioning the validity of marriage, proclaiming themselves agamists, free of outdated societal standards."

e. Ágamos ἄγαμος (Greek) unmarried.

AGAPE (AG-up-ee)

n. Unconditional love most commonly associated with spiritual or selfless love rather than erotic love. Volunteering one's time, money and efforts to help those less fortunate than oneself, the act of lovingly driving your child around to all their different training sessions regardless of how exhausting it is for you as a parent. Doing work for the benefit of others without seeking reward and adulation.

"In a world consumed with capitalism and egoistic pursuit, we need more acts of agape."

e. Agápi ἀγάπη (Greek) - love.

AGAPET (AG-ah-pette)

n. A man of pleasure who lusts and hunts after women. A philanderer; a 'whoremaster'; a player.

"His excessively promiscuous past finally caught up with him when he met the woman of his dreams, sadly his reputation preceded him and she was not at all interested in having an agapet as a partner."

e. Agapitós ἀγαπητός - man keeping a secret mistress, beloved; *agapiti* ἀγαπητή - secret mistress, darling (Greek).

AGENOCRATIA (ay-jen-oh-CRAY-shee-ah)

n. The opposition to using birth control.

"It wasn't because she wanted a baby that she had agenocratia but more the fact she didn't want to synthetically alter her hormones, so they used withdrawal method and condoms for prevention of pregnancy."

e. Its coinage is elusive as it is a new word suggestion. My suggestion of etymology would look something like prefix 'a' in English can indicate being *in* or *on* + *génnisi* Γέννηση - birth, *kratia* κρατία - state (Greek), 'in birth state' rather than a non-birth state would indicate not wanting to use birth control.

AGGRATE (ag-RATE)
v. To please somebody or express thanks towards them. To delight.
"To aggrate his wife also gave him innumerous pleasure, a sense of satisfaction at being her source of delight."
e. *Agratare* (Italian) to please, gratify.

AICHMOPHOBIA (AIK-muh-fo-bee-ah)
n. The fear of pointy or sharp things, being touched or prodded with a pointy object such as a penis perhaps? "Ay caramba!" Is the first thing that came to mind - Spanish interjection for surprise meaning "Oh geez!" a softer version of "Ay carejo" meaning "Oh fuck!".
"Eternal celibacy and sexual frustration was the result of her infliction of aichmophobia."
e. *Aichmí* αιχμή (Greek) - peak, point, spearhead, *phobos* φοβοι - fear.

ALGOLAGNIA (al-goh-LAG-nee-uh)
n. The practice of experiencing pleasure or being turned on by inflicting or receiving physical pain (also known as sadomasochism), "active algolagnia" signifying Sadism and "passive algolagnia" signifying Masochism. Of a person, an algolagniac (a masochist or sadist).
"Many sexual fetishes exist where the inclination is towards algolagnia rather than fornication."
e. *Algolagnie* (German), *álgos* ἄλγος - pain, *lagneía* λαγνεία - lust (Greek).

ALLOSEXUAL (al-oh-SECK-shoo-uhl)
n. The regular experience of sexual desire towards others.
"It is little spoken about but many women peak in their allosexuality after hitting forty, contrary to a lot of their male counterparts who often begin to lose sexual drive at that age."

e. Coined by the asexual community to reduce the presumption that feeling sexual is 'normal' and not feeling sexual desire or attraction (asexuality) is 'abnormal'.

ALOPECOID (al-oh-PEE-koid)
adj. That resembles a true fox. Fox-like; vulpine. Foxy.
"They always sent Alevtina to the bar to order food and drinks as her alopecoid charms worked their magic every time to get them a discount."
e. Alópix ἀλώπηξ (Greek) fox, -oid - having the nature or form of.

AMARITUDE (ah-MA-ree-tewd)
n. Anguish that is felt when someone or something breaks your heart, leaving a bitter taste in your mouth and your mind, an acrimonious sense of resentment or distress.
"He was overcome with amaritude after she left him."
e. Amaritude/Amartume (French) - emotional pain, bitterness of taste, amāritūdō (Latin) bitterness of expression, taste or feelings.

AMATORCULIST (a-muh-TOR-kew-lest)
n. One who pretends their affections are genuine but is really only semi-invested in the tryst, a trifling and insignificant or unreliable lover.
"The question is whether one wants to take a risk and put in an effort to make a relationship work or if one is satisfied being an amatorculist that floats from one lover to another."
e. Amātorculus (Latin) little lover, related to amateur (French) originally - someone who loves, amour - love.

AMARULENT (uh-MAR-yoo-luhnt)
adj. To be consumed with bitter feelings. Of a spiteful or malicious intent.
"The jaded lover easily turns amarulent when there are no apologies or forgiveness."
e. Amarulent (French) bitter, amārulentus (Latin) of a sour disposition.

AMATORY (AM-ah-tor-ee)

adj. Of a nature or with intention to invoke romantic, sexual or loving feelings. That has an inclination towards love. Also at one point, something related to the pubic region.

n. A potion or drug with the capacity to excite desire. A love poem.

"*Amatory advances simply have no effect on someone who is not interested in reciprocating them towards the giver.*"

e. Amatorius (Latin) of lovers, that causes loving feelings.

AMBISEXTROUS (am-bee-SECK-struss)

adj. When one is of ambiguous sexual orientation, displaying both male and female characteristics or being romantically or sexually attracted to either sex. Androgenous, bisexual. Of an object, something that is suitable for either sex.

"*If we attach specific behavioural, physical and intellectual traits to one sex or the other, are we not then all inherently ambisextrous?*"

e. Ambō (Latin) meaning both or both sides, + sex.

AMBOSEXUAL (AMB-oh-SECK-shoo-ul)

adj. That includes both men and women. Comprises of female and masculine traits. Characteristic of sexual maturity.

"*Her choice of bed buddies was ambosexual, you never knew who would come out of her room in the morning.*"

e. Ambō - both, sexualis - being either male or female (Latin).

AMORIST (AM-uh-rist)

n. A person whose preoccupation is flirting and an incessant infatuation with desire, sex and love. A promiscuous lover.

adj. Relating to love and desire, a writer of sensual poems.

"*Social media makes known many a frustrated amorist that could perhaps benefit from channelling their sexual energies into more productive pursuits.*"

e. Amor (Latin) love. Also remodelled from *amour* (French) into *amourist*.

AMOURETTE (Ah-moo-ret)

n. When you encounter an exciting person and embark on a lusty and passionate tryst that is short in duration. A short lived love affair, a fling.

"The secretive amourettes of their youth, made for delicious storytelling."

e. *Amourette* (French) a minor love affair, (also another word for love-grass).

ANACAMPSEROTE (an-ah-CAMP-seh-roat)

n. A herbal concoction that is believed to have the power to reconcile lovers. A root or plant capable of reviving a lost love. Something that acts as a healer of broken feelings. A love potion.

"The mutual effort they were putting into reconnecting as a couple was working as a strong anacampserote encouraging love to bloom again in their household."

e. *Anacampsérote* (French), *anakámptein* ἀνακάμπτειν (Greek) to bend back, recovery. The botanical name *anacampseros* describes a small succulent plant native to South Africa, parts of Australia, Ethiopia and Latin America. Known for its resilience, an ability to thrive in tough conditions is perhaps how it became a symbol for healing broken love.

ANAGAPESIS (un-Ah-GUP-eh-siss)

n. No longer feeling any affection towards the one you once loved; falling out of love.

"Her anagapesis didn't happen all of a sudden but rather slowly over time as the connection between them whittled away."

e. The prefix *an* - without, *agápi* αγάπη (Greek) - love, -sis - in a state of the first element. (When I first saw this word I pronounced it an-ag-ah-PEE-siss - which makes you think of being in agony and pieces).

ANANKE (an-AN-kee)

n. An irresistible chemistry that drives one towards a particular person as if by fate is said to be the work of the Greek goddess of compulsion, inevitability and necessity *Ananke*. A destined encounter that impacts your life so greatly that you cannot help but contemplate whether it was all planned for you by some greater power.

"The circumstances by which they met were so uncanny, Ananke must have been at work."

e. In Ancient Greek mythology, Ananke is the Orphic personification and most powerful dictator of fate and circumstance. *Ananki* ανάγκη (Greek) - necessity/ need, *écen* (Old Irish) necessity, *ananke* (Maori) anyway.

ANDROMANIA (an-droh-MANE-ee-ah)

n. Overt sexual desire and behaviour of females towards males. A madness for men. Nymphomania.

"She found it amusing that every time she went out with this particular friend, she became a type of andromaniac, obsessed with catching a man for the night."

e. *Anír* ανήρ - man, *manía* μανία - excessive desire for (Greek).

ANEABIL (a-NAY-buhl)

n. One who has no spouse. An unmarried or single person.

"In the chaos of rearing children, housework and marital expectations it is tempting for the married person to long for the life of the anaebil."

e. Of an old Scots term *anelape* ánlépix - solitary, *ane* - one, a single person or thing.

ANHEDONIA (an-hee-DOH-nee-uh)

n. The inability to feel pleasure or take an interest in anything once deemed pleasurable. When no activity brings you joy.

"No longer aroused by physical touch, finding enjoyment in food, exercise or social engagements, she wondered whether she was suffering from a form of anhedonia."

e. In psychology it is a symptom of depressive disorders and mental health conditions. The prefix *an* - without, *idoní* ἡδονή (Greek) - pleasure.

ANILINGUS (an-ah-LIN-guss)

n. Oral stimulation or 'rimming' of the anus with the mouth or tongue to attain sexual pleasure for the recipient (and the conductor). Asslicking.

"She yelped in surprise when he began analingus on her, then became worried he may try to kiss her straight afterwards."

e. *Anilingus* (German); *ānus* - posterior opening of the alimentary canal, *lingere* (Latin) to lick.

ANORGASMIA (an-or-GAZ-mee-ah)

n. An inability to achieve orgasm despite being aroused by foreplay, or desiring intercourse and enjoying coitus.

"The man was well versed in cunnilingus and the foreplay a woman desires, which led to his partner overcoming her anorgasmia."

e. *An ἀν* (Greek) - without/not, *orgasmus* (Latin) - excitement or violent action in a body part.

ANTIPELARGY (an-tee-peh-LAR-jee)

n. Love and mutual care particularly from children towards their parents. Reciprocal tenderness and kindness.

"Their children were grateful for the wondrous childhood and incredible opportunities their parents provided them, displaying an antiperlargy that was authentic and appreciated by all the family."

e. *Antipelargie* (French), *antipelargosis* (Latin) reciprocal kindness, *antipelárgosis ἀντιπελάργωσις* (Greek) return of benefits.

ANUPTOPHOBIA (an-up-tuh-FOH-bee-yah)

n. An irrational fear that one will forever remain single and alone. An intense fear of being wedded to the wrong person.

"It's weird how some misguided men believe women to experience anuptophobia as much as they do when statistically the happiest women are single."

e. A neologism that gained traction on the internet around the late 2010s from *an* - without + *nuptial* - wedding/marriage, *phobia* - fear.

APODYOPSIS (A-poh-dye-op-siss)
n. The act of picturing someone naked, mentally removing their clothes.
"*She had to ask him to repeat his order because she was busy with apodyopsis when he first spoke.*"
e. Apodýo ἀποδύω (Greek) - take off, ópsis ὄψις - sight, see.

ATAVISM (AT-ah-viz-um)
n. To be closer in resemblance to one's grandparents or further distant relatives or ancestors.
"*A mysterious atavism must be the cause of his orange hair and tan skin because his immediate family of the last three generations were of Asian descent.*"
e. *Atavisme* (French), *atavus* (Latin) ancestor, great grandfather's grandfather.

ATTINGENT (a-TIN-jent)
adj. To be in physical contact with another. Touching.
v. To *attinge*. To touch or affect. To come into contact with.
n. An *attingent*. That which comes into contact with.
"*They were attingent all evening just waiting for a moment to slip away and enjoy each other in private.*"
e. *Attingĕrei* - to touch on, *tangĕre* - to touch (Latin).

ATTRAHENT (A-trah-hent)
adj. That draws one towards itself. That is attracting, that draws in.
"*His attrahent display of strength and chivalry was a major draw card for the romance deprived women of the countryside.*"
e. *Attrahĕre* (Latin) to draw towards.

AURICOMOUS (or-ICK-uh-muhss)
adj. In possession of golden or blonde hair.
"*They nicknamed her Rapunzel for her luscious and long auricomous locks.*"
e. *Aurum* - gold, *coma* - hair (Latin).

AUTARKEIA (or-TAR-kee-yah)

n. A philosophy where one finds contentment in not desiring another person, relationship or material possessions. A belief system that centres around not needing anyone or anything. From Aristotle who defined it as "freedom from all things", a state of contentment in which no aid or support is needed. An idea that one truly only needs themselves and their beliefs, moving away from material possession and desire or reliance on other people.

"Can anyone live truly in autarkeia in this modern world?"

e. *Aftárkeia* αὐτάρκεια (Greek) - self sufficiency.

B.

BAISEMAINS (bez-MAN)
n. A paying of respect or compliments. Literally a kiss or kisses placed upon the hands.
"Giving his baisemains was done with words these days as kissing a hand felt rather old fashioned and even creepy to some."
e. *Baise* - kiss, *mains* - hands (French).

BALLOTTEMENT (bah-LOT-ment)
n. An archaic method of diagnosing a pregnancy by tapping on the cervix or abdomen to observe if there is a reaction from the fetus. Checking if you're preggers.
"There was no need for a ballottement as she was wretching her guts up every morning and night, had an extremely sensitive sense of smell and hadn't had a period for several months, she just knew she was pregnant."
e. *Balloter* (French) to toss, to move.

BASIATION (bay-zee-AY-shun)
n. When two people engage in the locking of lips (and tongues). Kissing.
v. To basiate. To kiss.
"They both sported sore lips and had to catch their breath after an intense basiation that lasted several hours."
e. *Bāsiāre* - to kiss, *bāsium* (Latin) - kiss.

BASOREXIA (baz-oh-REX-ee-ah)
n. An overwhelming urge to kiss, such as when one sees a person who they are extremely attracted to or who is in possession of incredible lips.
"He was consumed with basorexia every time he laid eyes on her luscious lips."
e. *Bāsium* (Latin) - kiss, *orexis* -craving, *un baiser* (French) - a kiss.

BEATIFIED (bee-AT-if-eyed)

adj/v. To have been made extremely blessed or happy. Feeling blissful or heavenly. A woman who is as such is known as a *beata*, and a man a *beatus*.

"*It was a chance meeting, a rare connecting of souls that caused them to feel beatified in each other's company.*"

e. *Béatifier* (French), *beātificāre* (Latin) to make happy.

BEBLUBBERED (buh-BLAH-bird)

adj. When you have been crying so intensely that your eyes are puffy, you are blowing your nose and just generally look a mess. A little disfigured from crying profusely. A blubbering mess.

"*Her cruelty and selfishness rendered him beblubbered on a regular basis, it was high time to leave her.*"

e. Formed within English from *be* - all over + *blubber* - to sob noisily + *-ed* indicating past tense.

BEGUIN (BAIR-gwin)

n. A fanciful infatuation. When your heart beats quickly if a certain person is around and you realise you have feelings for them. An instant crush.

"*She had a beguin on the new recruit at work, it was hard to tell if his personality was engaging when his good looks were so intoxicating.*"

e. *Béguin* (French) - a crush. Coming from the name of a bonnet religious women wore in the 1200s, from the 1600s onwards the word was used in reverse based on the idea that devout women would suddenly be consumed by a passion of impure thoughts due to their abstinence.

BELLIBONNE (bel-EE-bone) and BONNIBEL (bon-EE-bel)

n. An archaic term for a beautiful and good woman, a fair maiden, a bonny lass, an attractive girl.

"*On the hunt for an innocent and beautiful young lady, he hoped that learning to dance would be a way to attract all the bellibonnes.*"

e. A formation from (French) *belle* - beautiful and *bonne* - good.

BENEDICT (BEN-uh-dikt)

n. A man known for being a perpetual bachelor who surprises everyone by getting married. A newly wed man.

"He made numerous claims of never getting 'tied down' to a woman when he was fancy free in his 20s, 30s and even 40s, but when he travelled abroad he came back a Benedict."

e. *Benedictus* (Latin) blessed. After the character Benedick in Shakespeare's *Much Ado About Nothing*, who arrogantly vows never to get married but transforms into a loving and committed partner to Beatrice.

BENTHIC (BEN-thick)

adj. That which exists at the deepest level. Pertaining to the depths of the ocean.

"It was a benthic love, a profound connection of twin flames, a miraculous joining of two wonderful souls."

e. Vénthos βένθος (Greek) depth of the sea. *Benthos* is the name given by German zoologist Ernst Haeckel to plants and wildlife that live in the deepest depths of the ocean.

BERSATRIX (BERSS-a-tricks)

n. One who rocks the cradle of an infant or cares for the children in lieu of the parents not being present. A babysitter.

"When I said to my children that the bersatrix would be looking after them, they looked at me frightened and asked if she would try to hurt them like she did with Harry Potter. I had to clarify that it wasn't Bellatrix from the books but an ancient name for a babysitter."

e. *Berseaux* (French) a cradle, *-trix* - implies a feminine.

BIDUOUS (BID-yoo-uss)

adj. That is only for the duration of two days.

"It was a biduous love affair, a sexy weekend away never to be spoken of again."

e. *Bīduum* (Latin) in a space of two days.

BILLYNOODLE (BILL-ee-NOO-dil)

n. A man whose self confidence is so inflated as to believe that all women are susceptible to falling madly in love with him due to his incredible attractiveness and charm. One who considers himself 'Gods' gift to women'.

"*It was hilarious to watch that billynoodle of a man work the room and get fully rejected by all the women present.*"

e. American slang from *Billy* - a generic name for a man + *noodle* - slang for head. A 'man-head' like a 'dickhead'.

BINATELY (by-NATE-lee)

adv. Things arranged in couples. Arranged in pairs.

"*It seemed she was the only single person at the party as everyone was arriving binately.*"

e. *Bīnātus* from *bīnī* (Latin) twin, double.

BLANDILOQUENT (blan-DIL-oh-kwent)

adj. That is smooth-talking; charming. Flattering chat. Also *blandiloquos* and *blandiloquious*.

n. *Blandiloquence*. A type of speaking that uses flattery and charm to attract, influence or entice.

"*She used her blandiloquent humour to win over the finest men and women at the party.*"

e. *Blandus* - bland, *loquens* - speech (Latin). Which seems contradictory from its meaning as charm is far from bland however, bland also implies smooth or soothing in quality which would apply to this sense as in 'smooth talking'.

BLISSOM (BLISS-uhm)

adj. Subject to having strong lustful desires. To be in heat (of a ewe).

"*She'd decorated the place with candles and fresh flowers, a delicious meal could be smelt from the kitchen and red and purple lights were increasing her blissom mood.*"

e. *Blœsma* (Old Norse) in heat.

BOVARISM (BOH-va-riz-em)

n. An exaggerated and glamorous, unreal or romantic notion of oneself. To imagine oneself other than we are, to fantasise about being someone else.

"The impact of social media channels and a culture of comparison depicts many to live lives of bovarism, a sense that one's life is more glamorous or enchanting than one really is."

e. *Bovarysme* (French) from the central character in Gustave Flaubert's novel *Madame Bovary* (1857), enchanted by her own romantic illusions and dissatisfaction with life.

BREEDBATE (BREED-bate)

n. One who is notoriously known for inciting trouble; someone who likes to start arguments or pick fights. A trouble-maker.

"Within a couple of months I realised that he was really a breedbate, starting arguments over every little insecurity he had, just such a headache and too immature for me."

e. Formed within English from *breed* - to produce offspring, to create more of + *bate* - strife, trouble.

BREVIPED (BREV-ee-ped)

adj. Being in possession of short legs or small feet. A 'shorty'.

"Being of short stature himself, many assumed that he was into breviped women but in fact he desired himself an Amazonian warrior goddess of a woman."

e. *Brevis* - short, *pedi* - relating to the foot (Latin).

BRIAREAN (bry-AIR-ee-an)

adj. With a capacity to do many things at once; to have numerous projects or engagements happening simultaneously. Literally 'many-armed'. Capable of multi-tasking.

"To maintain a polyamorous relationship seems like a headache to me, one must be of a Briarean character to juggle all those personalities, emotions and date nights!"

e. Eponym of Briareus, a Greek mythological giant that possessed 100 hundred arms and fought against the Titans with Zeus.

BROMOPNEA (broh-MOP-nee-ah)
n. A foul smelling odour emitting from the aural orifice. Bad breath; a stinky bazoo; a smelly gob.
"For her, it doesn't matter how sexy, cute or charismatic you are, if you have bromopnea that is a total deal breaker."
e. A new word suggestion from *vrómos* βρῶμος - smelly, stench + *pnia* πνηα - breath (Greek).

BUGAROCH (BYOO-gah-rok)
adj. That is handsome, striking, good looking, pretty, comely.
"I'm not sure if someone would understand that they are very attractive to me if I said to them that I find them bugaroch."
e. An old Irish term found in English lexicographer Francis Grose's Dictionary of the Vulgar Tongue (1811).

BUMBASTE (bum-BAYSST)
v. To spontaneously strike in succession on another's caboose. To beat the buttocks. To smack that arse.
"It is important to communicate an interest in bumbasting before charging forth and doing so, not everyone is into that kink."
e. Formed with English from *bum* - a person's buttocks, *baste* - to thrash, beat or hit.

BUSS (buss)
n. A particularly noisy and vigorous kiss or kissing.
v. To *buss*. To kiss.
"He longed for a buss from his crush and kept imagining a time when their lips would lock."
e. Of uncertain origin but suggested to be related to another similar term of the era for kissing 'to basse', also related to *bāsiāre* (Latin) to kiss.

C.

CAFUNÉ (KA-foo-nay)

n. The act of tenderly running your fingers through a loved one's hair. The intimate action of using one's fingers as a hairbrush to caress your lover's locks.

"*Lying on the couch together engrossed in a film, he was simultaneously and perhaps unconsciously engaged in the act of cafuné.*"

e. Brazilian Portuguese, said to be derived from the Yoruban people who were forcibly transported from West Africa during the transatlantic slave trade, and said to have played a significant role in shaping the country's Afro-Brazilian culture.

CAGAMOSIS (kag-ah-MOH-siss)

n. A marriage that is lacking in sufficient happiness. An unhappy betrothal or marriage.

"*Studies show that who you marry is one of the key definers of one's overall health and wellbeing and therefore cagamosis should not be something one forces themselves to withstand.*"

e. Of unknown origin or coinage, a new word suggestion with no clear etymological roots. It could be inspired by *kagathos* καγαθος - good + *gámos* γάμος - wedding (Greek) + -osis - denoting a condition, disease, infection or disorder, so could be thought of as "good wedding disorder" implying a state of not being able to achieve a good marriage.

CALEFACIENT (ka-luh-FAY-shunt)

adj. To render something warm, to induce heat. Also *calorifacient*.

n. An agent that induces warmth.

"*His suggestive eye contact was so calefacient she had to run to the bathroom and splash down to settle her nerves.*"

e. *Calefacĕre* (Latin) - to make warm.

CALESCENT (kuh-LESS-uhnt)
adj. Glowing with warmth, radiating or increasing with heat.
"Her calescent feelings for him were hard to hide from their work mates."
e. *Calēscēntem* (Latin) - growing warm.

CALIGYNEPHOBIA (cal-ee-guy-nah-FOH-bee-yah)
n. The intense fear of beautiful women.
"He was apt at making conversation and being funny online when it came to talking to beautiful women, but in real life he was possessed by a type of caligynephobia."
e. *Kállos* κάλλος - beauty + *gyní* γυνή - woman + *phobos* φόβος - fear (Greek).

CALLIPYGIAN (kal-uh-PIJ-ee-an)
adj. Being in possession of beautifully shaped buttocks that beg appreciation. Bearing a bubble butt. Having a nice arse. Possesses a beautiful bum. Also *callipygous*.
"In the modern era, one of the most desired physical attributes in a woman is to be callipygian, a refreshing contrast to the 1990s fad of being uber skinny and waif-like."
e. *Kallípygos* καλλίπυγος - that has beautiful buttocks from *kállos* κάλλος - beauty + *pygí* πυγή - bum (Greek). Used to describe an Ancient Roman statue of the goddess of love known as Aphrodite Kallipygos or Venus Callipyge.

CALLISTEIA (kal-iss-TEE-yah)
n. Part of a festival in Ancient Greek times when women would compete in a contest that focuses on physical attractiveness. A beauty pageant.
"The men hovered in the corner of the night club observing the women and ranking them as though they were in a type of callisteia."
e. *Kallisteía* χαλλιστεῖα (Greek) beauty. *Callisteias* were often conducted in honor of *Hera*, sister of Zeus, goddess of women, childbirth, and marriage.

CAMSTEARY (kam-STAIR-ee)

adj. Unreasonably determined to be perverse or wild despite what anyone else says. To be titillated by breaking rules, having a twisted mind or pushing boundaries. Unruly.

"Was it any surprise that he was a bit camsteary after growing up in a brothel?"

e. Of uncertain origin but said to be derived from *cam* (Welsh, Scottish) crooked, twisted, bent.

CASANOVA (kass-uh-NOH-vah)

n. An allusive and irresistibly charismatic man who is known for being skilled at seducing women (or men) and having numerous lovers. A man who displays the same traits as the famous historical personality.

"She was drawn to the musings of Casanovas for entertainment value but never victim to their advances or charms."

e. Eponym of Gianomo Casanova, an 18th century Italian adventurer and author from Venice renowned for being very successful with the ladies.

CATAGLOTTISM (kat-ah-GLOT-iz-em)

n. A thrusting out of the tongue during kissing. Smooching with the tongue. French kissing.

"They were too busy indulging in cataglottism to notice the other debauchery happening all around them."

e. *Cataglottisme* (French) a kissing with the tongue. *Kataglóttisma* καταγλώττισμα (Greek) a lubricious kiss, swallowing.

CATAMITE (KA-tah-might)

n. The junior male lover of an older man, a boy used as a sexual partner for a man.

"A cult where many youths were catamites raised questions around the consensual nature of their sexual exchanges."

e. *Catamītus* (Latin) boy kept as a sexual partner by a man, also the name of Jupiter's cup bearer Ganymede in Greek mythology.

CATHEXIS (kuh-THEK-sis)

n. Concentrated intense mental investment and focus onto one particular person, idea or an object, sometimes in a potentially unhealthy manner. A sentimental attachment to a photograph, a lover's item of clothing, a family heirloom or other object. (Other impassioned attachments to belief systems or groups are also considered forms of Cathexis).

adj. *Cathectic.* That has significant emotional or personal attachment.

v. *Cathect.* To attach emotions to.

"Enamoured with his new girlfriend, he developed a strong cathexis towards winning her affections."

e. *Káthexis* κάθεξις (Greek) holding, the act of retaining, intended as a translation of *besetzung* (German) occupation, in the psychoanalysis of libido.

CELATION (sel-AY-shun)

n. The concealment of gestation or parturition. Not disclosing a pregnancy or the birth of a child. Hiding the fact that one is 'up the duff' or had an illegitimate child.

"Due to unwanted press and attention during what should be a personal time, celation is common in the entertainment business."

e. *Celāre* (Latin) to conceal.

CHAETOPHOROUS (kee-TOFF-uh-ruhss)

adj. In need of a shave, bearing spiky hairs.

"After many weeks apart from his lady, he was looking rather chaetophorous and she requested he smoothen out before he got busy on her."

e. *Chaetophora* (Latin), *chaití* χαίτη - mane, *fóros* φόρος - tax (Greek). In zoology, used to describe a particular type of invertebrate that has bristly hairs.

CHAGRIN D'AMOUR (SHA-gran-DA-moor)

n. An aching of one's heart, lovesickness, heartache, a broken heart, a sorrowful love or painful love affair.

"She resigned herself to refraining from long distance dating because it only seemed to end in a chagrin d'amour."

e. *Chagrin* - grief or sorrow, *amour* - love (French).

CHARIVARI (SHA-ree-VA-ree)

n. A cacophonous and discordant mocking serenade performed (on pots and pans) for immoral or unpopular wedding ceremonies.

v. *To charivari.* To welcome or greet someone with a charivari.

"He got married so soon after his first wife died that it was tempting for fans of hers to perform a charivari at his 2nd wedding in protest."

e. *Charivari* (France). Used in France to mock unharmonious nuptials and unpopular people in general. From 1832-1937 it was an illustrated newspaper that contained political cartoons and caricatures.

CHEILOPROCLITIC (KEE-loh-proh-clit-ick)

adj. Having an erotic desire for a person's lips. Attracted to lips in particular. In awe of sexy smackers.

"Is not everyone a little cheiloproclitic? The power and allure of a lovely pair of smackers is pretty universal, no?"

e. *Cheílo* χείλο - lip, *proklínein* προκλίνειν - to incline, lean forward (Greek), could be thought of as 'leaning towards the lips'.

CHIRAPSIA (kuh-RAP-see-ah)

n. An action that involves a friction of the hands against the skin. A massage.

"The best way to get her in the mood was with chirapsia."

e. *Chirapsia* (Latin), *cheirapsia* χειραψία (Greek) friction, handshake from *cheir* χειρ - hand + *aptein* άπτεῖν - to touch.

CHONES (CHON-ess)

n. Mexican slang for knickers, panties, underwear.

"He cheekily texted her to return without her chones when she went to the bathroom whilst they were dining with his boss and business partners."

e. Derivative of *calzones* (Spanish) breeches.

CICISBEO (CHICH-iz-bay-oh)

n. A cavalier male companion or lover of a married woman. A woman's male gallant who has specific access to her. (Not necessarily a sexual relationship but often implied to be one).

"Out of respect for her husband, she refrained from having any close single male friends mostly because it is generally assumed that a married womans' male friend is some sort of cicisbeo."

e. Of uncertain origin, it is suggested that perhaps an onomatopeic word implying 'like a whisper' or perhaps related to '(pois)chiche beau' - meaning beautiful chick(pea) in French. In 18th and 19th century Italy, *cicisbeos* or *chevalier servants* were common amongst bourgeois women and attended public events alongside their mistresses.

CINGULOMANIA (sin-gyoo-loh-MAY-nee-yah)

n. An irresistible urge to hold someone in your arms, whether known to you or not. A strong need to embrace someone dear to your heart. An intense desire to hug.

"Spending weeks on end out in nature on a solo camping expedition, he experienced cingulomania at the first sight of another person on the mountain."

e. *Cingō* - belt, encompass, surround (Latin), *manía* μανία - mania (Greek) madness. Also thought to have first been used by Jacob Edward Schmidt (J.E. Schmidt) in his *Lecher's Lexicon*, published in 1967 and again in 1984.

CLOYING (KLOY-ing)

v. To be excessively affectionate, overly sentimental or complimentary towards a love interest, to a point of disgust. To demonstrate an overwhelming display of intimacy that goes beyond what is pleasurable and becomes unpleasant. To be nauseatingly sweet in an attempt to lure but instead transforming the flirtation or sexual experience into a bore.

"The excessive gestures and flattery felt cloying and insincere, becoming a major turn off."

e. Accloy - to become lame, *clouer* - to nail (French).

CLOAKATIVELY (KLOKE-ah-tiv-lee)

adv. In a manner that is superficial. Skin deep; outwardly; existing only on a surface-level.

"She loved deeply and honestly, not cloakatively."

e. Formed within English from *cloak* - a garment worn to conceal or cover + *-atively* - implying the nature of the first element.

COEUR D'ARTICHAUT (KERR-dar-tee-show)

n. Used to describe one who has a tendency to fall in love easily and frequently. To easily give one's heart over or to have a soft heart behind a wall of steel. Literally meaning an artichoke heart, coming from the idea that the many leaves of an artichoke are attached to the 'heart', representing the many lovers that a person has had or that have easily attached themselves to that person's heart. (In French, it refers more to someone who is kind-hearted in general rather than to do with romance).

"Witnessing their close friend with yet another new lover on their arm, they pondered whether it was a belief in cinematic romance or a reluctance to persist during times of unpleasantness that caused them to have a coeur d'artichaut."

e. Coeur - heart, *artichaut* - artichoke (French).

COHERENTIFIC (koh-HERE-en-tiff-ick)

adj. To cause to make as one or bring together. To render coherent or cohesive. To make it clear.

"He didn't want him to have any doubts about his intentions or love for him so a marriage proposal was a coherentific way of demonstrating his commitment."

e. Formed within English from *coherent* - when all parts are harmoniously working together to form a whole + -ific from *ficus* (Latin) making, doing.

COITOPHOBIA (koi-toe-FOH-bee-ah)

n. Extreme apprehension around engaging in a sexual act. Abnormal and persistent fear around engaging in sexual intercourse. Fear of having sex.

"Coitophobia can present itself as a failing during sexual intercourse, such as erectile dysfunction or an inability to orgasm."

e. *Coitus* (Latin) to come together, *phobos* φόβος (Greek) fear.

COITUS INTERRUPTUS (KOI-tuhss-in-tuh-RUP-tuhss)

n. The practice of a man intentionally withdrawing his penis from the vagina right before ejaculation in order to prevent any sperm from entering the vaginal tract and therefore avoiding pregnancy. The *withdrawal method*; 'pulling out'.

"Using coitus interruptus had worked well for them throughout their whole relationship, only falling pregnant when they had intentionally wanted to, a fact her husband attributed to his great sense of timing."

e. A direct borrowing from Latin *coitus* - sex from *coīre* to go together + *interruptus* - interruption.

COMSTOCKERY (COM-stock-uh-ree)

n. The censorship of presumed immoral or salacious artistic materials such as visual art or literature. Excessive opposition to lewd or vulgar expression. Prudishness.

"With today's culture of attention seeking and over-sharing, the saturation of the internet with pornography, social media thirst-trap accounts and desperate attempts for attention through sexual exploitation, one wonders if a bit of comstockery could be useful in some domains."

e. An eponym derived from *Anthony Comstock* (1844-1915), a member of the *New York Society Suppression of Vice*, an organization that was committed to the supervising of the 'morality of the public'.

CONCOMITANT (kuhn-KOM-ee-tuhnt)

adj. That are side by side. That goes together. Compatible. Unseparated.

n. A person that accompanies another. A buddy; a companion.

v. *Concomitate.* To go with, to accompany.

"They were concomitant in their approach to tackling life's challenges, raising their kids and fulfilling their own personal goals, a true team of a couple."

e. *Concomitāri* (Latin) to go with, to accompany, similar to 'committed'.

CONCUBITANT (con-KYOO-bit-unt)

n. A person who is obligated to marry another out of duty or 'morality', such as a woman expected to marry her deceased husband's brother right after his death.

adj. Of a marriageable age.

"In many cultures, marriage is not based on romantic love but rather on duty and obligation, rendering many widows and young girls concubitants, often forced into marriages they do not want to be a part of."

e. *Concubine* - a woman who cohabits with a man as his wife, *concubīnus* (Latin) together.

CONCUPISCENCE (kuhn-KYOO-puh-suhns)

n. A vehement and libidinous desire or sexual appetite. A passionate and lustful need for carnal activities.

adj. *Concupiscent.* A condition of sensual longing or tendency to 'sin'. In a state of feeling 'horny' or 'toey'.

"Rather than embracing sexual desire as part of the human condition, the condemnation of concupiscence led them only to be more likely to participate in reckless and detrimental behaviours."

e. *Concupĕre* (Latin), to be desiring or longing for.

CONFARREATION (con-FA-ree-ay-shun)

n. Most esteemed and dignified matrimonials. A wedding ceremony. Marriage.

"Sadly because of the incongruous nature of their characters, the confarreation was short-lived."

e. *Confarreāre* (Latin) to unite nuptials by the offering of bread before the high priests of the Roman state. *Farreate* - united in marriage through the ceremony of spelt bread in ancient Roman times, *farreum* or *panis farreus* - translates as spelt bread although the grain used was *emmer*.

CONFRICATION (con-free-KAY-shun)

n. An act of rubbing together.

v. *Confricate*. To rub together.

"Flirty banter, lustrous looks followed by dancing and confrication were the greatest source of foreplay."

e. *Confricāre* (Latin) to rub together. *Confricatrice* - a lesbian.

CONNUBIALIZE (ko-NYOO-bee-al-eyes)

v. To commit via a ceremony of vows. To wed, to marry; to 'get hitched'.

n. *Connubiality*. The practice or right to marry.

adj. *Connubial*. Having gotten married. Wedded; hitched. Pertaining to wedlock.

"After a two year engagement that followed 10 years of dating, it was time to connubialize in front of friends and family."

e. *Co(n)nūbium* - wedlock, marriage, *nūbĕre* - to wed (Latin).

COQUET/ETTE (koh-KETTE)

n. A young man or woman who flirts playfully or teasingly often characterised by bashful femininity, cheekiness, delicate and whimsical energy. One who has an audacious tendency to seduce and flirt without genuine affection. One given to flirtatiously trifling with others affections. A 'cock-tease' or a 'cunt-tease'.

v. To *coquette*. The action of seducing, to act like a coquet/ette.

adj. *Coquettish*. Of a flirtatious, girly, cheeky, or seductively demure nature.

"Teen years and early womanhood are often characterised by coquettish behaviours as a means to learn about female agency and power."

e. *Coquet/ette* (French) - one who dresses well and presents well, flirtatious, one who is innocently eager to please; who has a playful behaviour and appearance.

CORDATE (KOR-date)
adj. Showing keen mental discernment and good judgement where matters of the heart are concerned. Heartfelt; sensible, sagacious, wise, cordial.
"She had a cordate affection for his parents who had been so generous and helpful towards them."
e. *Cordātus* - intelligent, prudent, sensible, *cor* - heart (Latin).

CORDIFORM (KOR-dee-form)
adj. Resembling the shape of the universal heart symbol. Heart-shaped.
"Around Valentine's day, every shop is filled with an array of cordiform gifts and decorations."
e. *Cordiformis* (Latin), *cordiforme* (French).

CORDOLIUM (korr-DOH-lee-uhm)
n. The intense torment and despondency of heartbreak. An achingly heartfelt grief or sorrow that results in melancholy. Heartache.
"After their divorce, he was consumed with a deep cordolium that seemed to weigh down his heart."
e. *Cor* - heart, *dolor* - pain, grief (Latin).

CORPULENT (KORR-pyoo-lent)
adj. Overly fat, large, big of body.
"He had a fetish for women of a corpulent body type and so encouraged her to eat plenty at every meal."
e. *Corpulent* (French) too fat, too big, *corpulentus* (Latin) from *corpus* - body + *lentus* - tough, *lent* (French) slow.

CORUSCATE (KO-russ-kate)

v. To brilliantly dazzle one's environment. To intermittently give forth flashes of light so as to shimmer, shine or sparkle. To glitter or flash in a quivering way.

"Conversations would silence and heads turn whenever she entered a room, demonstrating her power to coruscate."

e. *Coruscāre* (Latin) sparkle, glitter, gleam, vibrate.

COUVADE (koo-VAHD)

n. Symptoms of pregnancy and its associated discomforts and pains experienced by the male whose partner is expecting. When the dad involuntarily suffers from labour or abdominal pains in sympathy for his pregnant spouse. "Sympathy pains".

"When men experience couvade it is an interesting phenomena, almost surreal or supernatural that the father can be so attuned to his pregnant partner as to physically share some of her pain and discomfort."

e. *Couvade* (French) from *couve* - to hatch or incubate, *faire de la couvade* - 'do a couvade' - an outdated ridiculous custom in some provinces of France, whereby when a man's partner had delivered, he would take to his bed and undergo certain restrictions and rituals, behaving as though he himself were pregnant or had given birth.

COXCOMB/ COCKSCOMB (KOX-kohm)

n. A conceited man that is ostentatiously preoccupied with his appearance and extravasating pompous mannerisms or language. A male who conducts himself in such a way to resemble a "cock", a rooster - prancing about, head held high and kicking up the dirt onto lesser creatures.

"He paroused around the gathering like a sententious coxcomb, overly self-righteous and impressed with his own attributes."

e. *Cockomb* - the crest of a domestic fowl/chicken, also known as types of flowers that resemble a chickens crest, and a jester's hat.

CREELING (KREE-ling)

v. An old Scottish marriage custom in which a newly married man (often on the 2nd day after the wedding) was made to traipse around the village with a large whicker basket full of stones on his back, and he was not permitted to stop or put the basket down until his bride ran out from the house and gave him a kiss.

"The bridal party set about creeling the bridegroom much to the amusement of the bride's family who was unaccustomed to the Scottish tradition."

e. *Creel* - a large whicker basket.

CREEMASTER (kree-MASS-tah)

n. The small muscle by which the gonads are surrounded and suspended. The muscle that holds the testicles.

"After a vigorous sexual workout he somehow pulled his creemaster, most likely due to the contraction experienced from orgasm."

e. *Kremastír* κρεμαστήρ (Greek) hanger, suspender.

CROKINOLE (CROCK-ee-nole)

n. A way of styling one's hair in a wavy or curly fashion using a curling wand to heat and wind the hair. A wavy hairstyle.

"Every time she went to meet him she had a crockinole so it was a surprise to him when she came out of the surf with dead straight hair."

e. *Croquignole* (French Canadian) - a small dry or crunchy biscuit from *croquer* - to crack or snap. Croquignole as a colloquial term for a wavy hairstyle came about in the 1930s, *croquignolet/ette* meaning cutesy or pleasing looking.

CUBATION (kyoo-BAY-shuhn)

n. The undertaking of reclining. When one lies down. To lounge, repose or sprawl.

"They were both in need of a cubation after spending the day adventuring in and outside of the bedroom."

e. *Cubāre* (Latin) to lay down; recline.

CUCKOLD (KUK-old)

n. A man who knowingly has a partner or wife who is sexually unfaithful and is therefore usually the object of derision. Occasionally a woman whose partner is sexually unfaithful. A man who is aroused by his spouse having sex with another man (cuckoldry). Also sounds like cock hold as though that woman has "a hold of his cock".

v. *To cuckold.* To cheat, trick or betray, to cause a man to become a cuckold (by the wife/spouse having sex with another man).

"A woman with a cuckold must question why he may not be bothered if she openly takes other lovers, n'est ce pas?"

e. *Cucuault* (French) a man whose wife has sex with another man.

CUCKQUEAN (KUH-qween)

n. A female cuckold, a woman whose husband or partner is sexually unfaithful.

v. To make a cuckquean of someone.

"You would never catch me as a cuckquean, I would never settle for sharing my husband around like some free buffet."

e. *Cuckold* (see above) + *quean* - a queen, a female.

CUCUMIFORM (qyoo-QYOO-mee-form)

adj. Whose shape resembles the long dark green vegetable known as a cucumber.

"She had assumed all male members were cucumiform until she chatted with her friends and discovered their experiences of an array of different shapes."

e. *Cucumis* (Latin) cucumber, *form* - having the form of.

CURIOSA (kyoo-ree-OH-ssaah)

n. Books. Literature or oddities usually of an erotic or pornographic nature. Risqué art/books.

"He was a fan of literary curiosa more than of porn films and would read aloud to his woman as a form of foreplay, much to her arousal."

e. *Cūriōsus* (Latin) an eagerness to learn, desirous of acquiring something.

CYESIS (sigh-YEE-siss)
n. A medical term for being with child. Pregnancy.
"*Her cyesis was incredibly uncomfortable in the first two trimesters, with a constant nauseous feeling as though she were hungover.*"
e. *Kýisis* κύησις (Greek) pregnancy.

CYESOLAGNIA (sigh-YEE-soh-lag-nee-ah)
n. A fetish whereby one experiences a sexual attraction to pregnant women. The hots for ladies with a bump.
"*I never realised that cyesolagnia was a thing until I was pregnant and would sometimes get hit on when I went out.*"
e. A neologism derived from *cyesis* κύησις - pregnancy + *lagnia* λαγνεία - lust (Greek).

CYMOTRICHOUS (sigh-MO-trick-uss)
adj. Being in possession of wavy locks. Wavy-haired. 'Babe with the waves'.
"*After swimming in the sea she became a cymotrichous siren, emerging from the water like a mermaid.*"
e. *Kýma* κῦμα - wave, *trich-* τριχ- hair (Greek).

CYNOSURE (SIN-eh-shoor)
n. Something or someone with a brilliance and beauty that draws you in, becoming a central focus of attraction, allure, admiration or interest. Something that serves for guidance or direction. Also attributed to the northern sky constellation *Ursa Minor*.
"*When his wife walked in the room, she was the cynosure of all eyes and his affections.*"
e. *Χυνόσουρα* (Greek), *cynosure* (French), *cynosūra* (Latin).

CYPRIAN (SIP-ree-en)

n. One who overly indulges in sensual pastimes. A sexually liberated, promiscuous woman. A term for a prostitute; one who is considered licentious or lewd.

"*A woman well versed in pleasure giving and her own arousal may be considered Cyprian by some and in touch with her sexuality by others.*"

e. *Cyprius* (Latin) of Cyprus. An eponym of the island of Cyprus, known in ancient times for its inhabitants worshipping the goddess of love and lust Aphrodite (Venus) and therefore those who lived there were considered extravagantly sexual.

CYRENAIC (sigh-reh-NAY-ick)

adj. That adheres to the philosophy in which the main aim in life is to experience pleasure. To hold a hedonistic belief that pleasure is the highest good. To believe sex is God.

"*A young teen often becomes Cryenaic initially upon discovering their sexual drive, one hopes that they will develop other passions by which they may channel their sexual energy as they mature.*"

e. *Kȳrinaïkós Kūρηναϊκός* (Greek), *Cȳrēnaicus* (Latin). From Greek philosopher *Aristippus*'s school of philosophy founded in the city of *Cyrene*.

CYTHEREAN (sith-uh-REE-uhn)

adj. Of a beautiful temptress who engages in sex work. One devoted to the goddess Aphrodite. A general word given to prostitutes in Ancient Greece due to its association to the goddess of love and beauty Venus/Aphrodite. Pertaining to the planet Venus.

"*Modern day Cythereans can depend on the lust of men to earn a living, just as has always been the case since ancient times.*"

e. *Cytherēa* (Latin), *Kythéreia Κυθέρεια* (Greek) - another name for Aphrodite or Venus, *Kýthira Κύθηρα* (Greek) - a Greek island that was a centre of worship of Aphrodite.

CYTHEROMANIA (sith-uh-row-MAY-nee-ah)

n. An immoderate appetite for coition. Excessive sexual desire in a woman. An all consuming desire for fornication, copulation, sexual intercourse, making love, nookie, rumpy-pumpy, banging, fucking, intercourse, coitus. Nymphomania.

"After years abstaining from sexual relationships, she was overcome with cytheromania when she moved overseas."

e. *Cytherēa* (Latin), *Κυθέρεια* (Greek) - another name for Aphrodite or Venus; *mania* - madness, particularly in an excited or aggressive manner.

D.

DAMOISEAU (DAM-wah-zoh)

n. The male equivalent of a damsel. A mister, a sir, young man, chap, lad. Originally a young man born into a family of nobility and privilege who had not become a knight yet.

"*All this misinformation about the sexes on social media is causing many a damoiseau and damsel to be in distress about how to be a man or a woman.*"

e. *Damoiseau* (French), *dominicellus* (Latin).

DANGLEATION (dan-guh-LAY-shun)

n. Dallying with girls in a flirtatious manner with no intention of seriously pursuing them.

"*She knew herself to be heterosexual but she still rather enjoyed indulging in dangleation in the company of gorgeous women.*"

e. From *dangle* - which referred to 'following a woman without asking question' (Dictionary of the vulgar tongue, 1811), also to swing freely, hang loosely, to keep hanging on; and *dangler* - one who pursues women without commitment or attachment (see below).

DANGLER (DAN-glah)

n. A man who persistently flirts with women and hovers about them with no intention of settling down. A womaniser. Also an appendage.

"*A herd of danglers fluttered around her but she had eyes only for the quiet calm of her husband who had no need to flirt about gaining the attention of numerous women.*"

e. From the verb to *dangle* - swing loosely to and fro + -er - to do with the first action.

DAPATICAL (duh-PAA-tee-kuhl)

adj. A thing or person that is magnificently sumptuous or costly. A delicious feast (for the eyes).

"Her dapatical outfit had everyone turning their heads at the party."

e. *Dapāticus* (Latin) sumptuous, *dap-em* - feast, *dapáni* δαπάνη (Greek) - expenditure, cost, expense.

DAPHNEAN (daff-NEE-uhn)

adj. Characterised by a type of virgin timidity and shyness. Pertaining to Daphne, a forest nymphe in Greek mythology known for rejecting all lovers and hence maintaining her virginity. She prayed to her father to escape Apollo's advances and he transformed her into a Laurel tree which then became a symbol of victory and achievement in Greece.

"Bashful and innocent, her Daphnean demeanor drew curiosity from the youngest men in the room."

e. *Dafnaíos* Δαφναῖος (Greek), *Daphnæus* (Latin) - Laurel tree.

DAPOCAGINOUS (dap-oh-CAJ-ee-nuss)

adj. Perceived as cold and lacking in courage or compassion. That is small of heart. Low of spirit; heartless; lacking in value.

"All the sweet talk in the world could not make up for their dapocaginous nature which was revealed through their snobbery each time they visited new places."

e. *Dapocaggine* (Italian) lack of intelligence or ability.

DASYPYGAL (dass-ee-PIE-guhl)

adj. Being in possession of very hirsute buttocks. A furry, woolly, fleecy, whiskered or shaggy bum. A hairy butt or rough-bottomed.

"She wasn't averse to his dasypygal characteristics, after all we are part of the primate family so she had seen a hairy butt before."

e. *Dasýs* δασύς - shaggy/hairy, *pȳgí* πῡγή - rump/ anus/ bottom (Greek).

DEALATION (dee-ay-LAY-shun)

n. To lose a sense of self or one's *joie de vivre* after getting together with someone. To lose one's wings after mating. The removal of physical or metaphorical wings.

"His friends were concerned for his wellbeing after a sort of dealation had taken him over since he got together with his new squeeze."

e. An entomological term that specifically refers to insects that lose their wings via biting or rubbing after mating; *de* - without, *aile* (French) and *ala* (Latin) wing.

DEALBATION (dee-al-BAY-shun)

n. The action of rendering something whiter. The art of whitening. To bleach.

"The rise of teeth dealbation in the modern day can be attributed to its association with youthfulness and good health and therefore overall attractiveness."

e. *Dealbātiōnem, dealbāre* (Latin) to whiten, whitewash.

DECATHECT (DEK-ah-thekt)

v. The action of detaching feelings from someone or something as a means of self preservation. To withdraw oneself emotionally in preparation for heartbreak or loss. To remove attachment to a person or idea.

"Decathecting from him happened long before they finally broke up, it was a coping mechanism to gradually release the pain of losing twenty years of marriage."

e. Used in psychoanalytic theory by Sigmund Freud, from *de* - from, of the senses, remove + *cathect* - to attach emotionally, *kathektikós* καθεκτικός (Greek) to be apt in holding.

DELIBATE (DEL-ee-bait)

v. To delicately taste. To savour a small amount. To consume a little taste of something, to sip or kiss the edge (of a cup).

"She watched her lips as they delibated the wine, feeling aroused at the thought of what else she may savour delicately."

e. Dēlībāre (Latin) to remove a small portion of, to taste.

DELIQUESCE (del-ee-KWESS)

v. To melt away slowly, to dissolve and permeate into the atmosphere like the smell of a delicious meal. To disappear gradually without notice. To vaporise like an exotic perfume. To dissipate one's energy.

"Like a phantom, her robes seemingly deliquesced as she walked towards her lover."

e. Dēliquēscere (Latin) to melt away, dissolve.

DELIRIFACIENT (duh-leer-ee-FAY-shunt)

adj. Momentarily making a person behave in a giddy or extremely happy manner. That has an effect of rendering the recipient temporarily delirious, emotionally excited, distracted, or in a euphoric state. An ability to render someone into an altered or disordered state of mind or consciousness. That causes one to be in a delirium.

"The power of chemistry and sexual attraction to render the majority of people delirifacient continues to be a fascinating area of study."

e. Chiefly a medical term formed within English from *delirium* - a hazy or confused state of mind + *facient* - causing an action or state.

DEMIMONDAINE (dem-ee-mon-dayne)

n. A woman considered disreputable, of dubious social standing and existing on the fringes of conventional or mainstream society, typically artists and courtesans. A woman who lives in rejection of conventional culture. A woman supported by a wealthy lover. A sugar baby or trophy wife.

adj. Of the quality of one who exists in the "demi-monde".

"Fearful of rejecting societal norms are those most often envious of living as demimondaines, free of imagined moral codes and suppressed expression."

e. From the French *"demi-monde"* - middle world or half world (*lit*). In the 19th century, a class of women that was considered to be lacking in morality; specifically courtesans supported by rich lovers.

DEOSCULATE (dee-OSS-kyoo-late)

v. The action of kissing with great warmth and affection. To kiss fondly, respectfully, with sweetness.

n. *Deosculation.* Enthusiastic kissing.

"Does deosculating have to be a precursor to more sexual activities? Cannot a kiss be enjoyed simply as a warm embrace of someone we are fond of."

e. *Deosculārī* to kiss with affection, *osculum* - kiss (Latin).

DESAMOR (DESS-ah-moor)

n. A lack of affection, coldness, indifference, lack of love. A sense of not giving a shit.

"With the passing of time, a distance grew between them as their relationship became filled with desamor."

e. A Spanish word that can be broken down into *des* - negating/ not/ without, *amor* - love, literally "not love".

DESIDERATUM (diss-id-eh-RAY-tum)

n. A thing for which a desire or longing is felt. A person or object that is wishfully needed or required. That which one desires most. Also known as a *desiderata*.

"It was evident in the way he watched her move around the crowded room that she was his greatest desideratum."

e. *Dēsīderātum* (Latin) thing desired.

DESIROUS (duh-ZIGH-russ)

adj. Displaying romantic or sexual desire for someone. Wishfully wanting or longing for. That elicits desire, is beautiful, lovely or seductive. That is to be wanted, hoped or wished for. Ready, eager and zealous to fight for something or someone. Characterised by a desire to impress or to please.

"She couldn't help that the melodious tone and husky quality of her voice was unintentionally desirous."

e. *Désireux* (French) wishful, eager; *dēsīderāre* (Latin) to desire.

DEUTEROGAMY (dyoo-tuh-ROG-ah-mee)

n. A second nuptial after the death or divorce of the first spouse. The 'second time around'. A repetition of espousal. A remarriage.

"On average, deuterogamy happens within four years of the ending of the previous marriage."

e. *Defterogamía* δευτερογαμία (Greek) a second marriage.

DICACIOUS (die-KAY-shuss)

adj. Attractively lively and cheeky in speech. Naughtily talkative. Good at pillow talk, sexting, erotic or dirty talk.

"Is having a dicacious handle on a language a sign of fluency or specificity of study?"

e. *Dicāci* (Latin) talking sharply.

DIFFAREATION (duh–FA-ree-ay-shun)

n. The necessary processes conducted to terminate a marriage. A ceremonial ending of one's partnership. The dissolution of matrimony. Divorce.

"Despite the countless couples therapy sessions, their relationship ended in diffarreation."

e. *Diffarreātiō* (Latin) ceremony of divorce. Amongst ancient Romans the reversal of the *confarreation* (marriage), a ceremony that was conducted and witnessed by the high priests of the religious state, marked by a special sort of sacrifice that gave way to the dissolution of the relationship.

DIFFIBULATE (dif-FIB-yoo-late)

v. To unfasten; unbutton, ungirdle, to open up.

"After hours of flirtatious talk and touch, she was quick to diffibulate his trousers once they got into her apartment."

e. *Diffibulāre* (Latin) to unbuckle.

DILECTION (deh-LEK-shun)

n. An unbound spiritual love or affection. Deciding upon what or who one's desire or affection is set. The act of choosing what or who we will love or set our sights upon.

"Marriage survives not by some sort of dilection but rather through emotional maturation, consistent good communication, loyalty and dedication to making it work."

e. A French word from Latin *dīlectiōnem* - Love of God and *dīligĕre* to esteem highly, to select one from others.

DIONYSIAN (DIE-oh-nee-see-uhn)

adj. Characterised by uninhibited, orgiastic, wild, spontaneous or irrational behaviour. Representing passion, chaos of emotions and instincts. Being a "wild child."

"His notoriety for hosting Dionysian parties was well established amongst the rich and famous."

e. An eponym from *Dionysus*, god of wine, dance, pleasure and fertility (Greek mythology).

DIRIMENT (DEER-ee-ment)

adj. That renders something null and void. That which never existed; invalidated. In particular with reference to marriages that have *diriment impediments*.

"Consummation is not a legal requirement for rendering a marriage valid; however in many religious sects a lack thereof may be considered diriment."

e. *Dirimĕre* (Latin) to separate, frustrate.

DISBOSOM (diss-BOUZ-uhm)

v. To unburden oneself from a secret. To confess, to divulge a hidden sentiment. To reveal, to un-bosom. To remove an emotional weight that one has carried around. To "get off your chest."

"She couldn't help but to finally disbosom her feelings for him after months of flirtatious chatter and romantic dates."

e. Formed within English *dis* - to put out, dislodge, expel + *bosom* - a woman's chest.

DISCONSOLATE (diss-KON-soh-luht)

adj/n. Unable to be consoled. Characterised by despondency, unhappiness or heartbreak. Inconsolable, gloomy, depressed, tearful. People as a group who are inconsolable.

v. To render disheartened or dispirited.

"To be disconsolate after becoming a widower is the purest evidence of a true love."

e. *Disconsolatus* (Latin) comfortless.

DODRANTAL (doh-DRAN-tul)

adj. Nine inches in length. Three quarters of a foot.

"Lets be honest, a dodrantal penis is surely too much for most women."

e. *Dōdrāntālis, dōdrāns* (Latin) nine twelfths or three quarters of a measure.

DOLORIFICAL (DOL-uh-ri-fik)

adj. That causes much heartfelt sorrow and grief. Painful.

"Her actions of infidelity were dolorifical but paled in comparison to the treasonous years of lying and manipulation."

e. *Dolōrificus, dolōr-em* (Latin) pain; *douleur* (French); *dolor* (Spanish); *dolore* (Italian).

DOLOROUS (DOL-uh-russ)

adj. Affected by physical pain. Giving rise to distress or grief. Hurting, sorrowful, painful or sad.

"Though the separation was amicable, the mental anguish of having failed at marriage and keeping her family together was dolorous."

e. Douloureux (French), dolōrōsus (Latin) - full of sorrow, painful.

DONJUANIST (don-HWAH-nist)

n. One who is excessively focused on seducing women. One who treats women as though they are interchangeable, without importance to them. A man who carelessly uses women as sexual conquests. One who behaves like the character *Don Juan*. A womaniser.

"The irony of donjuanists believing themselves to be masters of seduction without realising that women who fall prey to their methods are only easily won."

e. Eponym of the legendary character Don Juan, known for his womanising ways, created by Spanish playwright Tirso de Molina.

DRACHENFUTTER (DRA-ken-foo-tah)

n. A gift used to appease someone who may be holding you in contempt. A present for one who is mad at you such as your spouse, mate, or in-law. A token of gratitude to smooth things over. A peace offering because you're in the "bad books."

"Don't forget to bring a drachenfutter because your spouse is well pissed-off with you!"

e. From German *drache* - dragon, *futter* - food; literally 'dragon food' as in to feed the dragon who is mad.

DRYGULCH (DRY-gulch)

v. To suddenly betray; to change allegiance. To have an abrupt change of heart. To join the 'other side'; to break trust. In some contexts, specifically to murder by pushing off a cliff.

"It wasn't simply the fact that he drygulched her, it was who he chose for his affair and the reasoning he gave as an attempt to justify his actions."

e. Originating in the American west, a *dry gulch* refers to a deep valley that is typically dry with a small river bed that is subject to flash flooding, implying an unpredictable change. It is thought that outlaws typically ambushed and killed in these areas and therefore 'drygulching' became synonymous with betraying.

DUENDE (dyoo-EN-day)

n. A captivating charm and charisma that embodies a person when they are passionate about what they are doing. A heightened emotionally authentic state. A type of magical aura; a magnifying presence.

"Their dancing radiated duende, an intense allure that was felt by all who gazed upon them at the wedding."

e. From Hispanic, Portuguese and Filipino folklore *duende* represents a magical creature or spirit, translating to pixie, leprechaun, elf or goblin. Derived from the saying 'dueño de casa' meaning 'master of the house'. Typically associated with the charisma of flamenco dancers that enables them to captivate an audience.

DYSPAREUNIA (diss-pah-ROO-nee-ah)

n. Sexual intercourse that is painfully unpleasant or abnormally difficult. Genital pain that occurs during sex. Uncomfortable sex.

"Experiencing regular dyspareunia with someone may be a sign that your body is telling you that that person isn't good for you."

e. From *dys* δυσ - 'difficult' + *pareunos* πάρευνος - lying with, bedfellow (Greek), παρά *pará* - beside + εὐνή *eunē* - bed.

DYSTOCIA (diss-TOE-see-yah)

n. Experiencing great difficulty in bringing forth a child. A complicated or difficult labour.

"Statistically dystocia is said to affect only 1% of births but when I speak with all the mums I have encountered, almost none have experienced easy births without any complications."

e. *Dystokía* δυστοκία from *dýskolos* δύσκολος - difficult, and *toketós* τοκετός - childbirth (Greek).

E.

EBULLITION (EB-yoo-li-shun)
n. An emotional outburst full of feeling. A strong burst of passion.
"Her ebullitions of jealousy were due to the fact that he paid her little attention when he went away for work and she questioned his interest in her."
e. Ebullicion, bouillir - to boil (French), ēbullīre (Latin).

ECBOLIC (ek-BOL-ick)
adj. That has the effect of expelling a foetus or placenta from a woman's womb. That assists in the birthing of a child or abortion.
n. An ecbolic. A drug or concoction that has this effect.
"During her labour she was vomiting frequently which actually had an ecbolic effect due to the contracting of her abdominal mussels whilst hurling."
e. Ekvolí ἐκβολή (Greek) ejection, expulsion.

ECCEDENTESIAST (ek-suh-den-TEA-zee-ust)
n. One who maintains a fake smile to disguise or hide the hurt within. One who gives the impression that everything is fine, while dying inside. Masking heartbreak whilst giving the impression of a cheerful outer appearance. Hiding one's true emotions by putting on a happy face. One who hides pain behind a smile.
"Despite the tragedy of losing her best friend and lover, she remained an eccedentesiast throughout the social gathering."
e. "Ecce dentes" (Latin) "behold the teeth". The term is thought to have been coined by Florence King, an American novelist and writer for The National Review. She used the term in her column "The Misanthrope's Corner" when discussing politicians and TV hosts, implying that no matter what, they maintain a plastered-on smile.

ECDYSIAST (ek-DIZ-ee-ast)

n. One who removes their clothing in a manner to seduce their audience. A strip-tease artiste. A stripping enthusiast. One who enjoys de-robing in front of people. A stripper.

"Addiction to being admired, desired and lusted over became a fixation of the ecdysiast."

e. *Ecdysis* ἔκδυσις - the action of stripping off, *enthousiastís* ἐνθουσιαστής - enthusiast (Greek).

ECDEMOLAGNIA (EK-dem-oh-lag-nee-ah)

n. A sense of lustfulness whilst away from home or on vacation. Feeling aroused after one changes up their surroundings. Being horny due to travelling.

"It was common for them to experience ecdemolagnia when travelling to tropical destinations, a type of sexual liberation overcame them when clad in bikinis and board shorts."

e. Of unknown origin and coinage but possibly derivative of *ecde* (Latin) from here, *dímos* δῆμος - municipality, town, *lagnía* λαγνία (Greek) lust.

ECSTASIATE (ek-STAY-zee-ate)

v. To render into an ecstatic state. To be consumed by ecstasy. Enraptured.

"Sensuous massage, a hot bath and a delicious meal were the perfect precursor to an evening of love-making, rendering them both extasiated."

e. From *s'extasier* (French) to demonstrate one's enthusiasm, admiration or rapture.

EFFLEURAGE (eh-FLOO-rahj)

v. To stroke the skin in a centrepetal fashion with the flat of the hand. To massage in a circular motion.

n. The act of massaging.

"She began to effleurage his limbs thinking it would lead to a sensuous state but instead he started giggling at every stroke."

e. *Effleurer* (French) to stroke with a lightness.

EGESTUOUS (eh-JESS-tyoo-uhss)

adj. That is in a state of neediness. Without wealth. Desperately poor.

"An egestuous state of mind could be remedied with a decision to take action on what is reducing a feeling of wealth in one's love and finances."

e. *Egestuōsus* - in an irregular fashion, *egestas* - poverty (Latin).

EIDETIC (eye-DET-ick)

adj. A vivid mental image or detailed memory recall. A strong vision that feels hallucinatory. In possession of a photographic memory.

n. A person who is capable of photographic memory.

"He made such an impression on her, the day they spent together an eidetic memory etched in her brain to recall at will."

e. *Eidetisch* (German), *eídos* εἶδος (Greek) form.

ELFLOCK (ELF-lok)

n. A lock of curled, tangled, twisted or matted hair. A dreadlock; a special lock of hair, a cute random curl.

"Captivated by her wild hair and elflock that stuck out behind her ear in a cute, zany fashion that endeared her even more to him."

e. Formed within English from *elf* - a mythological or folkloric creature + *lock* - a strand of a person's hair that bunches together. Attributed to the cheeky actions of elves, said to twist and play with people's hair.

ELUMBATED (ee-LUM-bate-uhd)

adj. A humoristic expression to describe being made 'weak in the loins', implying perhaps a little too much action in the pelvic area.

"The excitement from the night before, not having seen each other in a long time meant they were both a little elumbated and slow to rise in the morning."

e. *Ēlumbus* - having a hip that is dislocated, *lumbus* - loin (Latin).

ELYSIAN (uh-LIZ-ee-uhn)

adj. Describes something as belonging to, or coming from heaven. Belonging to the beautiful and glorious afterlife. Pertaining to the state or abode of the blessed after death. Resembling what one would expect to see or experience in heaven/the afterlife.

"*As in an Elysian dream, they floated down the river basking in the joy of having encountered each other at this moment in time.*"

e. *Elýsion pedíon* Ἠλύσιον πεδίον - Elysian Fields were a Greek conception of the afterlife that developed over time, also known as "The Fortunate Isles" or "Blessed Isles" and said to be located at the end of the Earth.

EMBERLUCOCK (em-BER-loo-cock)

v. To confuse one's head, to bewilder, to muddle.

"*Never let someone emberlucock your spirits or sense of self with their manipulations of your character and self esteem.*"

e. *Emburelucocquer* (French), a nonsensical word meaning to fill one's head with fantastical ideas.

EMBONPOINT (om-bon-PWANG)

n. A euphemistic way of saying someone is a little on the plump side, in a pleasing manner. Well nourished in appearance. Full of figure. Curvaceous.

"*Many millenial women feel that they aren't considered attractive unless they are super slim, having grown up with the idolised super skinny supermodels of the 90s, but in her experience most men didn't mind a woman embonpoint.*"

e. From the French phrase 'en bon point' meaning *in good condition*.

EMBRANGLE (em-BRANG-uhl)

v. To be entangled. To have the effect of perplexing a person; to confuse them.

"*Their young hearts were embrangled with thoughts of commitment and freedom, wanting to hold onto each other but also wanting to explore the world.*"

e. *Em* - to cause to be, into + *brangle* - to shake, to sway to and fro.

EMMENOLOGY (em-ee-NOL-uh-jee)
n. A written work of detailed knowledge on the female monthly cycle and menses. The study of menstruation and associated beliefs.

"It would be useful for both sexes to study emmenology in secondary school to better equip girls in a practical sense and to teach boys to develop perhaps a more compassionate understanding of what females endure each month."

e. *Émmina* ἔμμηνα (Greek) monthly bloods, menses.

EMPRESSEMENT (om-PRESS-mont)
n. An extravagant demonstration of emotion. An enthusiastic display of excitement towards something or someone. Affectionately eager.

"A new love affair is often filled with empressement, acts of devotion and undivided attention."

e. *Empressement* (French) excitement.

ENCRATY (EN-krah-tee)
n. An inner power giving one the ability to govern one's emotions, desires and actions so as to resist impulses or temptations. A state of self mastery where one holds faculty over one's own passions and instincts. Self-control.

"He demonstrated remarkable encraty when it came to the woman who was the object of his desires, he expressed his admiration for her without acting upon it, out of respect for her marriage."

e. *En'kráteia* ἐνκράτεια - restraint; *en* ἐν - in, *krátos* κράτος - (Greek).

ENGOUEMENT (on-gyoo-MON)
n. A state of admiration or awe. A condition of one who has an unreasonable fondness for something or someone. A lively fascination with a person or topic. An excessive enthusiasm or infatuation (often short-lived).

"The killer combo of personality, charisma, charm and good looks have the public in engouement."

e. *Engouement* literally an obstruction in the throat, from *engouer* (French) to choke, to be impassioned, momentarily enthusiastic.

ENGRAM (EN-gram)

n. A physical trace of a memory imprinted on the brain to demonstrate its existence. Something that has a lasting effect on one's memory. A mental imprint.

"It was hard to dispel the numerous engrams of their love and the subsequent heartbreak that had carved themselves into her brain."

e. *Engramm* (German), *en* ἐν -in + *grámma* γράμμα - letter (Greek).

ENIGMA (uh-NIG-mah)

n. A charismatic or talented person who is challenging to interpret. A mysterious person or thing that evades understanding at first. One who is difficult to decipher. A type of unsolvable puzzle or paradox.

"She embodied a sense of other-worldliness, a beautiful enigma for men to puzzle over."

e. *Aínigma* αἴνιγμα (Greek) to speak allusively or obscurely.

EONISM (EE-oh-niz-uhm)

n. The adaptation of dress sense and mannerisms that are typically associated with the opposite sex. To be a transvestite.

"Eonism has been around since the earliest civilisations, the act of non-gender conforming is not a new philosophy but perhaps seems novel to some because of the platforms social media provides."

e. An eponymous derivation from *Charles d'Éon*, a French diplomat and spy known for dressing in women's clothes.

EPHEMERA (eh-FEM-uh-rah)

n. Something which is short-lived or is a transitory experience. Something impermanent or temporary such as passionate fling or affair.

"Entranced by a type of romantic ephemera, Paris proved to be a sexually lucrative holiday destination."

e. *Efímeros* ἐφήμερος (Greek) lasting only for a day. An ephemeron is an insect that lives only for a day in its winged state.

EPICENE (EP-ee-seen)

adj. Suitable for any sex. Characteristic of both male and female style, behaviour or traits. Androgynous.

"Because they dressed in epicene garments, the couple shared clothes."

e. *Epicoenon* (Latin) a type of noun used in grammatical context for either male or female subjects.

EPIGAMIC (ep-ee-GAM-ick)

adj. Of colours or characteristics that specifically attract the opposite sex. Attractive.

"People always say that red has an epigamic effect on most men but she seemed to get the most attention when she wore a rich, velvety green."

e. *Epí* ἐπί - on + *gámos* γάμος - wedding, marriage, mating. In biology specifically the colours of animals that attract a mate.

EPITHYMETIC (ep-ee-thim-ET-ick)

adj. Of a burning desire or appetite. That is of the most soulful need.

"Many would argue that the most epithymetic aspect of human nature is to want to be understood, to connect deeply, to feel less alone."

e. *Epithymitikós* ἐπιθυμητικός - desirous, *epithymeín* ἐπιθυμεῖν - to wish, *thȳmós* θῡμός - appetite, soul (Greek).

EROTOGENIC (eh-rot-oh-JEN-ick)

adj. That induces sexual desire or gratification. That produces arousal. Also *erogenic*.

"An erotogenic effect was closely linked to a feeling of connection and understanding, a sense of safety with a man."

e. *Érotos* ἔρωτος - love, *genís* γενής - kind (Greek).

EROTOLOGY (eh-ro-TOL-oh-jee)
n. The study or science of how sex works. Descriptions and directions of sexual intercourse and love making in literature.

"*Their interest in erotology, revealed by numerous books on tantra and lovemaking on their bookshelves, led one to wonder if they would be good in bed.*"

e. Érotos ἔρωτος - love, logía λογία - words (Greek).

EROTOMANIA (eh-rot-oh-MANE-ee-ah)
n. A delusional belief that oneself is the object of a person's desires. A type of madness derived from loving passionately. Abnormal or excessive sexual needs or sexual drive.

"*So strong was his attraction to his neighbour, he was consumed with erotomania despite her not making any advances towards him.*"

e. Érotos ἔρωτος - love, manía μανία - obsessiveness (Greek).

EROTOPATHY (eh-rot-oh-PATH-ee)
n. A pathological sexual inclination. An abnormal sexual drive.

"*It is normal to experience a surge in sexual desires at the peak of one's hormonal growth and physical prowess, but to keep this sexual drive in check is important to avoid becoming overcome with erotopathy whereby sexual desires continuously consume one's thoughts.*"

e. Érotos ἔρωτος - love, páthos πάθος - passion (Greek).

EROTOPHOBIA (eh-rot-oh-FOE-bee-ah)
n. An extreme aversion or fear towards sexual love or activity.

"*Many who have experienced sexual violence and repeated betrayal are quite often inclined to develop a type of erotophobia, a total dislike of anything related to sexual activity.*"

e. Érotos ἔρωτος - love, phobos φόβος - fear (Greek).

ERUBESCENT (eh-roo-BESS-uhnt)
adj. Developing a redness in the cheeks. Growing red; reddening; blushing.

"He told himself he was cool, he would not be overwhelmed by his own attraction to her but the second he noticed her as she walked into the venue, he became noticeably erubescent."
e. Ērūbēscĕre (Latin) to blush.

ERYTHROPHOBIA (eh-RITH-roh-foh-bee-ah)
n. A fear of one's cheeks burning red with desire upon encountering or thinking about someone of interest. A morbid fear of blushing. A hypersensitivity to crimson shades. An aversion to the colour red.
"She developed erythrophobia after experiencing severe and uncontrollable blushing when faced with a boss she despised, concerned that it would be mistaken for admiration."
e. Erythos ερυθος -red, phobos φόβος - fear (Greek).

EUCRASY (YOU-krah-see)
n. The perfect combination of elements that creates a healthy, attractive and functional whole. A state of physical wellbeing.
"The perfect symmetry of a eucrasy that includes good communication, patience, emotional maturity, consideration, passion and sex appeal in a relationship is the main goal."
e. Efkrāsía εὐκρᾱσία (Greek) temperateness, of a good temperature.

EUDAEMONY (you-DEE-mon-ee)
n. Experiencing happiness, well-being and prosperity.
adj. Eudaemonic. That is instrumental in causing happiness.
"She felt a blissful harmony in her marriage, with her children and work colleagues, a type of eudaemony."
e. Evdaimonikós ευδαιμονικός (Greek) blissful, happiness.

EXOGAMY (ex-SOG-ah-mee)
n. The binding practice of marrying outside one's clan, social group, ethnicity, nationality, culture. A duty to outbreeding.
adj. Exogamous. Of a tendency towards breeding or coupling outside of one's culture and nationality.

"Exogamous bonds create genetic diversity and have the capacity to forge better interrelationships and understanding between cultures."

e. Éxo ἔξω - out, *gámos* γάμος - marriage (Greek).

EXOSCULATE (ex-OSS-kyoo-late)

v. The action of kissing in a frenzied manner. Passionate kissing.

"After months apart, they were consumed with exosculating at every given moment before they had to part once more."

e. Exosculārī, osculārī to kiss (Latin).

F.

FACETIAE (fah-SEE-shee-ee)

n. An indirect expression, a euphemism for pornographic, witty and humorous literature. Books of an inappropriately lewd nature.

"Little did anyone know at the school, but when this particular mum said she was an author, she didn't specify that it was of facetiae."

e. *Facētiae* (Latin) cleverness, wittiness, pleasantry (think *facetious* - making light of serious issues).

FAINÉANT (FEN-ay-on)

n. One who wishes to do nothing, who does not want to work at love or a job or personal growth. An idler. A royal lazy-ass.

adj. Characterised by laziness, that is indolent or does nothing.

"Her fainéante efforts at keeping the marriage alive led to the demise of their relationship."

e. *Fainéant* (m), *fainéante* (f) (French). In reference to the "do-nothing" Merovigian kings of the Frankish dynasty (5th-8th century) who were largely figureheads in name only. Initially known for conquests and expansion, their royal power declined due to internal conflicts and lack of leadership.

FAMICIDE (FAM-uh-side)

n. When a person intentionally destroys another's reputation; the slandering of the good name of another. The destruction of your honor or self-esteem. Publicly 'cutting someone down'.

"He became a ruthless master of famicide after discovering her betrayals, and one could empathise with his actions as she had conducted herself in such a grotesque entitled manner."

e. *Fāma* - fame, *-cīda* - killer, slayer (Latin).

FANTASTICATE (fan- TASS-tee-kate)

v. To fantasize about a desired event or happening. To fancify; to render more fantastical.

"Is fantasticating over one's object of desire a form of manifestation or pointless obsession?"

e. Formed within English from *fantastic* - that exists in one's imagination + *-ate* to make into the first element.

FANTOD (FAN-tod)

n. Occupying a condition of irritability. A feeling of uneasy restlessness. An emotional fit.

"The constant mixed messaging, a lack of communicating intentions and feelings, led her to experience a severe case of the fantods."

e. The origin of *fantod* is a mystery with some suggesting it is related to *fantigue* - a state of excited tension that could possibly be a combination of *fantastic* and *fatigue*, a term coined by English novelist Charles Dickens.

FATUOUS (FAT-yoo-uss)

adj. Of actions or chatter that is of a besotted nature. Displaying a lack of thought; foolish.

"His fatuous attempts at impressing were not so subtly disclosing his attraction to her."

e. *Fatuus* (Latin) silly, foolish.

FEATOUS (FEET-uss)

adj. Shapely and well made. Handsome, elegant, comely.

"Her featous attributes were all the more alluring because of her insanely witty sense of humour."

e. *Factīcius* (Latin) practical, *feat* (Old English) suitable, graceful, suitable.

FECUNDATE (FECK-uhn-date)

v. A biological term referring to the introduction of the male element to make the female fruitful or pregnant. To impregnate, to render fertile, to fertilise.

n. Fecundation - an impregnation.

"Statistics reveal that the most prominent fecundating must happen during the Christmas and new year festivities, seeing as September is globally the month with the most daily births."

e. Fēcundus (Latin) fruitful.

FELICIFIC (fee-luh-SI-fik)

adj. That produces a feeling of joy. That elicits happiness. That makes one happy. Also *felicificative*.

"His felicific efforts at dinner paid off because she agreed to see him again after spending the evening laughing and playing games."

e. Fēlīcificus (Latin) *fēlix* -happy, *ficus* -making.

FESCENNINE (FESS-uh-neen)

adj. Of a quality that is obscene or vulgar. Satirical, licentious and at times abusive verse.

"No need for fescennine verse to get one in the mood, but some tasteful erotic talk is a playful way to begin foreplay."

e. Derivative of ancient Italian poetry which consisted of rude and playful joking known as *Fescennia*. Also an ancient city from central Italy.

FIDUCIARY (fuh-DYOO-shah-ree)

n. One who is entrusted with private information or responsibilities. A trustee. A document or declaration, evidence that proves one's credentials and validity.

adj. Held in confidence. That depends on trustworthiness.

"The most difficult part about their separation was the great loss of losing her fiduciary, a person with whom she felt safe keeping her innermost thoughts and feelings for the longest time."

e. *Fīdūciārius* (Latin) most trustworthy. Related *fiduciaire* (French) trustee.

FLANEUR (flah-NER)

n. One "about town", one who wanders around aimlessly but for pleasure. One who is an aloof observer of society.

"Pens and pencils in hand, the urban flaneurs congregate to flirt amongst themselves steeped in the ambiance of dimly lit café lounges."

e. *Flâneur* (French) is one who likes wandering around, to promenade. From the verb flâner meaning to walk around with no particular aim but for pleasure.

FLATCOCK (FLAT-cock)

v. The act of two females rubbing their private parts up against each other for arousal. Lesbian sex.

n. An old slang term for a woman.

"Though she found women to be the sexiest, most beautifully alluring creatures on earth, she was not prepared to flatcock with one of them."

e. Appears in lexicographer Francis Grose's *Dictionary of the Vulgar Tongue* (1788).

FLESHLING (FLESH-ling)

n. One who is preoccupied with matters of the flesh. An enthusiast of sensual pursuits.

"After dropping MDMA, they became a pool of fleshlings, a bunch of bodies writhing up against one another."

e. Composed within English from *flesh* - the muscular or meaty parts of a body + *-ling* - a person concerned with the first element.

FORELSKET (FOH-rel-sket)

n. The state of experiencing a euphoric elation typically associated with falling in love. Mesmerised by a blissful, loving ecstasy.

"Walking through central park after their dinner date, he stopped to hold her chin in his palm, consumed by forelsket as he bent down to kiss her."

e. A Norwegian term that broadly means *in love*.

FRANGIBLE (FRAN-juh-bull)
adj. That is of a condition that is easily breakable. Fragile.
n. *Frangibility*. The quality of being easy to be broken. Fragility.
"Don't put me through your indecisive games for my frangible heart can take no more!"
e. *Frangible* (French) breakable, *frangĕre* (Latin) to break.

FRICATRICE (FRICK-uh-triss)
n. A woman who engages in dry humping with another woman. A lesbian. Also *fricatrix* and *confricatrix*.
"The erotic behaviour of fricatrices was a major turn on for many a man until their egos slightly faltered at the realisation that the women climaxed more intensely without their help."
e. *Fricāre* (Latin) to rub + -ice/-ix - indicating a female counterpart.

FROTTAGE (frot-AH-sheh)
n. Rubbing up against someone for sexual arousal. A desire to rub one's clothed body up against another (often non consenting person).
"In the heat of the summer on the Paris metro, she experienced her first unwanted frottage on the packed train, unable to move away."
e. *Frottage* - a rubbing or friction, from the verb *frotter* (French) to rub.

FROTTEURISM (FROT-er-iz-uhm)
n. The perversion of obtaining orgasm or sexual gratification by touching and rubbing up against a stranger in a public place without their consent. A *frotteur* being a person who does this.
"The attempted frotteurisms on female patrons was getting so numerous that they decided to make a female-only section of the night club where women could drink and dance in peace."
e. *Frottage* - a rubbing or friction, from the verb *frotter* (French) to rub.

FUGACIOUS (fyoo-GAY-shuss)

adj. Having a tendency to disappear, to run away or fall away too soon. Something that is evanescent, temporary, fleeting or of short duration.

"He was worried that he had a fugacious bride on his hands due to her tardiness to their nuptials."

e. *Fugĕre* (Latin) to flee.

FULGENT (FOL-junt)

adj. Of a radiance that is attractive. Impressively bright and shining. Dazzling.

"Her enthusiasm for various artistic passions and hobbies had a fulgent effect on his perception of her."

e. *Fulgēns* (Latin) brilliant, gleaming.

FULSOME (FULL-sum)

adj. Nauseatingly affectionate or complimentary. Excessive in admiration. Overdone, offensive, obnoxious; voluptuous, plump; in copious amounts.

"Let not one's attraction to another have a deterrent effect by being overly fulsome."

e. Formed within English from *full* - to its limit + *some* - of the quality of the first element.

FUSTILUGS (FUSS-tee-lugz)

n. A corpulent, beastly person with gross habits. A slovenly, slutty type. A fat dirty bastard/dirty whore.

"The crudest and most hateful comments on peoples profiles most often come from the greatest fustilugs of society."

e. Formed within English from *fusty* - having a bad smell + *lug* - implying something heavy.

G.

GALLIONIC (GAL-ee-o-nick)
adj. Marked by an uncaring attitude; indifferent in nature; dismissive or irresponsible.

"Nothing hurts greater than a gallionic response to a confession of romantic feelings."

e. An eponym of ancient Roman senator Gallio, specifically known for dismissing accusations against Paul the Apostle.

GALLOMANIAC (gal-oh-MANE-ee-ak)
n. A person with a crazed infatuation for French people and all things French.

"A self professed gallomaniac, she moved to Paris in search of love, lust, language and lengthy lunches."

e. *Gallo* (Latin) relating to all things from the ancient Gaul (modern day French territory) + *mania* - obsessive desires.

GAMIDOLATRY (GAM-ee-doh-lat-ree)
n. The worship of marriage.

"Previous generations engaged in a certain degree of gamidolatry, particularly those religiously inclined would idealise the notion of marriage, but today quite the opposite seems to be evident."

e. Of unknown origin, perhaps derivative of the ancient meaning of *gamic* - pertaining to marriage + *-olatry* - excessive worship.

GAMINESQUE (gam-ee-NESK)
adj. That is reminiscent of a child in appearance or behaviour. Innocently childlike; childishly playful; girlish/boyish.

"The gaminesque qualities of a damsel in distress type woman appealed to some, but for him it was the warrior femme fatale types he lusted for."

e. *Gamin/gamine* (French) boy/girl + *-esque* - of a quality of the first element.

GAMOGENESIS (GAM-oh-jen-eh-siss)

n. A biological term for procreation; when sexual reproduction occurs.

"It's wild to think about the different possibilities of gamogenesis when the division and combining of gametes to make custom made children is becoming more advanced."

e. *Gamo* γαμο - relating to sex and marriage, + *génesis* γένεσις - creation (Greek).

GAMOMANIA (gam-oh-MANE-ee-ah)

n. To have an outrageous obsession with marriage that often results in one making absurd or outrageous marriage proposals.

"None of these women were afflicted with gamomania as society would have everyone believe, but rather with ambitions of personal and professional development which inevitably raised the standard of men they would be willing to accept as partners."

e. *Gamo* γαμο - relating to sex and marriage + *mania* μανία - obsession with (Greek).

GAMOMORPHISM (gam-oh-MOR-fiz-um)

n. The stage at which a being attains sexual maturity.

"It feels a bit like a glitch in female development when girls are attaining gamomorphism as young as 8 years old, whilst still looking like children rather than young women, the human body should adapt to this not being possible until well after 16."

e. *Gamo* γαμο - relating to sex and marriage + *morphism* - having the condition of the first element, from *morfí* μορφή - form (Greek).

GAMOPHOBIA (gam-oh-FOE-bee-ah)

n. An intense feeling of adversity towards matrimony, nuptials, engagements and everything wedding related. The fear of marriage.

"With the record rates of divorce it's a wonder not more people have a bit more gamophobia."

e. *Gamo* γαμο - relating to sex and marriage + *fovía* φοβία - fear of (Greek).

GARÇONNIÈRE (gar-son-nee-AIR)

n. Quarters where single men conjugate. A flat, room, place for dudes. A bachelor pad.

"The men went away for a snowboarding 'boys weekend' but had plenty of female visitors to their garçonnière."

e. *Garçonnière* (French) from *garçon* - boy.

GELASIN (JEL-ah-sin)

n. A cute little dimple that appears in the cheek when one smiles.

"Most people agree that there is something charming about the sweet gelasin that appears in the throws of a happy giggle."

e. *Gelasínos* γελασῖνος - dimple, *gelán* γελᾶν - to laugh (Greek).

GELASTIC (jel-AST-ick)

adj. That provokes laughter through being silly. Capable of being risible. Pertaining to laughter.

"It is pretty common knowledge that women enjoy a man who has gelastic capabilities, but I would argue that most men enjoy this quality in women too."

e. *Gelastikós* γελαστικός (Greek) risible.

GENOPHOBIA (jen-oh-FOH-bee-ah)

n. Intense anxiety around having sexual intercourse. Extreme aversion to a coital act. Fear of sexual intimacy.

"Those who experience genophobia often withdraw from intimate or romantic relationships of any kind because they induce severe panic attacks and feelings of inadequacy or shame."

e. *Génos* γένος - offspring, sex, gender + *phobos* φόβος - fear (Greek).

GILLIVER (JIL-ee-vah)

n. A woman who is sexually promiscuous or has a great sexual appetite. A harlot; a jezebel.

"Many a woman is a gilliver at heart but maintains a mystique around her sexual endeavours, it is not something to be shouted from the rooftops but rather to elegantly and privately go about her sexcapades."

e. Eighteenth century slang from *gilliflower*, a type of wallflower or other plant that is spicy like a clove.

GLABROUS (GLAY-bruss)

adj. To have smooth skin, free from any hairs. Hair-free.

"The fetishising of women with almost completely glabrous bodies has made hair removal a very lucrative occupation."

e. *Glaber* (Latin) bald, smooth, without hair.

GLOZING (GLOW-zing)

adj. That which is coaxing, flattering in order to attain something. Persuasive; deceitful.

"His glozing tongue won him favour with many a young lady, but women ignored him and his transparent attempts at luring women to bed."

e. Formed within English from the verb *gloze* - to veil with compliments + *-ing* - actioning the first element.

GLUTITION (gloo-TISH-un)

n. The action of gulping something down. A swallow. Also *deglutition*.

"The question is whether one is comfortable with glutition or not really, many would say that it depends on the man and the taste."

e. *Glūtīre* (Latin) to swallow.

GNATHONIC (NAY-thon-ick)

adj. Attempting to attain favour in a cringey or overtly complimentary manner. Acting obsequiously to gain advantage, like a parasite. A sycophant.

v. *Gnathonize.* To flatter.

"Her gnathonic attempts at wooing worked on the lesser of the two men, the one who lavished adulation, who needed his ego to be constantly stroked."

e. *Gnathōnicus* (Latin) from a person who resembles the parasite character Gnatho of Terence, in 2nd century playwright Terence's comedy *Eunuchus (The Eunuch)*, which features a complex plot around rape and reconciliation.

GODEMICHE (goad-mee-SHAY)

n. An object in the shape of an erect penis. A penis looking thingamabob. A dildo.

"I don't really get the appeal of godemiches, vibrators are far more effective!"

e. *Godemiché* (French) and *gamache*- a type of leather material used to protect clothing from mud, *gaude michi* (Latin) delight me!

GOLIARDY (GOL-ee-yard-ee)

n. The practice of debaucherous and lustful behaviour. Riotous conduct. Later known as *goliardery*.

adj. *Goliardic*.

"To indulge in goliardy in your teens and twenties is pretty standard for many, though perhaps those who miss this evolutionary step may be found practicing goliardy well into their forties and fifties."

e. From *goliard* (French), a term given to wandering students and scholars throughout Western Europe predominantly between the 12th to 13th centuries, known for reciting poetry that praised drinking and debauchery. *Goliards* also came to be known as 'educated jesters' for their creative satirical use of Latin, living on the margins of the church and society, performing in taverns and public spaces.

GOLUPTIOUS (goh-LUP-shuss)

adj. That is delightful, sumptuous or luscious.

"Her goluptious figure was the talk of many when she visited in a skin-tight red frock."

e. An arbitrary formation derivative of voluptuous.

GORMLESS (GORM-less)

adj. Lacking ability to discern well; unintelligent, dull, stupid.

"Does not an emotionally mature man also seek an intelligent and capable partner to tackle the world with rather than a gormless subservient?"

e. *Gawmless* from *gaum* (Norse) wit, tact, attention, sense. Antonym *gaum-like* - having an intelligent look.

GRABBLE (GRAB-ul)

v. To forage with the hands in search of something. To grope. To feel one's way.

"She awoke to him grabbling her body, lustfully searching for a breast or bum cheek, which he later claimed to have no recollection of doing whilst sleeping."

e. *Grabbelen* (Dutch) grabbing.

GRACILITY (grah-SIL-uh-tee)

n. The state of being thin, lean. Having a simple elegance. Gracefully slender.

adj. *Gracile*. Graceful.

"He had the gracility of a ballerina, weaving from table to table, catching the eyes of both men and women in the cabaret bar."

e. *Gracilitās* (Latin) simple elegance, slenderness.

GRAPHOLAGNIA (graff-oh-LAG-nee-ah)

n. An intense liking for looking at obscene or sexually explicit images.

"Is grapholagnia better hidden today and perhaps more widespread due to the internet, versus the days of playboy and other sexually explicit physical magazines?"

e. *Grafikós* γραφικός - graphic, picture, *lagnía* λαγνία - lust (Greek).

GRAUSTARK (GR'OW'-stark)

n. An imagined place of idealistic romance and adventure. An intensely romantic piece of writing or writing that includes such a place. A fantasy.

adj. Graustarkian. Characterised by romance, melodrama and implausible situations, also the name of the fictional language.

"Should we not live our lives as though in Graustark, romanticising each mundane daily activity to experience joy and excitement as the main character of our own life?"

e. Eponym of *Graustark*, an imaginary country invented by American novelist George B. McCutcheon in his romance novel of the same title.

GRAVIDA (GRA-vee-dah)

n. A woman who is pregnant. A female who sports a baby bump. A medical term used in conjunction with a number that indicates how many confirmed pregnancies a woman has had.

"After a five course meal late in the evening, people stood to offer their seats on the train home thinking she was a gravida."

e. *Gravidus* (Latin) pregnant, laden. *Gravid* - full, teaming, heavy with young, pregnant.

GRISETTE (griz-ETTE)

n. Originally a young working class French woman; later becoming slang for a pretty, flirtatious and independent woman and those who also frequented prostitution on the side.

"The man was licentious in his Parisian activities and countless grisette adventures and expenditures."

e. *Grisette* (French) from *gris* - grey, indicating the inferior clothing fabric of the lower working class + *ette* - implying a female or a smaller version.

GUMFIATE (GUM-fee-ate)

v. To cause to enlargen, swell, puff up.

"Simply brushing her hand lightly against the side of his thigh seemed to encourage a certain part of his body to gumfiate."

e. *Gonfiare* (Italian), *gonfler* (French), to blow up, inflate, *conflāre* (Latin) to blow, fuse.

GYMNOPHOBIA (jim-no-FOH-bee-ah)

n. A prejudice against the naked form. An intense fear of nudity, being seen naked or seeing others in the buff.

"No sign of gymnophobia at Haulover Beach or Newborough Warren, or indeed a woman in the throws of labour."

e. *Gumnos* γυμνός - naked, *phobos* φόβος - fear (Greek).

GYMNOSOPHY (jim-NOSS-uh-fee)

n. The practice of deep contemplation performed while naked and abstaining from all indulgences.

"It is understandable that gymnosophy derives from India as the weather is mostly stinking hot everywhere, trying to sustain any sort of naked practice in the UK would be a death defying feat."

e. From *gymnosophists* - "naked philosophers", a name given to these types of Indian philosophers by travelling Greeks, from *gymnós* γυμνός - naked + *sofós* σοφός - wise.

GYNAECOMANIA (guy-neh-koh-MAY-nee-yah)

n. An irrational enthusiasm and sexual obsession towards women.

"One must be in control of their fixation on bedding women after becoming sexually mature, lest it not lead to gynaecomania."

e. *Gyneko* γυνεκο - woman, *manía* μανία - mania (Greek).

GYNAECOMAZIA (guy-neh-koh-MAZE-ee-yah)

n. The abnormal development of the mammary glands, the growing of breast tissue in men. Man boobs. Also *gynaecomastia*.

"A fear of developing gynaecomazia was his motivation for hitting the gym each morning, the only breasts he wanted in his life were his wife's."

e. *Gyneko* γυνεκο - woman, *mastós* μαστός - breast, *maziá* μαζιά - together (Greek).

GYNANDROID (guy-NAN-droid)

n. Primarily of a woman who is neither distinguishable as specifically female or male. One who combines elements of femininity and masculinity. Whereas *androgynoid/androgynous* applies more specifically to a male of such characteristics.

adj. *Gynandrous*. Resembling or being of both sexes; androgynous; hemaphroditic.

"Her gynandroid physique drew the attention of both men and women, of all sexual orientations."

e. *Gyneko* γυνεκο - woman, *andros* ανδρος - man, having male organs (Greek).

GYNIOLATRY (guy-nee-OL-a-tree)

n. Deep adoration, respect and devotion of women.

"Gyniolatry is sometimes described as 'excessive' devotion to women, can it ever really be excessive? Modern cultures have demonised chivalry and romance as though treating women with devotion is something to be considered cheesy and distasteful."

e. *Gyní* γυνή (Greek) woman + -olatry - worship of, from *idolatrie* (French) idolising.

GYNOPHOBIA (guy-no-FOH-bee-ah)

n. A debilitating fear of approaching women, or of being humiliated by them. Fear of females.

"Most often stemming from trauma or abuse by a woman, gynophobia, the fear of being humiliated by a woman is also the basis of misogyny - the hatred of women."

e. *Gunē* γυνή - woman, *phobos* φόβος - fear (Greek). Earliest known use is in 1886 by physician Oliver Wendell Holmes Sr.

GYNOTIKOLOBOMASSOPHILE (GUY-no-tik-oh-low-boh-MASS-oh-file)

n. One who finds immense pleasure in tenderly nibbling on the earlobe of a woman. One who enjoys sensually kissing a woman behind her earlobe on the neck. An ear or neck biter.

"One who is aroused by kissing on the ears and neck would be best paired with a gynotikolobomassophile."

e. *Gynos* γυνος - female, *ōtikós* ὠτικός - of the ear, *lobos* λοβός - earlobe, *masáomai* μασάομαι - to chew, *fílos* φίλος - friend, (Greek). Said to have been coined by American novelist and poet Alexander Theroux.

H.

HABILABLE (HAB-ee-lah-bull)
adj. That which is capable of being dressed.
"She started giggling uncontrollably after an epic love-making session when she rose to get dressed she discovered she was not habilable due to her legs still being shaky."
e. Habillable from se habiller (French) to get dressed, to clothe oneself.

HABILIMENT (ha-BILL-uh-munt)
n. One's outfit, personal attire, clothing.
"It never ceased to amaze him, the understated sexiness, the effect her habiliment had on him each time they met."
e. Habillement (French) clothing.

HALO EFFECT (HAY-lo-eh-fekt)
p. When one is dazzled or hoodwinked by beauty and charisma, failing to see the undesirable personality beneath the exterior. When one is viewed or perceived as more angelic, capable or accomplished than they truly are. Blinded by beauty.
"Social media has a halo effect on populations, creating an illusion of the existence of innumerable online desirable personalities."
e. Halo - a circle of light above one's head implying holiness. Halosis χάλωσης (Greek) to be captured, taken, breakdown. Effect - a change as a result of something.

HAMARTIOLOGY (ha-MAR-tee-olo-jee)
n. The study of how sin originated, how it affects humanity, the nature of it, how it is transmitted and how it affects one after death. A branch of Christian theology based on biblical doctrine of sin.

"Harmatiology considers sex outside of marriage or a monogamous committed relationship as a sin, a transgression."
e. *Amartia* ἁμαρτία - sin, *logos* λόγος - study, word, discourse (Greek).

HAMARTOPHOBIA (huh-MAR-toe-foh-bee-ah)
n. An irrational fear of committing acts considered morally or religiously wrong. A fear of sinning.
"*A strict Catholic upbringing instilled hamartophobia in them as children, becoming overly fearful of doing anything wrong at all, let alone giving in to any sexual urges.*"
e. *Amartia* ἁμαρτία - sin, *phobos* φόβος - fear (Greek).

HAPHEPHOBIA (HAFF-uh-foh-bee-ah)
n. An extreme dislike of being touched. Distress induced by the thought or act of coming into contact with another's skin. The fear of touching or being touched.
"*He avoided handshakes and hugs due to his haphephobia.*"
e. *Háptein* - grasp, sense, *phobos* φόβος - fear (Greek).

HAPTICS (HAP-tix)
n. The world of touch and tactile experiences.
adj. *Haptic.* Referring to the sense or stimulation of touch.
"*One must endeavour to be a master of haptics to be the greatest lover.*"
e. *Aptikós* ἁπτικός (Greek) tactile, able to be in contact with.

HARRIDAN (HA-ree-dunn)
n. A woman considered to be sexually promiscuous and foul-mouthed. Later came to mean ill-tempered, scolding and sharp-tongued.
adj. Also *Harridanical.* Aggressive, angry, disagreeable, of a bad temper.
"*It was impressive she hadn't become a complete harridan considering the torment and betrayals he had put her through, rather she chose to upgrade her life and forget he ever existed.*"

e. Borrowed from *haridelle* (French) a scrawny horse or female servant, implying one who is unable to work due to weakness.

HEAUTONTIMORUMENOS (hee-AW-ton-tim-oh-ROO-mee-nuhss)

n. The man who torments himself. The self-tormentor. One fixated on one's own pain or humiliation. A belief that one deserves to suffer.

"*After the painful end of his relationship, he wandered around like a heautontimorumenos, inflicting emotional torment upon himself by replaying memories of love lost.*"

e. *Eaftón timoroúmenos* Ἑαυτὸν τιμωρούμενος (Greek) self-punished. Also an eponym of a play written by Roman dramatist Terence (Publius Terentius Afer), said to be translated wholly or in part from an earlier Greek play by Menander.

HEDONICS (huh-DON-ix)

n. The science of pleasurable and unpleasant sensations or feelings. The observation of the degree of unpleasantness or enjoyability of a particular state or experience. The study of human pleasure.

adj. *Hedonic.* Pertaining to pleasure or pain.

"*Experiencing first hand the limitations and explorations of human pleasure and pain, her knowledge of hedonics was vast thanks to the many years she worked as a dominatrix.*"

e. *Idonikós* ἡδονικός - pleasurable, *idoní* ἡδονή - pleasure (Greek).

HEDENOPHOBIA (hed-uh-noh-FOH-bee-uh)

n. An intense feeling of guilt around enjoying oneself. A belief that life is better lived without enjoyment. An irrational fear of experiencing pleasure.

"*To better understand hedenophobia, one must observe circumstances of the individual's upbringing or environment that were extremely centred on punishment for "sinning".*"

e. *Idoní* ἡδονή - pleasure, *phobos* φόβος - fear (Greek).

HESTERNOPOTHIA (hess-TER-no-poth-ee-ah)

n. A deep yearning for what happened the day before. A nostalgia for yesterday.

"*On the train back home after spending the weekend together, he was overcome with hesternopothia and got to organising their next rendezvous.*"

e. Of unknown origin other than in *The Phrontistery – a dictionary of obscure words*, but derivative of *hesternal* from *hesternus* (Latin) yesterday.

HETAERA (huh-TEER-ah)

n. An Ancient Greek term for a concubine of the highest class. A female companion or prostitute. A high class escort. Also *hetaira*.

"*It is interesting to ponder the inner workings of a man who has a beautiful and intelligent wife yet engages the services of hetaeras at every opportunity.*"

e. *Etaíra* ἑταίρα (Greek) female companion, courtesan.

HETAEROCRACY (het-ee-ah-ROK-rah-see)

n. A governing by harlots. The ruling of concubines. Paramours in power. Also *hetairocracy*.

"*Imagine a hetaerocracy whereby prostitutes had political power and rich businessmen were mere sexual objects!*"

e. *Etaíra* ἑταίρα - female companion, courtesan + *aristokratia* ἀριστοκρατία - rule of the highest born, aristocracy (Greek).

HETAERISM (huh-TEER-iz-uhm)

n. A system whereby every man and woman are considered equally married to each other within a small tribe or community. Communal marriage or concubinage. Also *hetairism*.

"*It is believed that primitive man operated in hetaerism, whereby communities shared lovers and were considered equally in partnership with each person.*"

e. *Etaíra* ἑταίρα (Greek) female companion, courtesan + *-ism* – the practice of the first element.

HINDERMATE (HIN-dah-mate)

n. A spouse, partner, friend or companion who is a hindrance.
"Experience in love and heartbreak will usually offer one a better discerning eye for distinguishing between those who are good to have around and those who are hindermates."
e. After *helpmate*, formed within English from *hinder* – to hold back, to prevent from + *mate* – a fellow, friend, companion.

HIPLINGS (HIP-lingz)

adv. From the region of the pelvic area. From the hips.
"She strutted towards him, hiplings, tossing her hair side to side in a type of mating ritual that caught the attention of onlookers on the dancefloor."
e. Formed within English from *hips* – the place between the thigh and waist + *lings* – indicating condition or situation.

HIRCISMUS (her-SSIZ-muhss)

n. A powerful and malodorous axillary odour. Stinky armpits.
"He was painfully aware of his hircismus after doing a workout at the gym that he instantly hit the showers."
e. *Hircinus* (Latin) like a male goat.

HIRSUTE (her-SYOOT)

adj. Covered in hair or stubble. Relating to hairiness. Hairy, untrimmed, bristly, shaggy.
"She made a pillow of his hirsute chest as they canoodled on the couch watching a movie."
e. *Hirsūtus* (Latin) bristly, hairy.

HOARY (WHORE-ee)

adj. Of hair that is a pale silver. Greying or white hair. Silver-foxing.

"One of the greatest injustices towards women is the acceptance by society of hoary men and far less so of hoary women."

e. Hoar - a 16th century adjective for greyish white usually used of frost that turns things as such.

HORNWORKS (HORN-werx)

n. The unfaithful actions of cuckoldry. Sexual shenanigans.

"The hornworks of the garçonnière came as no surprise to the women who had known these men since adolescence."

e. Formed within English from *horn* - a permanent curve shaped growth + *works* - physical labour.

HOUGHMAGANDY (HOCK-mah-gan-dee)

n. Extramarital sex. Infidelity, fornication, adultery.

"She'd had enough of the houghmagandy and finally left him to his own devices."

e. A Scots term of uncertain origin though some suggestions of roots in *hough* - a leg of beef or behind the knee and *canty* - lively, cheerful, perhaps suggesting enjoying 'a lively piece of meat' as it were.

HOYDEN (HOI-duhn)

n. A person considered to be a bit of a brute. Typically of a girl or woman that behaves in a boisterous manner, a tomboy, but also a socially awkward, unsophisticated lad.

adj. Tomboyish, brash, badly behaved.

v. *Hoydening.* Of a girl or woman behaving in a boisterous, and uncouth manner.

"It seems inevitable that many women become a little hoyden when in environments that are dominated by men, a type of personality shift in order to be included or accepted more easily."

e. Of uncertain origins but may be related to *hoit* - to indulge in rowdy behaviour.

HUGGERY (HUG-uh-ree)

n. The practice of wrapping one's arms around another both literally or figuratively. A hugging.

"Scientific research states that for a human being to survive in a mentally sound state, they are in need of a regular huggery, something around 8 times a day!"

e. From a *hugger* - a person who hugs often.

HYMENEAL (high-muh-NEE-uhl)

adj. Relating to weddings: songs, rites, altars, consummation. Of wedlock.

n. *Hymeneals* (plural). A wedding.

"We all got carried away in their glorious hymeneals, witnessing the joining of two wonderful people."

e. *Hymenaeus* (Latin), *yménaios* ὑμέναιος (Greek) belonging to nuptials, a wedding, a wedding hymn.

HYPERAPHIA (high-puh-RAFF-ee-ah)

n. The condition of having an extraordinarily intense sensitivity to touch. A painful aversion to tactile sensations.

adj. *Hyperaphic*. With a morbid sensitivity to touch.

"Even very light contact is unbearably painful for those afflicted with hyperaphia."

e. *Yper* ὑπερ - exceedingly, overly, *epafí* επαφή - touch, contact (Greek).

HYPERGAMY (high-PER-gah-mee)

n. The practice of marrying a partner of higher social standing. 'Marrying up'.

adj. *Hypergamous*. Relating to the practice of *hypergamy*.

"If one seeks a hypergamous union, one must put the work in to evolve into a suitably matching partner."

e. *Yper* ὑπερ - exceedingly, overly, *gamía* γαμία - marriage (Greek).

HYPERHEDONIA (high-per-huh-DOH-nee-ah)

n. An overwhelming or excessive enjoyment of activities, emotional states or sensory experiences. A pathological increase in pleasure gained from an event or activity. A medical condition that refers to an increased sensitivity to enjoyable stimuli or pleasurable experiences. The opposite of anhedonia (see 'A').

adj. *Hyperhedonic.* Feeling a heightened level of pleasure gained from regular activities.

"After a few wines, the household chores became hyperhedonic as she romanticised her life, imagining herself in a movie whilst the music blared."

e. *Yper* ύπερ - excess, overly, beyond, *idoní* ἡδονή - pleasure (Greek).

HYPERTRICHOLOGIST (high-per-trik-OL-o-jist)

n. A beautician or barber who specialises in removing unsightly facial hair.

"He looked like a new man after visiting his hypertrichologist, whose skill made him look younger and more handsome."

e. *Yper* ύπερ - excess, *tríchosis* τρίχωσις - hairy (Greek). Hypertrichosis - a condition known as 'werewolf syndrome' where one experiences an abnormal amount of hair growth all over the body

I.

IGNESCENT (ig-NESS-ent)
adj. Capable of bursting into flames, emitting sparks. Volatile, fiery, scintillating. Ignitable.

"Their ignescent outbursts of passion were most often fueled by wine and arguing."

e. *Ignēscere* (Latin) to become inflamed, to ignite.

IGNOSCENCY (ig-NOSS-un-see)
n. Having a predisposition and capacity to be forgiving. Forgiveness.

"She felt no ignoscency after discovering his five year long affair, but rather a need to remove him completely from her life."

e. *Ignōscentia* (Latin) the act of forgiving.

ILLAQUEATE (ill-A-kwee-ate)
v. To take in one's clutches. To seize one in one's grasp. To entrap, ensnare, entangle, to catch in a noose. To take a hold of someone.

"Perhaps it was her independence, her aura of non-chalance combined with charisma and beauty that gave her an effortless ability to illaqueate men."

e. *Illaqueāre* - to snare, *laqueus* - noose (Latin).

ILLECEBROUS (ill-uh-SEE-bruhss)
adj. To be so alluring as to have the ability to capture one's attention. Attractive, sexually appealing, alluring, enticing.

"There was a plethora of physically attractive people at the party, lovely eye candy, but it was a quiet confidence, a type of charismatic aura that she found made a man truly illecebrous."

e. *Illecebrōsus* - charm, lure, enticement, *illicĕre* - to entice (Latin).

ILLINITION (ILL-ee-nish-un)
n. The action of rubbing against or into.
"The illinition of massage oil into the skin was so arousing, she left the treatment on a euphoric high."
e. *Illinĕre* (Latin) to smear.

ILUNGA (ee-LOON-gah)
n. One who is willing to forgive on the first account, tolerates a second indiscretion but never fooled a third time. A type of tolerance within reason until one reaches their personal boundary limit. The varying shades of emotion one feels during a progression of intolerance. The grey area sentiments that lead to "three strikes and you're out".
"It really depends on the person I'm dealing with whether my ilunga will allow for some initial indiscretions or whether my patience will be a short fuse."
e. Named the most difficult word to translate in 2004, an African word from the Bantu language of Congo.

IMAGO (ee-MAH-go)
n. A subjective idealized mental image that one creates of someone or oneself, which influences one's perceptions and attitudes towards them. A subconscious mental picture.
"The hero and prince imagos of older generations are swiftly being updated with more modern storylines of romance where women are successful and capable, looking for depth in connection rather than a saviour."
e. *Imāgō* (Latin) natural form, representation.

IMPUDICITY (im-pyoo-DISS-uh-tee)
n. The state of being immodest or lacking shame. To be without bounds. Not conforming to the norms of sexuality. Shamelessness.
"Her impudicity ruffled many feathers in her strict religious community."
e. *Impudicité* (French) impertinence, *impudīcus* (Latin) shameless.

INAMORATA (ee-nah-mo-RAH-tah)

n. A mistress, a female lover, a paramour, a sweetheart, a beloved.

"He had the tattoo of his previous inamorata removed out of respect for his wife to be."

e. *In(n)amorata* (Italian) mistress, sweetheart.

INAMORATE (ee-NA-mor-uht)

v. To inspire to fall in love. To induce feelings of love. To enamour, to influence with love.

adj. In love, enamoured.

n. One who is in love.

"He paid close attention to her interests, taking the time to become close, and planning wild adventures to inamorate her."

e. *Inamorare* (Italian) to enamour, to fall in love.

INAPPETENT (in-AP-uh-tuhnt)

adj. To be without desirous inclination. To have no appetite, urges or impulses.

"It is perfectly normal in a long lasting relationship or marriage that one experiences inappetent phases towards one another, the trick is to make an effort to work together out of those ruts."

e. *In -* to negate the following element, *appetĕre* (Latin) to long for, desire.

INCALESCENT (in-kah-LESS-uhnt)

adj. Becoming hotter, increasing in heat.

"The fact he became incalescent whenever she came near was evidenced in the slight flush of red in his cheeks."

e. *Incalēscĕre* (Latin) to grow hotter.

INCHOATE (INK-oh-ate)

v. To take the first steps towards. To commence.

"She was tired of inchoating first dates and found it attractive when a man initiated spending time together."
e. *Incohāre* (Latin) to start.

INCICURABLE (in-see-KYOO-rah-bull)
adj. One that cannot be disciplined or domesticated. Chiefly in biology of plants being incapable of being cultivated or introduced to new habitats. Unable to be tamed.
"Known as a wild child, her tendency towards non commitment was considered incicurable by some."
e. *Incicurābilis* from *cicurāre* to tame (Latin).

INCIPIENT (in-SIP-ee-uhnt)
adj. In its early stages. Just beginning.
"Their relationship was incipient, in the honeymoon phase, colluded with feelings of euphoria and excitement."
e. *Incipĕre* (Laton) to begin.

INCOMPOSSIBLE (in-com-POSS-uh-bull)
adj. That are utterly incapable of existing together. Incompatible.
"Once the children had flown the nest they soon realised that in fact they were incompossible."
e. *Incompossible* (French), *incompossibilis* (Latin) incapable of coexisting.

INDISCERPTIBLE (in-di-SERP-tee-bull)
adj. Incapable of being separated. Inseparable.
"All that they had experienced together had forged their bond on a deep level, making them indiscerptible."
e. *In* - opposite of the following element + *discerpere* (Latin) to tear apart.

INDURATE (IN-dyoo-rut)

adj. Of a person's character that is morally hardened. Cynical, jaded, unfeeling.

"It takes strength of character to endure many years of failed dating, heartbreaks and disappointments without becoming indurate."

e. Indūrāre (Latin) to make hard.

INFANDOUS (IN-fan-duss)

adj. That one cannot speak of. Nefariously wicked. Unmentionable, unfathomable.

"How does one sleep at night knowing that one is so infandous, so at ease with betraying their spouse?"

e. Infāndus (Latin) unspeakable.

INGUINAL (IN-gwan-ull)

adj. That is located in or belonging to the crotch area. In your private parts.

"An inguinal throbbing could be felt across the audience when the sexiest burlesque performer began her strip-tease."

e. Inguinālis from inguin (Latin) the groin.

INHAUST (in-HORST)

v. To drink up or inhale. To receive and retain into one's mind.

"An unconscious smile spread across his face as he was inhausting the energy of the cute girl who walked into his coffee shop."

e. In - with the sense of towards, into + haust from haurīre (Latin) to draw in.

INTERNUNCIO (in-tuh-NUN-see-oh)

n. A messenger that goes between two parties.

"Divorce attorneys, the internuncios for jaded ex-spouses."

e. Internunzio (Italian) intermediary.

INVEIGLE (in-VEE-gull)
v. To use allurement to blind judgement and draw in under false pretences. To seduce.
"*The notorious stripper used her body, her lustrous curves to inveigle rich men and fleece them of thousands.*"
e. Aveugler (French) to blind.

INVERECUND (in-VEH-ruh-cund)
adj. Unapologetic, audacious, unashamed, brazen.
"*Her inverecund and fierce personality was one of her finest attributes according to her husband.*"
e. Inverēcundus (Latin) shameless.

IRRECUSABLE (i-rah-KYOO-za-bull)
adj. Incapable of being rejected. That one has to accept. Irrefuseable.
"*Ones that think their advances are irrecusable are often, in fact, the ones most easily refused.*"
e. Irrécusable (French) irrefutable, *irrecūsābilis* - unable to be refused from *recūsāre* - to refuse (Latin).

IRREDIVIVOUS (ee-red-ee-VEE-vuss)
adj. Incapable of being repaired or revived. Unrevivable.
"*The final blow was the nastiness that insured after separating which ensured their love was irredivivous.*"
e. *Irredivīvus* (Latin) irreversible from *redivivous* - to become active again, revive and *vivus* - alive. Vivre (French) to live.

IRREMIABLE (ee-REM-ee-ah-bull)
adj. Which is incapable of being returned. Irrevocable, irreversible. Of a state of no return.
"*Be under no illusions, it should go without saying that infidelity is irremiable and requires a great deal of emotional maturity from both parties to work through should you decide to.*"

e. *Irremeābilis* from *remeāre* (Latin) to return.

IRRESPECTUOUS (ee-russ-PECK-tyoo-wahss)
adj. Lacking in respect, disrespectful, dismissive.
"An irrespectuous tone or behaviour is a major turn off for most people."
e. *Irrespectueux* (French) without respect.

IRROBORATE (ee-ROB-oh-rate)
v. To make stronger together. To strengthen.
"Nothing like travelling, a child, a loss or financial pressures to irroborate a relationship or break it off."
e. Interestingly *irrōborāre* means to shine and *rōborāre* once meant to strengthen but today means to rob (Latin).

ISANGELOUS (iss-AN-juh-luss)
adj. That is equal to an angel. Angel-like.
"Her waist length blonde hair created an isangelous aura about her, an illecebrous glow."
e. *Isángelos* ἰσάγγελος (Greek) angel, like an angel.

IVRESSE (IV-ress)
n. A state of intoxication or drunkenness.
"Ivresse will surely affect the performance of most men, or lack thereof."
e. A direct borrowing from French.

J.

JACTANCY (JAK-tuhn-see)
n. Cockiness, arrogant boastfulness, conceited bragging, vainglory, egotism.
"A display of jactancy can be fun in moderation but generally found to be a major turn off for most."
e. *Jactāntia* (Latin) from *jactāre* to throw, toss about.

JACTITATION (jak-tee-TAY-shun)
n. An ostentatious public declaration. A tossing, twitching or jerking of the body; a false claim. Also *jactation*.
"Proceedings against the jactitation of marriage were abolished in 1986, however one can still order an injunction if a person is claiming to be married to them but are in fact not."
e. *Jactāre* (Latin) to throw, toss about.

JAUK (jork)
v. The action of delaying or wasting time. To trifle, dawdle, or shuffle. To toy with.
"To jauk with another's feelings, is to be rife with indecision and mixed messages."
e. A Scottish term of unknown origin. Alternative: *jank*.

JAMPHING (JAM-fing)
n. The act of a man abruptly and unkindly ending a romantic tryst with someone. Dumping a lover without consideration or warning. A male jilt. Also a *jampher*.
"There is no more painful a jamphing than one that is conducted over text or by ghosting."

e. *Jamph* (Scots) to mock, to make game of, to make false pretences, to tire or fatigue.

JEJUNE (jeh-JOON)

adj. Of little stimulation to the mind or body. Lacking in substance, dull, uninteresting, naive, childish. Literally starving.

"*His attempts at wooing were jejune at best until he met the one who inspired him to step into his inner hero, making a true effort and winning them over.*"

e. *Jējūnus* (Latin) fasting.

JENTACULAR (jen-TAK-yoo-lah)

adj. That belongs to or resembles breakfast or is of the time of the morning meal.

"*As part of their Sunday morning ritual, they took turns preparing a jentacular spread of croissants, fruits and coffee while the other had a little lay-in.*"

e. *Ientāre* (Latin) to breakfast.

JILLET (JIL-utt)

n. A flirtatious, coquetish or promiscuous woman. A giddy lass entering puberty. A flirt.

"*Many referred to her as a Jillet, but she couldn't help that everything she said came out smooth as butter.*"

e. From the name *Gillot* and the pet form of the female forename *Juliane* or *Giliane*, now a Scots term.

JISM (JIZZ-uhm)

n. Known most commonly as semen "jiz" but may also be used to describe energy and strength. Though today that would probably be avoided due to its more familiar use.

"*Worn out simply by his eager display of interest, the man was full of more jism than she'd anticipated.*"

e. Of unknown origin but recorded as first appearing in the mid 1800s.

JOINTURE (JOIN-chuh)

n. An estate or land granted to the wife, becoming her property, in the event of her husband's death. A plot of land owned by two people. Also synonymous with dowrie.

"Were it not for their jointure, she would have been a penniless widow."

e. Jointure (French) a join, *jungĕre* (Latin) to join.

JOSS (joss)

n. In the sense of luck or fate.

"The superstition that it is bad joss to see the bride in her dress before the wedding day comes from a time when marriages were mostly arranged and the fear around wanting to ensure one's son would follow through with his commitment to the arranged wedding."

e. An archaic English term for a Chinese figurine or statue of a deity often placed in homes on altars and in temples, used in prayers and offerings along with *joss sticks* (incense) and the burning of *joss paper*.

JOUISSANCE (shjoo-ee-SONSS)

n. Overwhelming erotic euphoria. Intellectual or physical ecstasy. Pleasure; orgasm.

"The abstinence from jouissance is a subjective choice based on individual beliefs and experiences, with numerous perceived benefits and drawbacks."

e. Jouissance - enjoyment, *jouir* - to enjoy (French).

JUBATE (JOO-bit)

adj. To be in possession of pendant hairs. Maned; having a fringe.

"He had a penchant for jubate jezebels, something about that 60s vibe just drove him bonkers."

e. A zoological term from *jubātus*- maned and *juba* - mane (Latin).

JUGATE (JOO-gate)

v. To get together as a couple, to pair up.

adj. That which is side by side; in pairs; overlapping.

"*It was obvious from the electric chemistry, the prolonged eye contact and the way they maintained close physical contact all evening that they would joogate.*"

e. Jugāre (Latin) to join, connect or yolk together.

JUNKETACEOUS (junk-uh-TAY-shuss)

adj. Given to entertaining, feeding, banqueting. Of one who enjoys trips, feasts or events of pleasure and indulgence. Frivolous, like a social butterfly.

"*Her junketaceous personality proved to be too overwhelming for his more introverted, peace-loving character.*"

e. From a junket - a festive and social affair.

JUNOESQUE (JOO-no-esk)

adj. Having a stately or queenly air about them. A woman considered statuesque and regal in beauty. A dignified, majestic and awe-inspiring presence and figure. Of or pertaining to the goddess Juno.

"*The room silenced as she sauntered in, Junoesque, instantly intimidating both men and women in with her indubitable charisma.*"

e. From Juno, the Roman goddess of adult women, love, childbirth and marriage, protector of Rome. Iuvenes (Latin) young.

JURAMENT (JURE-ah-munt)

n. An attestation of truth to abide by. A formal and sincere promise. An oath.

"*During the wedding ceremony, they made their juraments of commitment and loyalty.*"

e. Jurer (French) to swear to, iūrāre (Latin) to swear.

JUVENESCENT (joo-veh-NESS-unt)

adj. That renders one more youthful. Becoming younger or more juvenile.

"*The juvenescent powers of a relationship that is healthy, compassionate, communicative and emotionally mature becomes evident in the wellbeing of the two partners.*"

e. *Juvenēscĕre* (Latin) to attain an age of youth.

K.

KAINOTOPHOIA (kay-noh-toh-FOH-bee-ah)
n. To experience an intense aversion to change.
"The way an abuser can manipulate their victim into a sort of kainotphobia, whereby they stay no matter their torturous treatment is one of the greatest hurdles to overcome when a victim of domestic violence attempts to leave their situation."
e. *Kainótis* καινότης - newness, novelty, modernity + *phobos* φόβος - fear (Greek).

KAKIDROSIS (KAK-uh-droh-siss)
n. A secretion of malodorous bodily perspiration. Disagreeable body odour. Stinky sweat.
"When the person is exceptionally attractive and fun to be around, how does one broach the subject of their kakidrosis?"
e. *Kakídrosis* κακίδρωσης (Greek) perspiration; (sounds like caca (French) pooh).

KALOKAGATHIA (ka-loh-kuh-GA-thee-ah)
n. An ideal of one who embodies both physical beauty and moral integrity emphasising a type of harmony between aesthetics and inner goodness. A combination of the good and the beautiful in someone. A virtuous and kind nobility of character. The perfect person, a paragon.
"She valued kalokagathia in others, a philosophical concept encompassing both inner and outer character with an aim to achieve a balance of physical beauty and moral excellence."
e. *Kalokagathía* καλοκαγαθία (Greek) kindness, nobility. From the phrase 'kalós kaí agathós' καλὸς καὶ ἀγαθός beautiful and good or good and kind. *Kalós* καλός - good, beautiful, honorable, *agathós* ἀγαθός - good, virtuous.

KALOLOGY (ka-LOL-oh-jee)

n. The philosophical study of human attractiveness and how it impacts society. The study of beauty.

"Those interested in kalology may study how people deemed aesthetically beautiful engage with, experience and are received in different world, societal and romantic contexts."

e. *Kalós* καλός - good, beautiful, of fine quality, *lógos* λόγος - words, study (Greek). A relatively new word suggestion though it is unclear who coined it, in circulation in studies of medical humanities and social sciences.

KALON (ka-LON)

n. An ideal of beauty and goodness. Morally beautiful and of the highest good. Values and priorities established in an ethical way known as *summon bonum*. Beauty that is more than skin deep.

"To do what is necessary and morally right is to take possession of kalon, such as giving one's relationship the commitment and loyalty it deserves."

e. *Kalos* καλός - beautiful. *Tó kalón* τὸ καλόν "the beautiful" or "the good" (Greek).

KALOPSIA (ka-lop-SEE-yah)

n. A delusional condition where people and things give the impression to be more beautiful than they truly are. A pleasant state where all appears beautiful.

"It is common for night clubs and bars to be full of people high on kalopsia, fuelled by alcohol and drug consumption, their perceptions of reality skewing the appearances of fellow clubgoers."

e. *Kalopsía* καλοψία from *kalos* καλός - beautiful, *ópsis* όψης - appearance, sight, vision (Greek).

KAREZZA (kah-REZ-ah)

n. The practice of sexual intercourse that deliberately controls and abstains from reaching ejaculation or climax with a goal of the maintenance and intensification of desire for one's partner. Prolonged sex that focuses on pleasure and union, avoiding orgasm. Also known as *coitus reservatus*.

"*The practice of karezza seems to open up more of a debate around men's ability to abstain from ejaculation rather than women's ability to abstain from climax during sex, considering the vast amount of women that claim they are incapable of reaching orgasm or have never experienced it altogether.*"

e. American obstetrician and gynaecologist Alice Stockholm coined the term for this practice from *carezza* (Italian) caress. The practice appears in Sanskrit and Hindu literature and is akin to *maithuna* in Hindu Tantra, and ejaculation control in Chinese culture *caiyin buyang* 採陰補陽 (for men- taking yin to replenish yang) *caiyang buyin* 採陽補陰 (for women- taking yang to replenish yin).

KATZENJAMMER (KAT-sun-jam-ah)

n. The experience of undesirable physical effects from an overindulgence in drinking the night before. A hangover.

"*Many profess that coitus is one of the greatest cures for a katzenjammer.*"

e. *Katzen* - cats + *jammer* distress, wailing (German), perhaps implying that a hangover is as unpleasant as listening to cats wailing.

KELDER (KELL-dah)

n. The prenatal chamber in which a foetus resides and grows. Another word for a woman's womb.

"*A tiny star ignited in the celestial darkness of her kelder, a seed of hope resulting from their tryst of limerence.*"

e. A borrowing from *kelder* (Dutch) a cellar, of which 'Hans-in-kelder' used as an expression to mean an unborn child.

KENODOXY (ken-ODD-ox-ee)

n. The study or love of egotism, cockiness and braggadocio; researching vainglory.

"*His attraction quickly faded after realising she was more interested in kenodoxy than becoming a deeper, self-aware version of herself.*"

e. *Kenódoxos* κενόδοξος - vain-glorious, snobby, *kenós* κενός empty, blank + *dóxa* δόξα - glory (Greek).

KERASINE (keh-RAH-seen)
adj. Feeling in need of some sexual gratification. Horny.
"*The subtle flirting, eye contact and shared humour was encouraging a kerasine chemistry between the pair.*"
e. *Kéras* κέρας - horn, *kerátinos* κεράτινος - horny (Greek).

KETUBAH (kuh-TOO-bah)
n. A Jewish marriage contract that stipulates rights and obligations and monetary provisions for the wife after the death or divorce of her husband. A pre-nuptial agreement.
"*They were both keen for a ketubah considering that each had amassed a considerable fortune before getting together as a couple.*"
e. *Ketūbbāh* כְּתוּבָה (Hebrew) written statement, contract.

KINBAKU (KIN-bah-koo)
n. A Japanese bondage artform that involves erotic fantasy play whereby one consensually and respectfully ties a partner up with very intricate rope knots and patterns, often for visual or sexual pleasure. Historically used as a type of trust building exercise between two people. Also known as *Shibari* or a 'rope kink'.
"*She found Kinbaku to be very sensual and vulnerable, a super sexy way to become closer with her partner.*"
e. 緊縛 (Japanese) tight binding, bondage.

KICKIE-WICKIE (KIK-ee-WIK-ee)
n. A humorous slang term for a wife. A wife's nickname like *wifey* today.
"*Always the life of the party, keeping everyone in high spirits, they couldn't get enough of his little kickie-wickie.*"
e. Derivative of the arbitrarily formed *kicksey-winsey* - a whimsical and unpredictable fancy, (topsy-turvy), later becoming *kicksey-wicksey*.

KINCHIN (KIN-chin)

n. A child. A term used by neighbourhood tramps and now prison slang for referring to a boy or a girl of one's community.

"For one week, she was without her kinchin to enjoy the spoils of what Jamaica could offer her."

e. *Kindchen* (German) baby; *kindeken* (Dutch) child, kin from *cyn* (Old English), *ken*, *kon* (Germanic) related by blood.

KINSEY SCALE (KIN-zee-scale)

n. A rating system whereby one evaluates their sexual orientation based on their sexual responses and experiences at a given time. Rating oneself from 0 (heterosexual), to 3 (equal attraction to both sexes, bi-sexual) to 6 (homosexual), with numbers in between denoting varying levels of attraction to or experience with both sexes and X implying no reaction or attraction (asexuality).

"The Kinsey Scale teaches us that many people have a spectrum of attraction and are not strictly or consistently heterosexual or homosexual."

e. An eponymous term coined by American sexologist Alfred Kinsey (1940) and his colleagues after developing the model to better understand the spectrum of human sexuality.

KIRKING (KER-king)

n. The first appearance at church of a newly wedded couple.

"Because they went directly on their honeymoon on the evening of their wedding, their kirking only happened upon their return."

e. *Churching* - the public appearance of a woman at church after bearing offspring and *kirk* (Scots) a church building.

KISMET (KIZ-met)

n. Providence, destiny, in the stars, fate.

"She couldn't help but wonder if it was a type of kismet that they met under such unusual circumstances."

e. *Kizmet* (Turkish), *qismet* (Persian).

KOI NO YOKAN (KOI-no-yoh-kahn)

p. A Japanese phrase that describes the feeling of when you first meet someone and you experience a premonition of eventually falling in love with that person. An instinctual and foreseeable sense of inevitable future love. A calm knowing of future loving rather than an impassioned 'love at first sight'.

"Because they lived in different countries it seemed impossible to pursue a love affair but they couldn't help the sense of 'koi no yokan' about their intimate and strong connection."

e. 恋 の 予感 (Japanese) premonition of love.

KOUROS (KOO-ross)

n. A sculpture of a nude (usually young) male.

"Her gay uncle had filled his garden with spectacular kouros, exotic flowers and bird houses, an absolute delight for the eyes."

e. Ionic dialect formation of *koros* κόρος (Greek) boy. *Kore* κόρη (Maiden, daughter) being a statue of a young clothed woman.

KRAUROSIS (kror-OH-siss)

n. A condition that causes the shrinking or shrivelling of the skin of the vulva.

"Kraurosis is most common in post-menopausal women, but less common in those who maintain an active sex life."

e. Borrowed from Latin, derived from *kravros* κραῦρος (Greek) dry, brittle.

L.

LABASCATE (LAB-iss-kate)

v. To commence falling or sliding.

"*He contemplated whether it was a ridiculous notion to be labascating for someone he barely knew on the internet, though the intensity of their connection was so illecebrous.*"

e. Labascere (Latin) to fall to pieces, to slip.

LABROSE (LAY-brohss)

adj. To be in possession of plump, luscious or voluptuous lips. Large or thick-lipped. One who has 'big smackers'.

"*She got a lot of attention for her naturally labrose lips, chiefly because she was a white-skinned Nordic girl, not typically associated with being in posession of a big pout.*"

e. Labrōsus (Latin) forming a rim or lip.

LACHRYMOSE (LAK-ruh-mohs)

adj. That is characterised by tearfulness or weeping. That induces crying or feelings of sentimental gloominess or sadness. That brings tears to the eyes.

n. Lacrimation. The act of shedding tears

"*A tear inducing activity such as cutting the onions was perfect to hide the fact she was lachrymose after discovering her partner's infidelity.*"

e. Lacrimōsus (Latin) tending to provoke tears, weeping, tearful.

LACKADAISICAL (lak-ah-DAY-zee-kull)

adj. Of a propensity to cry often. Deficient in good feelings, languishing. Overcome with a feeling of emptiness.

"The breakup had been hard on him but after several months he was determined to get out of his lackadaisical state and begin the healing process."

e. *Lack-a-day, lackadaisy* - an interjection used to express regret, grief or concern similar to *alas!* or *oh no!*

LA DOULEUR EXQUISE (lah-DOO-lerr-ex-KISS)

n. The excruciating yet exquisite pain of wanting someone you cannot have or cannot attain. Getting a kick out of attempting to pursue someone you know you may never have. A tortuous wanting of someone out of your league. Unrequited love.

"Upon seeing him with his wife, *la douleur exquise* set in and forced a nostalgic reminiscing of personal moments they had shared but now she realised would never eventuate into something more."

e. Literally "the exquisite pain" (French), *la* - the (feminine), *douleur* - pain, *exquise* - exquisite.

LAETIFICATE (luh-TIF-ee-kate)

v. To induce higher spirits; make joyous again. To cheer up, revive or stimulate.

adj. *Laetificant*. With a capacity to render cheery. Stimulating.

"There is nothing quite like a surprise encounter with an attractive stranger to laetificate the senses."

e. *Laetificāre* (Latin) to make happy or glad.

LAIRWITE (LAIR-wight)

n. A charge given to adulterous men or women, particularly for fornicating with one who is bound to servitude. A fine for having sex with a slave.

"Divorce settlements could be considered some of the greatest lairwites where the reason for divorce is infidelity."

e. An Old English term *legerwite* from *leger* - lying, + *wite* - fine.

LAMBITION (lam-BISH-un)

n. The act of lapping, licking or lightly touching with the tongue. A tonguing, a lapping.

adj. *Lambitive.* Consumed by lapping up with the tongue (of medicines).

"Skills at cunnilingus are directly correlated to one's sense of intuition with the lambition of one's lover."

e. *Lambĕre* (Latin) to lick.

LAPLING (LAP-ling)

n. One who immensely enjoys lounging between the thighs of a woman. A person who likes to lie in a lady's lap.

"He enjoyed being his wife's lapling on a Sunday afternoon whilst watching movies and having his hair stroked."

e. Formed within English *lap* - the front side portion of a seated person between the hip and the knee, *ling* - belonging to or connected with the first element.

LASCIVIOUS (luh-SIV-ee-uhs)

adj. Inclined towards being lusty, unrestrained in the amount of sexual relationships one accrues. Driven by the enjoyment of luxuriousness, sex and desire. Immodest, wanton, lewd, slutty.

"To be lascivious is one's own choice, to make a display of it may act as a deterrent to some or be attractive to others. The question is what do YOU want in a partner?"

e. *Lascīvus* (Latin) sportive, lusty.

LAUTITIOUS (lor-TISH-uss)

adj. Attractive and impressive through being splendidly sumptuous. Magnificent; resplendent; luxurious; elegant.

"She looked good enough to eat, lautitious in her white bath robe after a delicious soak in the hot tub."

e. *Lautitia* - magnificence, *lautus* - bathed, neat (Latin).

LECTUAL (LECK-tyoo-ul)

adj. In need of bed rest or to be confined within the bed chambers, usually of a person who is unwell.

"Though she was in good health, she was in a lectual mood each time her boyfriend came around if you know what I mean."

e. *Lectus* (Latin) bed, couch and interestingly *lectio* or *lecture* (French) a reading, it could be thought of 'as a place where one reads'.

LEIOTRICHOUS (lie-OT-rick-uss)

adj. To be in possession of smooth and straight hair. Also *lissotrichous*.

"He looked like a gorgeous Mongolian warrior with his leiotrichous mane and tanned skin."

e. *Leio* λειο - smooth + *thrix* τριχ - hair (Greek).

LEMAN (LEE-mun)

n. A sweetheart, beloved or lover. Also of a mistress, a paramour, in a more negative sense. (Also pronounced 'lemon').

"Newly coupled, his little leman was constantly by his side, going wherever he went like a lovesick little puppy."

e. *Leofmon* (Middle English) a dear man, *léof* (Frisian) - beloved, precious, dear.

LENTIGINOSE (len-TIJ-uh-nuss)

adj. That is covered in minute dots resembling freckles. Related to *lentigo* - a pigmented deposit on the skin. Freckled. (Also *lentiginous*).

"There's something beautifully leopard-like about a lentiginose face when the pigment is quite strongly contrasted with the skin colour."

e. *Lentīgo*, *lens* (Latin) lentil.

LEUCOMELANOUS (loo-koh-MEL-ah-nuss)

adj. Of a fair complexion, sporting dark hair.

"Her leucomelanous beauty was even more dazzling because she was Junoesque in stature with a husky growl of a voice."

e. *Lefkós* λευκός - white, *melan* μελαν - ink (Greek).

LEUCOUS (LYOO-kuss)
adj. Of a pale complexion with blonde hair. Albino.

"*He was self conscious of his leucous complexion, but she found him to be a person of beauty and was in awe of the contrast they made skin to skin.*"

e. *Lefkós* λευκός (Greek) white.

LEVERET (LEV-uh-ret)
n. A type of woman seen as a pet; a mistress.

"*The misguided assumption of immature women seeking or claiming they can steal a woman's husband, unbeknownst to them that a good wife is not threatened by their escapades. Why keep a man who enjoys leverets over a grown-ass woman?!*"

e. Of a hare strictly in its first year, implying something that is new, childish. From *levrette*, a small version of a *lièvre* (French) hare.

LEVIRATE (LEE-vuh-rut)
n. A Jewish custom of a compulsory marriage of a widow to the brother of her deceased husband or the next of kin.

"*Levirate law was designed to protect women in a society where women depended on men but in modern day could be seen as more of an imposition to the widow.*"

e. *Lēvir* (Latin) husband's brother, brother-in-law.

LIBERTINAGE (LIB-er-teen-ij)
n. A behaviour that displays an overindulgence in sensual pleasures; free-thinking promiscuity. Demonstrating a reduction in boundaries or morals. Debauchery.

"*She rocked up at the party in west Hollywood expecting a civilised networking event but instead was greeted with chaotic libertinage.*"

e. *Libertin* (French) a freed man; *lībertīnus* (Latin) member of a class of freedmen.

LIBIDINIST (luh-BID-uh-nist)

n. A person with an abnormally high sexual drive and appetite. A promiscuous, hypersexual and horny individual.

"*The expectation was that female escorts were required to behave as types of libidinists, but in reality many clients craved a more natural girl-next-door or girlfriend type experience.*"

e. *Libīdo* (Latin) sex drive.

LIBKEN (LIB-kuhn)

n. A place where one can lay down to rest or sleep. A bed, house or lodging.

"*After years of dating and broken relationships, the one thing she craved more than anything was to have her libken to herself, to work on her peace and tranquility.*"

e. Formed within English from *lib* - to sleep + *ken* - a house where the disreputable meet or sleep.

LICKERISH (LICK-uh-rish)

adj. Eager to taste or enjoy. A desirous longing or appetite for something or someone. Sweet, tempting, attractive, lusty, greedy to swallow. Sexually keen.

"*They positioned themselves near to the entrance so as to cast their lickerish eyes upon all those who entered the room.*"

e. *Lickerous* (Anglo-Norman) pleasing or tempting to the palette, sweet pleasant, delightful.

LIMERENCE (LIM-uh-ruhnss)

n. The condition of being romantically besotted with someone and having an overwhelming desire for the feeling to be reciprocated. An involuntary initial rush of obsessive desire for another. Having "the hots" for someone. Romantic infatuation.

adj. *Limerent*. Experiencing strong feelings of limerence. Feeling in love or infatuated.

"Is it often difficult to know the difference between true compatibility or simply being affected by limerence. Spending good and hard times, travelling and living together will most likely reveal the true chemistry of a partnership."

e. *Limer* - apparently arbitrary, *-ence* - of the quality of the first element. Interestingly *limer* means *adhesives* in Norwegian which could be thought of as "stuck to a person".

LIPOTHYMY (luh-POTH-uh-mee)

n. A temporary state of unconsciousness. To experience swooning, fainting.

"His long distance girlfriend showed up unannounced to his graduation party, looking like a million dollars and shocking him into lipothymy, perhaps because he suddenly realised how much he truly loved and admired her."

e. *Lipothȳmia* (Latin); *lipothȳmía* λιποθῡμία (Greek) faint.

LORETTE (lor-ETTE)

n. A 19th century high-class French prostitute that operated in the vicinity of the Notre Dame de Lorette church in Paris. A high-class hooker. Their lifestyle became known as *lorettism*.

"The fashionable Lorettes of Paris were unlike 'kept' courtesans but relied instead completely on prostitution to earn an income, usually with numerous regular clients."

e. A direct borrowing from French proper noun *Lorette*, derived from *laurus* (Latin) laurel plant - also meaning 'crowned in laurel'.

LOVELORN (LUV-lorn)

adj. A feeling of being rather upset that one is not experiencing requited love. Unhappy as a result of a breakup. Pining for love. Lovesick.

"Though he put on a brave face and smiled at the gathering, his lovelorn eyes were apparent even hidden behind his sunglasses."

e. Formed within English, *love* - a disposition of deep affection for someone, *lorn* - lonely, bereft, left alone.

LUBENCY (LOOB-uhn-see)

n. A pleasurable willingness in action. A pleasantness, amusement.

"They flirted with such ease and lubency that their attraction was evident for all in attendance."

e. *Lubentem* - happy, *libent-em* willing (Latin).

LUBRICIOUS (LOO-bruh-kuss)

adj. Describes that which is slippery, slimy or oily. Something or someone that is unstable, shifty, sneaky, elusive, wonton or lascivious.

"She had to repeatedly and physically peel off his lubricious hands whilst trying to dance at the concert."

e. *Lūbric* (Latin) wanton, smooth, slippery, *-ous* characterised by the first element. (Think of *lube-like*).

LUCENCY (LOO-sun-see)

adj. The state of being radiant, luminous. To shine with brilliance.

"The light of the moon evoked a sensual lucency on their skin through the glass ceiling of their bedchambers."

e. *Lucent* - bright, luminous from *lūcēre* (Latin) to shine.

LUCTUAL (LUCK-tyoo-uhl)

adj. Of a feeling that is sad, full of sorrow, in mourning.

"He asked the heavens that the next relationship be only full of kindness, compassion and loyalty so as to revive his luctual heart."

e. *Luctus* (Latin) mourning.

LUDIBUND (loo-dee-BUND)

adj. That is full of playful attributes. Fond of light-heartedness, curiosity; playful.

"Who can resist the charms of one who is not only physically attractive and sporty, but also ludibund in nature? The perfect combo for having a great time."

e. *Lūdibundus* - playful from *lūdĕre* to play (Latin).

LUGENT (LOO-junt)

adj. To be lamentful. Demonstrative of weeping or mourning. Crying your eyes out.

"The lugent effects of her marriage breaking down had caused her to become a recluse and avoid almost any human interaction due to the redness and soreness of her eyes."

e. Lūgēre (Latin) to mourn.

LUPANARIAN (loo-pah-NAIR-ee-uhn)

adj. Anything that derives from or is related to a whorehouse, bordello, brothel and by extension associated with promiscuity.

"She was shocked into silence upon entering his home for the first time due to the lupanarian decor that depicted numerous nude sex scenes."

e. In Ancient Roman times, sex workers were referred to as *lupa* - shewolf (*lupus* - wolf) and therefore a brothel was a *Lupanar* - a house of shewolves (Latin).

LURDAN (LER-den)

n. A person that comes across as lazy, dull, incapable and a little stupid. One who is disinclined to work or exert themselves. A sloth.

"The greatest of lurdans hide behind their internet screens lurking and lusting over people they could never attain, critiquing the slightest imperfections with the greatest of righteousness without ever considering the ludicrousness and hypocrisy of their position."

e. Lourdin - a heavy fellow from *lourd* - heavy (French).

LUSORIOUS (lyoo-SAW-ree-uss)

adj. Used as a hobby, a pastime, in sport.

"The way she discarded men was lusorious, in one aspect her friends found her escapades amusing and on the other hand they genuinely felt a little disgust at her level of narcissism and unaccountability for her actions."

e. Lūsōrius (Latin) belongs to a player, gamer.

LUXURIA (luk-ZJOO-ree-ah)

n. Absolutely self indulgent erotic longing for sexual gratification. An excessive addiction to indulging in sexual pastimes and a fixation on collecting high value foods and drinks or glamorous items such as perfumes. Sinful lusting or overindulgence.

"*The spectrum of luxuria is based upon one's own predisposed assumptions on active sexuality and desire, what seems excessive to one may seem minimal to another.*"

e. *Luxuria* (Latin) excess, extravagance. In Ancient Rome, luxuria was used to describe living in rebellious and sinful excess. In English "luxury" originally meant "lust" or "lechery".

LUXURIST (luh-KSHOO-rist)

n. One who revels in and is preoccupied with all that is luxurious, fond of sensual and indulgent pleasures. A luxury-loving person.

"*Does not a capitalist regime incite us all to be luxurists?*"

e. *Luxury* - the habitual indulgence in things that are choice or costly, *ist* - denotes a person of.

LYCHNOBITE (LICK-nuh-bite)

n. One who lives fast in the night time and sleeps all day. A night-dweller.

"*Their drug-fuelled sexcapades made them verifiable lychnobites, the night-walkers of the vegas strip.*"

e. *Lychnóvios* λυχνόβιος, from *lýchnos* λύχνος - lamp, *víos* βίος - life (Greek) in other words 'lamp life' (which would imply it is night time).

M.

MACARISM (MACK-uh-riz-um)
n. The pleasure found in witnessing another's joy or success. The experience of happiness due to a specific person or thing.
"Macarism came easily to her as she felt a great depth of beauty in the love others shared, the tenderness that they might display, a sweet reminder of the good in the world."
e. *Makarismós* μακαρισμός blessing; *makarízein* μακαρίζειν - to rejoice (Greek).

MACROTOUS (muh-KROH-tiss)
adj. Being in possession of rather large or long earlobes. Big-eared.
"The surgeon was changing the lives of the macrotous individuals, pinning back and reducing their ears was drastically enhancing their attractiveness."
e. *Makrós* μακρός - long, large; *oús* οὖς - ear; *makrótis* μακρώτης - length, (Greek).

MADEFY (MAD-uh-fie)
v. To render moist, to make wet, to induce a dampness.
adj. *Madescent.* That is moist.
"Every woman seeks true foreplay that leads to a madefied state before engaging in sexual intercourse."
e. *Madéfier* (French), *madēre* - to be wet and *facere* - to make (Latin).

MAMIHLAPINATAPAI (mum-ee-luh-PEE-nah-tah-pie)
n. A quiet moment between two people looking at each other in the hopes that the other will take action on a thing desired but that neither are willing to do.

"The chemistry between them was palpable but as both of them were married, there remained a type of mamihlapinatapai between them."

e. The Yaghan language (Argentina), on the verge of extinction, in Thomas Bridges' *English-Yaghan Dictionary*, *ihlapi*, 'awkward', from which *ihlapi-na*, 'to feel awkward'; *ihlapi-na-ta*, 'to cause to feel awkward'; and *mam-ihlapi-na-ta-pai*, suggests 'to make each other feel awkward' as a literal translation.

MAMMIFEROUS (mam-IF-uh-russ)

adj. That which has mammary glands, breasts. In possession of boobies.

"He wasn't mad about the fact that he was the only male amongst the other mammiferous attendees as he got a huge amount of attention."

e. *Mammifère* (French) of the Mammalia animal group who nourish their young with milk; *mamma* (Latin) a breast, udder + *iferous* - bearing.

MAMMIFORM (MAM-ee-form)

adj. Shaped like a breast, dome or cone. Looking like tits. Boobie-like.

"They cracked up laughing when they pulled the cookies out of the oven because rather than being heart-shaped, they looked rather more mammiform."

e. *Mammiforme* (French) that has the shape or is reminiscent of an udder; *mamma* (Latin) a breast, udder + *iform* - having the shape of the first element.

MAMMILLIFORM (mah-MIL-ee-form)

adj. That bears a resemblance to the shape of a nipple, a *mamilla*.

"The print on her top was rather accidentally mammilliform and therefore quite distracting for the teenage students."

e. *Mammilla* (Latin) breast, nipple.

MAMMOSE (mah-MOSE)

adj. In possession of large boobs. Full or big-breasted. Big-titted.

"Her brother actually broke his nose from a stripper motor boating him because she was so mammose and clearly underestimated the power of those chesticles!"

e. *Mammōsus* (Latin) breast-shaped, having big boobs, having a protuberance.

MAMZER (MAM-zah)

n. A child considered to be conceived illegitimately, outside of a marriage. A bastard child.

"Where it was once frowned upon to be a mamzer, the occurrence is so common today for children to be born out of wedlock that old laws around nationality and citizenship need to be changed."

e. In Judaism, *mamzēr* (Hebrew) a child of an illicit union; *mamzer* (Yiddish) bastard, thief.

MANTRAP (MAN-trap)

n. A man or woman likely to intentionally entrap, ensnare, or trick another, such as into marriage. Also another term used humorously for marriage.

"A perpetual seducer, a type of mantrap, you would be wise to steer clear."

e. *Man* - adult human male, *trap*- a device for catching game or noxious animals.

MANUSTUPRATION (man-uh-STYOO-pray-shun)

n. The act of arousing oneself sexually, masturbation.

"With pornography so easily accessible online, it's easy to conceive that many a teenager is frequently engaged with digital manustupration."

e. (Latin) *Manus* hand, *stuprate* - to degrade, debase, pollute.

MARITURIENT (ma-ree-TYOO-ree-uhnt)

adj. One who is keen to marry. Eager to get hitched. Looking for a wife/husband.

"We live in a time where many countries are becoming less and less mariturient, people are waiting until they are older, living together first and perhaps not settling for the minimum as much."
e. *Marītāre* (Latin) marry.

MATA HARI (mah-tah-HA-ree)
n. A temptress doubling as an informant or spy. A woman who uses her skills of seduction to extract highly classified information for the purpose of informing the enemy.
"Her seductive qualities had all the men in the room in the palm of her hand, bending to her will, much like a Mata Hari."
e. The stage name of an infamous Dutch exotic showgirl who spied for the Germans, executed by the French in 1917. She adopted her stage name from Malay *mata* - eye, *hari* - dawn, day = eye of the dawn or sun.

MATROCLINOUS (ma-troh-KLIGH-ness)
adj. That has inherited more of the biological mother's characteristics rather than the biological father's. That resembles the mother or has a tendency to inherit only the mothers traits. More like mum.
"Her matroclinous beauty was evident when he first met his mother-in-law to be, who still maintained a dignified and serene allure about her."
e. *Māter* (Latin) mother; *klínein* κλίνειν (Greek) to lean.

MAUDLIN (MORD-lin)
adj. Of a tearfully sentimental disposition such as when one is overly drunk. Given to crying. Exaggeratedly emotional.
"It was time to take her friend home as he was becoming increasingly maudlin, trying to drown the sorrow of his recent breakup."
e. *Maudelain*, relating to depictions of Mary Magdalene crying and an alternative (Middle English) form of the name *Magadalene*.

MEGAPROSOPOUS (meg-ah-PROSS-op-us)
adj. With a large face.

"He was teased in school for being megaprosopous, but his glow up occurred when he reached young adulthood, as his large face was endowed with a chiselled jawline transforming him into a well-built handsome man."
e. Mégas μέγας - great, large ; prósopos πρόσωπος - person (Greek).

MEGASCOPIC (meg-ah-SCOP-ick)
adj. Visible to the naked eye.
"Even after 20 years of marriage, their love for each other was megascopic."
e. Mégas μέγας - great; skopos σκοπος - watching (Greek).

MELLIFLUOUS (mel-IFF-loo-us)
adj. That sounds as sweet as honey. That resembles honey in taste and texture. Honeyed; sweet.
"It is hard to define and hard to resist one with a mellifluous quality to their voice."
e. Mellifluus (Latin) like honey, honey flow.

MERETRICIOUS (MEH-ruh-trish-uhs)
adj. Superficially attractive but in fact lacking in real depth or integrity. An alluring but false show. Looks good on the outside but lacks personality. Has the qualities of a bimbo or himbo. Deceptively alluring.
"She felt that popular summer destinations were full of meretricious types; great bodies but not much personality or charisma."
e. Meretrīx (Latin) a prostitute. Traditionally insinuating one that has the characteristics of a prostitute (demonstrative of the diminutive ways they have been viewed historically).

METAGNOSTIC (met-ag-NOSS-tick)
n. That is impossible for the human mind to comprehend or decipher. Beyond your wildest dreams, ineffable, incomprehensible.

"The power of chemistry between two individuals is a metagnostic force that the human mind will forever contemplate; why are we so crazy about some people and not others? What are the factors that turn us on so specifically with that one person?"

e. Metá μετά - after + gnostikós γνωστικός - cognitive, relating to knowledge (Greek). Could be thought of as The knowledge of 'after'.

MICROPODAL (my-KROP-uh-duhl)

adj. In possession of very small feet. Tiny tootsies.

"Unbeknownst to her, he actually had a micropodal fetish and was delighted at her size 3 shoe size."

e. Mikrós μικρός - small, pod ποδ - foot (Greek).

MINAUDERIE (min-ORD-uh-ree)

n. A display of obvious flirtations. Disingenuous, coquettish or unnatural behaviours designed to impress. A flaunting.

"He was not easily hoodwinked by the minauderies of the loud young women who came to flaunt themselves at him, but rather intrigued by the quiet presence of nerdy types."

e. Minauderie - simpering, minauder - to make a display of affection, simper (French).

MINESTRA RISCALDATA (me-NAY-strah-risk-uhl-DA-tah)

p. Refers to a situation that is doomed, hopelessly making repeated attempts to make something work. Such as a couple getting back together after one or several breakups. The "same old story", "old news", "a pointless reunion".

"Seeing their friends break up and get back together repeatedly without facing any of their underlying issues was a true minestra riscaldata."

e. (Italian) literally means "reheated soup", minestra - soup, riscaldata - heated. Implying that when something is "reheated" it won't be as delicious as the first time around.

MINIMFIDIAN (min-um-FID-ee-an)
n. A person that has the least amount of faith in something.
adj. That has the smallest degree of faith. Faithless.
"A *minimfidian* of love no longer believes that it is possible to fall in or feel love ever again."
e. *Minimus* - smallest, *fidēs* - faith (Latin).

MIRIFICENCE (my-RIFF-uh-sunss)
n. The working of wonders. The action of making something appear miraculous.
adv. *Mirifically/Mirificously*. That acts in a wondrous manner. Wonderfully; marvellously; magnificently. Like a miracle.
adj. *Mirific/Mirifical/Mirificent*. That makes extraordinary. Wonder-working; marvellous; awe-inspiring.
"Despite breaking up and getting back together numerous times over a decade, it was with *mirificence* that they found their way back together at the right time in their lives."
e. *Mirificentia* (Latin) miracle, amazingness.

MISACCEPTATION (miss-ax-ep-TAY-shun)
n. The act of misinterpreting or misunderstanding; taking in a wrong sense of something.
"Frustratingly, the *misacceptation* of one's kindness for attraction is quite common, rather than the realisation that some people were raised with a sense of politeness and friendliness."
e. *Mis* - wrongly + *acceptation* - receiving something favourable.

MISBESEEM (miss-beh-SEEM)
v. To be unbecoming; unflattering; unsuited to. To act in an inappropriate, unfitting or unattractive way.
"It started out as a bit of a laugh but very quickly his drunken dancing and flirtatiousness *misbeseemed* his otherwise wonderful character."
e. *Mis* - wrongly + *beseem* - appear.

MISQUEME (miss-KWEEM)

v. To act in an unacceptable manner. To ungratify; to displease; to offend. Also *misqueam*.

"Though he tried to justify his infidelities, it was clear that his lack of accountability completely misquemed her and her unwavering commitment to their relationship."

e. Mis - wrongly, + *queem* - act in an acceptable fashion; *cwēming* (Old English) pleasure.

MISTETCH (miss-TETCH)

n. Something which is a flaw, an unhealthy habit, a bad trait, a vice.

v. To teach bad practices; encourage bad habits.

"The mistetch of going back to a lover that is an incredible bedfellow but treats you as expendable is really one that you should seek to grow out of quickly."

e. Mis - wrongly + *teche* from *tache* (French) a distinctive mark, trait.

MITESCENT (me-TESS-ent)

adj. Becoming milder. Softening, diminishing, weakening, declining.

"It's perhaps easy to confuse the comfortability of familiarity in a long term relationship with the feeling that one's love is becoming mitescent."

e. *Mītescere* - to grow mild; *mītis* mild (Latin).

MISYOKE (miss-YOKE)

v. To have married the wrong person. To be inappropriately matched.

"The unfortunate realisation that they were desperately misyoked dawned on her after travelling together for the first time."

e. Mis - wrongly + *yoke* - to attach.

MOLLITIOUS (mol-ISH-uss)

adj. Of a soft, sensual, sultry, luxurious or sumptuous quality.

"The added excitement to the senses of a mollitious bed can never be underestimated."

e. *Mollitiēs* (Latin) softness. (Perhaps akin to *mollycoddle* - to' wrap in cotton wool', also sounds a lot like *malicious*).

MOLROWING (MOL-row-ing)
n. The habit of engaging with a disreputable woman. Hanging out with a hustler's wife or girlfriend, particularly while that gangster is imprisoned. The practice of cavorting with prostitutes. Out on a noisy spree.
"He was on a molrowing with the boss's wife under his strict orders to keep her out of trouble."
e. *Moll* - the sweetheart or female accomplice of a gangster + *rowing* - to make a commotion.

MONANDRY (MON-an-dree)
n. The practice of marrying only one man at a time. A wife who has only one husband (as opposed to *polyandry*). Mating with only one male.
"While there is some evidence to suggest that women are more inclined towards monandry, it's really a personal preference and perhaps women are less likely to kiss and tell."
e. *Monandría* μονανδρία (Greek) having one husband.

MONOTHELIOUS (mon-oh-THEL-ee-uss)
adj. Several males serving to fecundate a female. Of a woman with more than one husband or lover. Polyandrous.
"Hats off to the monothelious woman she thought to herself, as she couldn't in her wildest dreams imagine trying to negotiate more than one penis in her life!"
e. A zoological term from *mónos* μόνος - single + *thílys* θῆλυς female (Greek).

MORDACIOUSLY (more-DAY-shuss-lee)
adv. In a biting manner.
adj. *Mordacious*. With a tendency to bite.

"After their mordacious kissing escapades, they were both covered in hickies."

e. *Mordāx* (Latin) given to biting; *mordre* (French) to bite, *morder* (Spanish) bite.

MORGANATIC (mor-gah-NAT-ick)

adj. Of a spouse of lower rank or social standing. Of a marriage where the spouse and children don't have any legal claim to the possessions of the higher ranking spouse.

"The pretentiousness of deeming one's spouse morganatic in the modern era is of great distaste and can only be conceivable to most in extreme cases of disparity."

e. *Morganaticus* (Latin); *morganaticum* - a morning gift - traditionally, an example in this sense was of land being gifted from a husband to the wife on the morning of their wedding but she is then entitled to nothing further.

MORSURE (mor-SHUH)

n. A little nip. An act of munching. A bite.

"The excruciating teasing of placing soft morsures on her neck was almost enough for her to climax in that moment."

e. *Morsure* (French) bite.

MOTRIX (MOE-trix)

n. A woman who is the first to instigate something. A female instigator.

"Once she decided not to be a motrix of dating, she began attracting men who would actively pursue her."

e. *Motrix* (Latin) feminine form.

MULIEBRAL (myoo-lee-EB-rull)

adj. Of the nature of a woman. Characteristic of womanhood. Womanly; feminine.

n. *Muliebrity*. Womanhood.

"Her muliebral curves were enough to drive a man to insanity."

e. *Muliebris* (Latin) unmasculine, characteristic of a female.

MULTIPARA (mull-TIP-ah-rah)

n. A woman who has given birth numerous times to healthy offspring. A female who has birthed several children. A mummy of many kids. Also *multiparous*.

"Some still find it surprising that a multipara can be even more beautiful after rearing children."

e. *Multiparus* (Latin) *multi* - implying numerous, *parus* -producing young, bearing.

MURKLINS (MURK-linz)

adv. Of a night time; in the dark.

"It was particularly of preference to make love murklins after they became parents, for fear of two little munchkins coming bursting in at any moment."

e. *Murk* - deficient in light + *lings* - indicating a condition.

N.

NAKEDIZE (NAY-kud-eyes)

v. To go without garments. To go nude.

"*They liked to nakedize in the sunlight so as to avoid any major tanning lines.*"

e. Naked - no clothes on the body + ize - to make into the first element.

NANTAIMORI (naan-TIE-maw-ree)

n. A Japanese practice of serving sushi or sashimi on the naked body of a willing male model. Less commonly practiced than its female counterpart Nyotaimori (see below).

"*The audience watching Magic Mike wondered if perhaps they should include a segment of nantaimori for VIP ticket holders.*"

e. Nantaimori 男体盛り (Japanese) - man's prime, Nantai 男体 - male body, mori 森 - forest.

NATES (NAY-teez)

n. An alternative term for the buttocks. The bum; the butt.

"*He was hypnotised by the effect of her denim jeans on her nates, making them look perky and round.*"

e. Natēs (Latin) the bum cheeks.

NATIFORM (NAT-ee-form)

adj. Resembling the form of one's gluteus maximus. Having the shape of a buttocks. Butt-shaped.

"*The classroom of primary school kids erupted in fits of giggles when one of them whispered under their breath that the new teacher's end of nose looked natiform.*"

e. Natēs, natis (Latin) buttocks. Nóton νῶτον - "south", noto νωτο (Greek) tergum, dorsal, relating to or situated on the back.

NATURISM (NAYT-yoo-riz-um)

n. The belief that living a natural way of life includes communal nudism.

"Though they were keen on the idea of 'a natural way of life', naturism was only possible in warmer countries."

e. *Nature* - the phenomena of the physical world of plants, earth and animals + *ism* - naming the condition of the first element.

NEANIC (nee-AN-ick)

adj. Pertaining to adolescence. When a youngling develops adult-like characteristics.

"In the neanic stages of human children, boys' voices break and girls get their periods."

e. A zoological term from *neanikós* νεανικός (Greek) juvenile.

NECTAREAN (neck-TAIR-ee-un)

adj. That is sweet like nectar. Also *nectareal* or *nectareous*.

"Her nectarean lips could destroy any feelings of inadequacy or tension."

e. *Nectareus* (Latin) nectary.

NEOGAMIST (nee-OG-am-uhst)

n. One who is just recently married; a bridegroom. Also *neogam*.

"The neogamists set off on their honeymoon to travel and hike in Peru."

e. *Neógamos* νεόγαμος (Greek) newlywed.

NEOLOCAL (nee-oh-LOH-kal)

adj. Of a dwelling for a newly married couple that is independent of either spouse's parents or family.

"It is strongly advisable to live neolocal before marriage to get a sense of what it is like to live with your future spouse, to not do so feels a little mad."

e. *Néos* νέος (Greek) new; *local* (French) of a particular space, *locālis* (Latin) relating to a place.

NEONATE (NEE-oh-nate)
n. A newborn child. A baby of under four months of age.
"When she travelled to remote parts of Asia, many locals wanted to see her neonate as it was the first time they had seen a caucasian baby in person."
e. Néos νέος (Greek) new; nātālis (Latin) belonging to birth,

NEOTENY (nee-OT-uh-nee)
n. Retention of child-like characteristics in a sexually mature adult. Also juvenile sexuality; the development of sexual maturity earlier than normal.
"The school uniform fetish and obsession with looking overly youthful, a type of neoteny of the modern era."
e. Neotenie (German); néos νέος young, new + teínein τείνειν to extend, tend (Greek).

NEPENTHE (neh-PEN-thee)
n. A special drink designed to help one forget their grief and suffering.
"Too many nepenthes makes a sad man frolick only to return to his despair the following day."
e. From nēpenthes (Latin); nipenthés νηπενθές (Greek), a drug described as having the capacity to free the mind of all worries (Homer's *Odyssey*). Nepenthe was once an alcoholic concoction that also contained opium and morphine.

NEXAL (NEX-ull)
adj. That causes or enables two parts to join. Of the quality of a *nexus*; being connected or linked.
"Their nexal attraction had a visceral effect on other bystanders at the concert."
e. Nexus (Latin) the action of binding.

NIDIFICATE (nid-IF-uh-kate)
v. To build a nesting place. To fabricate a nest. To nest. Also *nidify*.

"With her belly in full bloom, growing her first child, she was absolutely ready to nidificate."

e. *Nīdificāre* (Latin) nidify, to nest.

NIPLET (NIP-luht)

n. The bump at the tip of the areola on a breast or chest. A nipple, a small nipple.

"It wasn't cold outside but her niplets were clearly high-beaming through her top as they chatted, making it challenging to focus."

e. A variant of the word nipple, recorded as early as 1648 but most frequently in use in the early 1900s.

NIYOGA (nee-YOG-ah)

n. The practice of appointing a brother or next of kin to have a child with their deceased brother's widow if they were childless, to ensure the family's lineage and as a way to mitigate the social and financial hardship a childless widow may face.

"A child born from the practice of Niyoga was therefore considered the child of the deceased husband, not the designated male who copulated with the widow."

e. *Niyunakti* नियुनक्ति - appointment; *niyog* नियोग - employment (Hindi).

NOCTIDIURNAL (NOK-tee-die-ER-null)

adj. Comprising of one day and a subsequent night. Of a 24-hour duration.

"Their tryst was noctidiurnal, a sleepless love fest before parting again with sweet sorrow."

e. *Noctus* - the night + *diurnal* - day (Latin).

NOLI ME TANGERE (nolli-may-TAHN-juh-ray)

p. "Touch me not," "Don't touch me," "cease holding onto me." A person that mustn't be touched or interfered with. A warning against involvement or meddling. Indicating a dislike or fear of being touched.

"I told my friend that I was setting a 'noli me tangere' on her for the next year, in the hopes of splitting with the cycle of unsuccessful love affairs she seemed addicted to embarking on."

e. *Nōlle* - to be unwilling + *mē* - me + *tangere* -to touch (Latin). Said to be words spoken from Jesus to Mary Magdalene when she recognised him after resurrection. *Noili-tangere* is the scientific name of a yellow touch-me-not balsam plant, named as such because their seed pods burst open when touched.

NUCHA (NYOO-kah)

n. The back of the neck; the nape. Also *nuque*.

"He nervously kissed him lightly on the nucha as a subtle invitation which resulted in his crush turning around with a big smile on his face."

e. *Nucha* (Latin) spinal chord. *Nuque* (French) nape of the neck.

NUDNIK (NOOD-nik)

n. One who is of a pestering, nagging or boring nature. An irritating person.

"He accused his wife of being a nudnik without considering how his lack of effort with the daily house chores were the primary basis for her discontent."

e. Yiddish, stem of *nudyen* - to bore, pester. *Nuda* (Russian) - boring or tedious, boredom. *Nudziarz* (Polish).

NULLIGRAVIDA (null-uh-GRAV-ee-dah)

n. A female who has never been 'with child'. A woman who has never experienced pregnancy.

"She lived her life nulligravida by choice, preferring instead the company of cats."

e. *Nulli/nūllus* - chiefly scientific meaning a sense of 'having no-', *gravida* - pregnant (Latin).

NULLIPARA (null-IP-ah-rah)

n. A woman who has never borne offspring.

adj. Nulliparous. Never given birth.

"Many societies need to catch up to the fact that numerous women are happier being nullipara, enjoying a life filled with friends, lovers, work and a social life."

e. Nulli/nūllus - chiefly scientific meaning a sense of 'having no-', -parus - bearing, producing (Latin).

NUNCUPATE (NUN-kyoo-pate)

v. To orally express a vow to someone. To dedicate a work to a specific person.

adj. Nuncupative. Declared orally.

"Before placing rings on fingers, they looked each other in the eyes intently whilst nuncupating their love for all to hear."

e. Nuncupāre (Latin) to consecrate.

NUPTIALITY (nup-she-AL-it-ee)

n. The marriage rate within a population. Also another term for weddings, nuptials or a couple about to be wed.

"Across the globe, nuptiality rates are in decline due to the rise of contraceptives, better female education and higher rates of participation in labor markets and the transformation of legislation allowing unmarried couples more rights."

e. Nuptial (French) nuptial; Latin nuptiālis (Latin) bridal, wedding.

NUPTURIENT (nup-TYOO-ree-unt)

n. One who is desirous of getting married. A person with a strong desire to get hitched.

"It used to be that maidens were desperately nupturient as they had so little choice to be otherwise, but these days it actually seems a lot more men are also of this disposition."

e. Nuptos - married + ūrient - creating the present participle of desiderative verbs (Latin) implying 'in the present moment'.

NYCHTHEMERON (nick-THEM-uh-ron)

n. Of a duration of twenty four hours. That takes a day and a night.

"The wedding celebrations began at lunch time and continued across the nychthemeron."

e. *Nychthímeros* νυχθήμερος (Greek) night and day.

NYMPHOLEPT (NIM-fuh-lept)

n. A person who is affected by an intense yearning for someone unattainable. One who is affected by nympholepsy.

adj. Afflicted with an irrational passion for an unobtainable object of desire.

"Physical beauty combined with sexual charisma is enough to send a person nimpholept, the test is to find another outlet for redirecting that intense energy."

e. *Nymphóleptos* νυμφόληπτος - possessed by nymphs, enraptured, frenzied; a belief that individuals could be controlled or possessed by the actions of nymphs (Ancient Greek).

NYMPHOLEPSY (NIM-fuh-lep-see)

n. An obsessive fascination with young, beautiful women. An overwhelming enthusiasm or desire for someone or something unattainable, an irrational ecstasy and frenzied state arising from seeing a nymph. Historically known as a passionate desire aroused in men by young girls.

"The societal state of nympholepsy is only strengthened by Hollywood, the music industry, social media, pornography and popular cultures."

e. Formed within English (from Greek lexicon), *nypmh-* a class of semi-devine spirits taking the form of a maiden + - *lepsy* - denoting a state of possession.

NYMPHOMANIAC (nim-fuh-MAY-nee-ack)

n. A woman obsessively preoccupied with copulating. A lady with an uncontrollable sexual appetite. A chick who spends a lot of her time thinking about or having sex. Sometimes men are referred to as such though the male equivalent is a *satyriasist*.

"*Many women who exude a lot of sexual energy are automatically assumed to be nymphomaniacs however, one may observe that they often channel their sexual energy into artistic projects or exercising rather than the physical act.*"

e. *Nympha* (Latin) labia minora, semi-devine spirit, maiden, *mania* -μανία (Greek) excessive desire, mental illness, *maniaque* (French) *maniacus* (Latin) - one afflicted with mania.

NYOTAIMORI (nee-yo-TIE-maw-ree)

n. A forest of food served on a naked female body (typically sushi), for the degustation of guests (the food not the woman). Stemming from the ancient art of *Wakamezake*, a practice of drinking booze from a woman's crotch (see 'W'). Also referred to as *body sushi*.

"*One of her sexual fantasies was to be a nyotaimori model*".

e. *Nyotai* 女体 - female body, *mori* 森 - forest (Japanese). Traced back to the fetishism of food play during the *Edo* period in Japan (1603-1868) and fuelled by Japan's economic growth in the 1960s.

O.

OBJURATION (ob-joo-RAY-shun)
n. The act of binding with a deep promise. An oath. A binding agreement.
v. *Objure.* To bind with an oath, to urge, to swear to.
"His objuration to his partner was to protect and care for her and their children."
e. *Obiūrāre* (Latin) to bind by an oath.

OBLECTATION (ob-leck-TAY-shun)
n. An instance of delight, enjoyment, pleasure, satisfaction.
v. *Oblectate.* To pleasure, to please, to rejoice, to make glad.
"They covered one another's naked body in fruit salad and spent the afternoon snacking on each other for their own oblectation."
e. *Oblectātiō* action or quality of giving delight; *oblectāre* to delight, to amuse (Latin).

OBREPTION (ob-REP-shun)
n. Seeking to attain things by intentionally concealing the truth. Obtaining gifts under false pretences.
adj. *Obreptitious.* That contains a falsehood.
"Her stomach churned at the obreption of his professions of love, little did he know her feelings no longer endured for him after discovering he had a mistress."
e. *Obreptiō* (Latin) the act of creeping up unseen, stealth.

OBSOLAGNIUM (ob-so-LAG-nee-um)
n. A diminishing sexual desire that most often accompanies the aging process. A loss of interest in sex. No more "urge to merge".
"Obsolagnium suggests that it is inherent to lose a sexual appetite as one ages; however health experts say that it is rarely age itself that

accounts for a decline in libido. Rather, desire and sexual satisfaction are immensely impacted by circumstances that challenge one's health, environment and emotional wellbeing."

e. A neologism from *obsolescere* (Latin) to become obsolete, to fall into disuse, *lagneía* λαγνεία (Greek) lust.

OCULOLINCTUS (ok-yoo-loh-LINK-tuhss)

n. The practice of licking eyeballs to experience sexual arousal. Being turned on by licking your partner's eyeball. An eyeball licking fetish, also known as oculophilia and 'worming'.

"Eyeballs are really meant for admiring and communicating rather than the practice of oculolinctus, I imagine it would feel rough as sandpaper for the recipient."

e. A neologism from *oculus* -eye, *linctus* - a licking, *lingĕre* - to lick (Latin). *Linctus* - a medicine to be licked up with the tongue.

ODALISQUE (OD-ah-lisk)

n. An exotic, sexually alluring woman. A sexy female slave in a harem.

adj. That intimately resembles a sexually attractive woman.

"When he asked the universe for more women in his life, he had imagined himself surrounded by odalisques but instead finds himself overrun with five daughters."

e. Odalisque (French) a concubine of the Sultan of Turkey, oriental theme of the lounging naked woman.

OEILLADE (err-YARD)

n. A meaningful and amorous look. A secret loving glance as a sign of affection. A wistful glimpse with the eyes, a knowing look, an ogling.

"They had only just met but they spent the dinner with arbitrary acquaintances exchanging oeillades across the length of the table."

e. Oeillade also oeyliades from oeil - eye (French).

OIKONISUS (oi-kuh-NIE-suss)

n. A burning desire to begin procreating and establish a household. A longing for family life.

"A wistful lust to be head of a household had not occurred to him previously, but suddenly he was consumed with oikonisus after seeing his brother happily chasing after his kids and wife."

e. Of uncertain origins but most likely from the root *oikos* οἶκος (Greek) house and *nīsus* (Latin) effort, tendency, endeavour. Interestingly, *oikonisus* means correctness in Finnish.

OIRAN (OI-rahn)

n. A courtesan of the highest ranking, the historical Japanese *Oiran* were considered superior to the common prostitute *yūjo* "woman of pleasure", due to their refined entertainment skills and artistic abilities.

"I wonder what the act of modern day stripping would look like if they adapted the artistic traits of the Oiran".

e. *Oiran* is taken from the Japanese phrase "*oira no tokoro no nēsan*" (おいらの所の姉さん) translating loosely to *"the lass at one's place"*. Originating in *Yoshiwara*, a famous red light district in the 1750s *Yukakau* of what is now known as Tokyo.

OLAMIC LOVE (oh-LA-mik-luv)

n. Referring to a deep and everlasting love that feels as though it encompasses the eternal universe. 'Cosmic love'.

"Is olamic love possible between human beings or is it more a sense of spirituality that one can only feel in connection to life and the universe itself?"

e. *Olam* ōlām (Hebrew) world, universe; *olamic* - belonging to a vast period of universal time.

OLFACTOEROTOCISM (ol-FACK-toe-eh-ROT-uh-siz-um)

n. Erotic arousal stimulated through smelling or from odours. Using the nose as a sex organ.

"It isn't hard to believe in the likelihood of a sexual receptor up the human nose, especially if you are one to be very affected by the scent someone carries."

e. *Olfactology* - the study of the sense of smell. Interestingly, many scientists claim that we have a sexual organ up our nose; the *vomeronasal organ* strongly resembles a structure in mammals that plays a key role in sexual attraction.

OLISBOS (OH-liz-buss)

n. A self-pleasuring device shaped as a phallus. A penis-shaped sex toy. A dildo.

"The anxiety accrued when travelling with an olisbos in one's carry-on luggage is not for the easily embarrassed or one who is ashamed to be caught with sex toys."

e. *Olisbos* (French), *olisthein* ὀλισθεῖν (Greek) - to slip, to glide.

ONANISM (OH-nah-niz-um)

n. Coitus interruptus, fornication with the self. Masturbation.

"The benefits of Onanism include reduced stress, better understanding of one's own sexual needs, better sleep, immune function and self-esteem, how ridiculous to condemn it in the name of spiritual superiority."

e. From the biblical story of *Onan* who refused to father children who would not belong to him, so he did not complete copulation with his deceased brother's wife but instead allowed his semen to fall on the ground, for which God punished him with death. This was consequently interpreted in Christianity and Judaism as divine condemnation of masturbation.

ONEIRATAXIA (oh-NAY-rah-tax-ee-ah)

n. When one creates a collection of illusionary thoughts in their mind's eye, getting so carried away in the fantasy that they are no longer able to distinguish it from reality. An inability to differentiate between dreams and the real world.

"He realised it had been a type of oneirataxia he had been maintaining when the bubble finally burst on his perception of her."

e. *Oniro* όνειρο (Greek) - dream, -*taxis*: a sense of. (It is unclear who coined the term or how long it has been in use).

ONOLATRY (oh-NOL-uh-tree)
n. Historically, the worship of "ass" as in donkey, meaning a preoccupation with something foolish. Figuratively it could be a *double-entendre*: the practice of foolishly worshipping one's own ass, obsessing over its size and neglecting to develop other personality traits; or could be the worship of other peoples' curvaceous tooshies, rumpuses, backsides.

"The practice of onolatry has dramatically increased since the popularisation of the bubble-butt."

e. *Onos* ὄνος - moon, όνος - donkey (Greek), -*olatry* - excessive worship of a thing.

OPHELIMITY (off-uh-LIM-uh-tee)
n. Nothing is "off limits" when one has the capacity and capability to produce complete satisfaction. Ability to please sexually. A drive to satisfy a desire, fulfilling a want or a need.

"A bedroom filled with ophelimity is a bedroom filled with orgasms."

e. *Ophélimité* (French), oféllein ὀφέλλειν (Greek) - benefit, enlarge, increase, strengthen, *Ophelia* - Greek goddess of total satisfaction.

OPSIGAMY (op-SIG-ah-mee)
n. Marrying later in life.

"Opsigamy should be seen as a societal virtue, where people take their time to choose a partner and hopefully have a better emotional maturity and wisdom to choose one of high compatibility."

e. *Opsígamos* ὀψίγαμος μία (Greek) late-married.

OPTASIA (op-tah-ZEE-yah)
n. Exhibiting oneself to be viewed, an apparition, a sight, a vision.

"When he laid eyes on her for the first time, an optasia, he knew she was the one."

e. *Optasía* ὀπτασία (Greek) - vision, optasia features in bible writings.

ORCHIDACEOUS (or-kid-AY-shuss)

adj. Exceptionally flamboyant, exotic or eye-catching as though it resembles an orchid. Ostentatious, fancy, flashy, showy.

"He made such an orchidaceous display of his attraction towards his love interest that it was impossible for anyone not to notice."

e. Orchidaceae (Latin) the botanical family of orchid flowers.

ORECTIC (oh-REK-tik)

adj. Characterised by an acquiescence of one's sensual impulses. Something that stimulates one's desire. Giving in to one's gratification, desires, appetites.

"The way they danced was orectic."

e. Orecticon, orecticus (Latin), orektikós ὀρεκτικός (Greek) - appetising.

ORGIOPHANT (orj-ee-oh-FANT)

n. Someone who presides over people engaging in communal sexual activities. An overseer of group sex. An orgie-master.

"An orgiophant was present at all times at the private party to ensure all participants were treated with respect whilst enjoying their sexual activities."

e. Orgiofántis ὀργιοφάντης from órgia ὄργια - orgies + faínein φαίνειν to make known (Greek).

OSCULANT (OS-kyoo-luhnt)

adj. When two organisms connect in a lips embrace. Kissing, suggestive of pashing, smooching, french kissing.

v. Osculate. To kiss.

"Their passionate reunion was osculant, locking lips as frequently as possible oblivious to their surroundings."

e. Ōsculānt, Ōsculāns from Ōsculāre (Latin) to kiss.

OSCULAR (OSS-kyoo-lah)

adj. Designed for pashing. Pertaining to the mouth and kissing; kissable.

"He had the most oscular lips she had ever seen, two perfect pillows she imagined pressed against her own."

e. Ōsculum - kiss from ōs - mouth, *culum* - denoting small structures (Latin).

OSCULUM (OS-kyoo-luhm)

n. A kiss, a little mouth, an opening or orifice.

"*Proceeding an afternoon of flirtation and teasing, they finally shared an osculum before saying goodbye.*"

e. Ōs (Latin) - mouth, *culum* - denoting small structures.

ỌṢUNALITY (oss-oo-NAL-it-ee)

n. The study of post-colonial sexualities with a focus on creating an empowered, non-phallocentric view of sexosophy inclusive of diverse forms of sexual pleasure and eroticism. An affirmation that normalises sexual pleasure and eroticism, with a focus on pleasure and fulfillment rather than orgasm.

"*Many would benefit from studying philosophies such as Osunality, that center around positive sexual experience with a primary focus on fulfillment rather than the phallicle dominance and orgasm centredness of pornography.*"

e. An African term derived from Nigerian philosopher Nkiru Nzegwu, appearing to be derivative of *Osun* - the Yoruba goddess of sensuality, love and beauty.

OUTRECUIDANCE (oo-tra-kwee-DONS)

n. When a person is so full of themselves, they act like mother nature's gift to humanity. Unrestrained self-confidence, egomania, conceit, arrogance, presumption, immoderate self-esteem.

"*The woman was a rare beauty proliferated by the fact she didn't show an ounce of outrecuidance.*"

e. Outrecuidance (French) from *outre* - beyond, excessive, *cuider* - to plume oneself.

P.

PAEDOTROPHY (peh-DOT-roh-fee)
n. The theoretical practices associated with rearing children. The art of raising kids.
"When one is going to have a child, there is a great emphasis on the labour and birth itself with little education of paedotrophy. It's really up to parents to do a lot of research themselves into different aspects of raising children."
e. Paedotrophia (Latin); *paidotrofía* παιδοτροφία (Greek) raising children.

PAIZOGONY (pie-ZOG-ah-nee)
n. Necking; playing kissy-face; love-play; the act of kissing.
"Did you know that a bit of paizogany is said to actually improve your immunity because of the introduction to new bacteria?"
e. A new word suggestion of unclear origins but my suggestion would be a relation to *paízo* παίζω - play + *ogónos* ογόνος - ogenous (Greek) + -ogony - denoting a study or development of the first element 'the study of play'. Also *gónos* γόνος - offspring.

PALPEBRATION (pal-puh-BRAY-shun)
n. A wink; winking or blinking.
v. *Palpebrate.* To wink repeatedly
adj. *Palpebrate.* That has eyelids.
"Some studies show that people are subject to palpebration when they are flirting or talking with someone they are attracted to."
e. Palpebratus - blinked; *palpebra* - an eyelid; *palpāre* - to touch (Latin).

PALPEBROUS (PAL-peh-bruss)
adj. Having large and thick eyebrows. Bushy brows.

"Her palpebrous face made for rather striking eyes, the way they were framed with those dark hairs."

e. Said to be a misinterpretation of the meaning of *palpebra* (Latin) eyelid + *-ous* abounding in.

PANDEMIAN (pan-DEE-mee-un)

adj. Of a love that is considered the most common or normal. A sensual Venus-like love. Human love.

"An ordinary sexual attachment sounds much more romantic, described as a pandemian love."

e. *Pandímios* πανδήμιος (Greek) belonging to all of the people.

PANEGOIST (pan-EE-go-ist)

n. A self absorbed person. An ego-maniac. One who believes only the self truly exists. A subscriber of the theory of solipsism, a solipsist.

"The filters on social media platforms that fuel the inflation of panegoists who developed a sort of limerence with themselves, an infatuation with their own falsehood and shallowness."

e. *Pan* - all encompassing, universal + *egoist* - one who is egotistical, who only talks about or is concerned with themselves. Could be thought of as "an egomaniac in every way".

PANEROTICISM (pan-uh-ROT-iss-iz-um)

n. The belief that anything and everything can have erotic value.

"The theory of paneroticism explains why today we hear of so many weird and wonderful fetishes, it is interesting to ponder what experiences change one from panerotic, to instigating a super specific erotic desire."

e. American psychologist and sexologist William Stayton believed that we all relate to the world in a panerotic sense and used the term *panerotic* to describe having a capacity for a broad erotic attraction or interest from birth, and therefore scholars of his work describe his theory as paneroticism (though it is an unofficial coinage). From *pan* - all encompassing, universal + *eroticism* - a sexual state, desire, arousal.

PANGAMY (PAN-guh-mee)

n. The inhibition of having selective choice in a sexual partner. Unrestricted, random mating. Random fucking.

"She liked the fact that he had been very selective in his choice of sexual partners rather than be victim to pangamy."

e. Pan πᾶν - all + gamía γαμία -marriage (Greek); "marriage or joining of all".

PANMIXIA (pan-MIX-ee-ah)

n. The blending of genetic inheritance. Unrestricted cross-breeding, mixing of races and ethnicities.

adj. Panmictic. Mixed-race, ethnicity, nationality or heritage.

"With travelling becoming so accessible over the last century, it's inevitable that large parts of the global population have become a panmixia."

e. Pan πᾶν - all + míxis μίξις - mix, mingle (Greek).

PANPHARMACON (pan-FAR-mah-kon)

n. Something that is reputed to cure all things. A universal remedy; a panacea. A cure-for-all.

"Whilst contemplating what really makes a person happy, she wondered if anything but love and connection could be a true panpharmacon."

e. Pan πᾶν - all + fármakon φάρμακον - medicine, drug (Greek).

PANTAGAMY (pan-TAG-ah-mee)

n. A system by which all the men and women of a household or community are considered married to one another. Universal bachelorette and bachelorhood. A system of 'free-love'.

"A system of pantagamy or 'complex marriage' may sound appealing to those inclined towards promiscuity, the fantasy of unrestrained choice in sexual partners, but the realities of such adventures usually differ greatly to the imagined freedoms."

e. Panto παντο - everything + gámos γάμος - marriage (Greek). Easily remembered by thinking of it as a 'pantomime of marriage'. Formerly practised by the 19th century *Perfectionist* religious commune at Oneida, New York State (1848–79).

PAPILLIFORM (pah-PIL-ee-form)

adj. Of the shape of a papilla. Nipple-shaped.

"*She noticed that people kept looking at her girlfriend when they were walking down the street and suddenly clocked that it was the mauve paint splodges on her t-shirt that looked rather papilliform.*"

e. *Papilliformis* from *papilla* - nipple (Latin).

PARACOITA (pah-rah-KOI-tah)

a. A slang term for a sex doll or robot; a female sexual partner. *Paracoitus* being the masculine equivalent.

"*Studies state that one of the most beneficial advantages of having a sex doll is the improvement of sexual technique.*"

e. Its origins are unclear though it appears in the online source The Phrontistery - a dictionary of obscure words. Its roots most likely being *para* (Spanish) for + *coitus* (Latin) intercourse - "for sex".

PARANYMPH (PA-ruh-nimf)

n. A bridesmaid or bridegroom, best man or maid of honour. One who advocates for another.

"*Their paranymphs came to their sides to sign the wedding documents as witnesses of their elopement.*"

e. *Paranymphe* (French) a mediator; *paranymphus* - a male wedding attendant, best man and *paranympha* - bridesmaid (Latin); *para* παρα - beside + *nýmfi* νύμφη - bride (Greek).

PARAPHILIA (pa-rah-FIL-ee-ah)

n. Sexual desires regarded as perverse such as attraction or interaction with abnormal sexual objects or practices. Abnormal sexual attraction.

"*My brother works as a doctor in ER and he's very tired of the paraphilia that leads to misplaced objects in anuses or elsewhere.*"

e. *Pará* παρά -other, beside, alongside, despite, *philia* φιλία - friendship, tendency to, love of (Greek). Coinage of the term was accredited to Croatian sexologist Friedrich Salomon Krauss in 1903.

PAREUNIA (pah-ROO-nee-ah)

n. Erotic contact involving the penetration of the penis into the vagina. A posh word for sex ya'll.

"He knew that pareunia was on the cards the second they got a moment alone and she was all over him."

e. *Párevnos* πάρευνος (Greek) bedfellow, lying beside.

PARI PASSU (PA-ree-PAH-soo)

adv. To be side by side. In equal or simultaneous step; in sync.

"They lingered pari passu at the reception, welcoming all the wedding guests as they arrived."

e. *Parri passu* (Latin) simultaneously.

PARLOUS (PAR-luss)

adj. That which is forbidden, dangerous, precarious, full of risk.

"He had a parlous air about him that was truly irresistible seeing as she was a bit of a daredevil herself."

e. Perilous from *perillus*, *périlleux* (French) dangerous.

PARNEL (PAR-nuhl)

n. A woman considered ready to engage in casual sex. Also a man considered effeminate or more characteristic of a woman. A wanton woman. A prostitute; or a mistress of a priest.

"A woman with natural seductive prowess, she was often mistaken for a high class parnel."

e. From the forename *Pernel* derivative of *Petronilla*, and considered the female version of *Peter*.

PARTHENOLOGY (parth-un-OL-oj-ee)

n. A branch of gynaecology that involves the observation and theory of the state of virginity. The study of virgins.

"She was interested in parthenology to study the science of sexual chemistry between humans, how and when it begins, when it is strongest, how long it lasts and the impact it can have on an individual."

e. Parthenologia (Latin); parthenología παρθενολογία; from parthénos παρθένος - virgin + logía λογία - words (Greek). "Virgin words".

PARTHENOPHOBIA (parth-un-oh-FOH-bee-yah)

n. An intense anxiety felt around virgins; particularly a fear of young girls. A fear of virgins.

"The young men joked about experiencing a type of parthenophobia when they were teenagers, however some admitted that they still were scared of girls."

e. Parthénos παρθένος - virgin + phobs φόβος - fear (Greek).

PARTURITION (par-tyoo-RISH-un)

n. That which has been brought into being, born or created usually with immense effort. The act of giving birth, physically or metaphorically.

"After such a long period of gestation, it may be easy to assume that parturition feels short or easy in comparison, but the insurmountable effort required to bring forth a life is equal to the months of growing it inside of you."

e. Parturitio (Latin) childbirth.

PASSIUNCLE (PA-see-unk-ull)

n. Emotions that exhaust the soul and heart rendering one incapable of true emotion; a trifling or insignificant passion; a thing that is of little fervor; passionless.

"Some thought her to be incapable of true emotion because she treated men and relationships as passiuncles, until of course she met a man who deeply inspired her and spiked her curious mind."

e. A term coined by English writer Thomas De Quincey; *passion* - intense feeling or emotion + *-uncle* - as a suffix denotes a smaller amount of the first element.

PECCAMINOUS (peh-KAM-uh-nuss)
adj. That consists of sin; sinful, lewd, lascivious, full of sin.
"When she discovered that they had a similar outlook on life, conversating about the universe, the arts, writing music and novels she was overcome with longing and full of peccaminous thoughts of lust and desire."
e. *Peccāre* (Latin) to sin.

PEGGING (PEG-ing)
v. A modern slang term for sexual activity of a woman penetrating a man anally with a strap-on dildo.
"As a professional escort, she experienced some rather strange requests but pegging was surprisingly frequent."
e. *Peg* - a short bolt made of wood or plastic + *-ing* denoting a noun in action.

PEIGNOIR (pen-WAHR)
n. A woman's lacey slip, a sexy robe, light dressing gown, negligée.
"She showed no embarrassment of being uncoiffed and strolling around in her black peignoir in the garden, but the neighbour flushed red when he noticed her."
e. *Peignoir* (French) a light dressing robe from *peignouer* - a garment worn whilst combing one's hair; *peigner* - to brush or comb.

PELURIOUS (peh-LOOR-ee-uss)
adj. That which is covered in fuzz or hair; furry, hairy.
"The injustice of society accepting pelurious men and not women can be partly attributed to pornography and its impact on shaping aesthetic standards."
e. *Pelure* (French) - skin, fur, coat.

PENECTOMY (pen-EK-tom-ee)

n. Surgical removal of the penis or some part of it. The amputation of the manhood.

"When penile cancer is present, surgeons fastidiously consider the benefits and risks of a penectomy due to the significant psychological implications it may have."

e. Pēnis (Latin) - the male genital organ + -ectomy from ektémnein ἐκτέμνειν (Greek) to cut out/off.

PENELOPIZE (peh-NEL-uh-pize)

v. To bide for time in the hopes of deterring potential suitors. To act like a Penelope - a virtuous wife. To delay.

"While numerous men were vying for her attention and affection, she Penelopyzed by keeping busy with numerous projects, work and running her household."

e. Pēnelopē (Latin), Pinelópi Πηνελόπη (Greek) of the Greek poem Homer's Odyssey, she who is the wife of Ulysses known for her unwavering loyalty to her husband, her intelligence and perseverance.

PENTAGAMIST (pen-TAG-ah-mist)

n. A person who has gotten hitched five times. A person with five spouses.

"We listen and we do not judge but... who in their right mind would become a pentagamist? How can anybody afford it financially, but also emotionally? She thought to herself."

e. Penta πεντα - five + gámos γάμος - wedding (Greek).

PERFERVID (peh-FER-vid)

adj. That is wholeheartedly dedicated to. Enthusiastic; ardent; impassioned; eager.

"He had a perfervid desire to please her, a quality she found very attractive after years of lazy lovers."

e. Perfervidus, praefervida (Latin) impassioned, fervent.

PERICLITATE (peh-RICK-lit-ate)

v. To endanger something; to jeopardise; to expose it to risk.

"*Only a fool would periclitate the affections of a good spouse, adulation and infatuation are temporary distractions of lust compared to a loyal and trustworthy partner.*"

e. Perīclitārī (Latin) in danger.

PERNOCTATION (per-nok-TAY-shun)

n. The act of spending the night; to sleep-over; an 'all-nighter'.

"*The excitement of seeing each other in the flesh for the first time led to a pernoctation of conversation and sensuality.*"

e. Pernoctatio (Latin) overnight, the action of passing the night in prayer.

PERVICACIOUS (per-vee-KAY-shuss)

adj. To be resolute, stubborn or inflexible despite persuasion or argument. Asserting one's will; headstrong; determined. (Sounds like someone with a tendency to be pervy though).

adv. *Pervicaciously.* To do in a stubborn manner.

"*It was difficult to watch their friend pervicaciously vie for their crush's attention despite their warnings of a very bad track record.*"

e. Pervicāx - stubborn, pervincere - to prevail (Latin).

PETHERAPHOBIA (peth-air-ah-FOH-bee-ah)

n. A fear of one's mother in law. *Pether*o*phobia* - a fear of one's father in law.

"*He developed a type of petheraphobia, a fear of his mother-in-law coming over at any moment because she was overbearing, meddling in their personal affairs and manipulative of his wife.*"

e. Petherá πεθερά (Greek) mother-in-law + phobia - fear of. *Many sources on the internet state the fear as pe*n*theraphobia however I cannot find the reason for the 'n' to be there, so I assume it is an oversight/spelling mistake to whoever originally coined the term.

PHALLEPHORIC (fal-uh-FO-rick)

adj. Describing the carrying or inclusion of phallic emblems, objects or shapes. Something that consists of dick-shaped things.

n. *Phallophoria.* Carrying an erect penis, a phallus.

"*The gathering of women were losing their minds with laughter when they attempted pottery class because everything they spun on the potter's lathe was turning out phallephoric.*"

e. *Fallifória* φαλληφόρια - a festival in which a phallus is carried during the procession; *fallós* φαλλός - penis (Greek).

PHILANDERER (fil-AN-duh-rah)

n. A professor of the fine art of flirtation with sexual intent. One who spreads his romantic and sexual affections towards numerous women. A man who frequently enters into casual sexual relationships, cannot help but be flirtatious, a serial flirt.

v. To *philander.* To 'sleep about'.

"*Many a male becomes a philanderer in their formative sexual years.*"

e. *Filandros* φιλανδρος (Greek) - with love for people, *phil* - loving, *anēr* - man, male, husband.

PHILEMATOLOGY (fil-uh-ma-TOH-loh-jee)

n. The study of the art of kissing. A practitioner of such is known as a *philematologist.*

"*Fascinated by romantic and sexual human behaviours, they decided to take up philematology.*"

e. *Filí* φιλί (Greek) - kiss + *-ology* -the discipline or science of something.

PHILEMATOPHOBE (fil-uh-MAT-oh-fobe)

n. A person who greatly dislikes or is fearful of kissing, from *philematophobia.*

"*The act or even the mere thought of kissing can turn a person into a philematophobe, particularly if they have an anxiety around bad breath and germs.*"

e. *Fílima* φίλημα - kiss + *phobos* φόβος - fear (Greek).

PHILOCALIST (fi-LOH-kal-ist)

n. A person who seeks out and is enamoured with the most beautiful and attractive people, who adorns their home with beautiful artworks, furniture and objects. One who cherishes the beautiful in all things, a lover of beauty.

"*His choice in women and home décor revealed him as a philocalist.*"

e. *Filókalos* φιλόκαλος (Greek) loving beauty, friendly + -ist - forming a noun derived from a Greek verb.

PHILOGYNY (fil-OJ-uh-nee)

n. The admiration, appreciation and love of women; a doating of women. A *philogynist* being a person who loves women.

"*A society is truly imperilled when there is a loss of philogyny, if not at the very least to have a respect for the givers of life.*"

e. *Filogynía* φιλογυνία (Greek) love of women.

PHILOPHOBIA (fil-oh-FOH-bee-yah)

n. A fear that is developed after repeated attempts at emotional intimacy, only to have failed and be left with a sense of emptiness and regret. A fear of getting too close to someone. A fear of love.

"*After so many failed relationships, they were overcome with philophobia.*"

e. *Philo* φίλος - loving, fond of, dear, beloved, friend, *fovia* φοβία - fear of (Greek).

PHILOPORNIST (fil-oh-PORN-isst)

n. One who enjoys spending time with and appreciating sex workers. A lover of prostitutes.

"*The dichotomy that many sex workers face when feelings of love threaten to cloud judgement during intimacy, is that of trying to determine genuine love and affection from those who are simply philopornists, an impossibly challenging distinction.*"

e. *Filo* φιλο - friend + *pórni* πόρνη prostitute (Greek).

PHILOPROGENITIVE (fil-oh-pro-JEN-eh-tiv)

adj. Pertaining to instinctive love of offspring. Describes having a great love for, giving great attention and care to one's children.

"In some areas, modern relationships and parenting styles seem to have spawned a generation of more philoprogenitive fathers in comparison to previous generations."

e. Filo φιλο (Greek) friend, *prōgignere* (Latin) to procreate.

PHILTER (FIL-tuh)

n. A magical concoction or charm said to produce feelings of sexual desire and lust towards a particular person. A love potion.

"Her perfume invoked a particular primordial desire within her girlfriend, an irresistible philter of sorts."

e. *Philtre* (French) once meant a love potion; *philtrum* (Latin) love potion, groove between the nose and upper lip; *fileín* φιλεῖν (Greek) to love, befriend.

PHIMOSIS (figh-MOE-siss)

n. An inability to retract the foreskin of the penis. Having an uncomfortably tight prepuce.

"Having phimosis made intercourse painful for him until he got circumcised."

e. *Phīmōsis* (Latin) contraction of the foreskin.

PHOENICEOUS (fin-ISS-ee-uhss)

adj. That which is scarlet coloured. Of a vibrant crimson colour. Hot red.

"Her phoeniceous lips and viridescent eyes instantly caught his attention even amongst the crowd."

e. *Phoenīceus* (Latin) bright red.

PHRENESIS (fruh-NEE-siss)

n. A type of delirium, frenzy, madness.

"There is no greater force than the phrenesis of love and desire, the delirium caused from falling into it, having a lack of it or being utterly consumed by it."

e. Phrenēsis (Latin) frenzy, delirium; *frénisis* φρένησις (Greek) frenzy.

PICKTHANK (PIK-thank)

n. One who tries to gain favour by imbuing someone with compliments and bad-mouthing other people. A sweet-talker; a flatterer; a sycophant.

adj. Of the quality of a pickthank; that is insincerely complimentary.

v. Pickthanking. To act like a pickthank; to act in such a way that is disingenuously flattering.

"His reputation for pickthanking was transparent, which made it difficult to be taken seriously when he had a genuine interest in someone."

e. From the old saying 'to pick a thank', meaning to try to earn favour.

PILOERECTION (pie-lo-ee-REK-shuhn)

n. When one has a strong emotional experience towards someone or something and experiences an involuntary reaction to a particular stimulation. For example, a feather being brushed against the skin on one's back. A physical reaction to cold, fear or excitement. Goosebumps.

"His gentle caress sent a sensuous shiver down her spine, inducing piloerection."

e. Pilo - of or relating to the hair, erection - the action of rearing.

PLURENNIAL (ploo-REN-ee-ell)

adj. Of a duration of several years; or occurring only every few years.

"Though their relationship had been plurennial, neither felt ready to get married."

e. Plūri (Latin) several, more, plural; the suffix *-ennial* denoting recurrence.

POLLICITATION (puh-liss-ee-TAY-shun)

n. An honourable pledge that has not yet been formally accepted. A promise.

"She kept her pollicitations of love, loyalty and fidelity to herself until he showed a genuine interest in her character and the consistency to win her over."

e. Pollicitārī (Latin) to promise.

PORNERASTIC (porn-uh-RASS-tick)

adj. Excessively inclined to frequent brothels, sex workers, or watch too much pornography. Lecherous; overly sex-driven.

"Her pornerastic tendencies started to wear off when she became obsessed with working out and refocusing her sexual energy into something more productive."

e. *Porno* πορνο - porn + erastís ἐραστής - lover (Greek).

POSTCONNUBIAL (post-keh-NYOO-bee-ul)

adj. Happening after the wedding. Post nuptials. After tying the knot.

"A type of postconnubial bliss is expected to last for roughly the first year of marriage, according to studies."

e. Post - that happens after + *connūbium* (Latin) marriage.

PREFULGENT (preh-FUHL-jent)

adj. Shining with a more beautiful radiance than others. Lustrous, incomparably radiant. Later also *profulgent*.

"In his eyes, she was the most prefulgent woman he had ever known and was convinced she was made of a large portion of stardust."

e. *Fulgēns* - lightning, *profulgentissimus* - brilliant (Latin).

PRIAPISM (PRY-a-piz-uhm)

n. An erect penis. In medicine, an abnormal and persistent erection of the penis, without sexual arousal. A phallic image, symbol, object or sculpture. A dick-pic.

"The ease at which many men think it appropriate or arousing to send women priapisms is truly astonishing."

e. *Priapismus* (Latin) persistent erection of the penis, *Priapus* - Greco-Roman god of fertility.

PRIAPIZE (PRY-a-pies)

v. To engage in sexual activity, have sexual relations, intercourse. To behave in a licentious, libidinous, or lustful manner. To have sex.

"*Studio 54 in New York was famous for its horny clientele priapizing in the basement and on the balcony*".

e. *Priapiser* (French) to have sex with a woman, Πριαπίζειν (Greek) to behave like Priapus, god of procreation and fertility.

PRIAPUS (PRY-a-pess)

n. A literary or physical representation of an erect penis. The Graeco-Roman god of fertility and procreation commonly represented as a small figure with a giant and erect member. An obvious erection.

"*The entrance to the night club had an eclectic array of sculptures, all with their priapus proudly on display.*"

e. *Priāpus* (Latin) - any object of phallic shape, a statue to ward off unwanted cretins in one's garden, Príapos Πρίαπος (Greek) - male god of procreation and fertility who is depicted as having a large and permanently erect penis.

PRIMIFLUOUS (prim-ee-FLOO-uss)

adj. That is the first to flow forward. That trickles first.

"*His attraction to her was a primifluous stream of desire that he hesitated to act upon until she gave a clear indication of reciprocating.*"

e. *Primifluus* (Latin) the first stream, that flows first.

PRIMIGRAVIDA (pree-mee-GRAV-ee-dah)

n. A woman experiencing pregnancy for the first time or who has only been pregnant once.

"*Did you know that the medical industry used to refer to all primigravidas over the age of thirty five as geriatric pregnancies?*"

e. *Prīmus* - main, principle, first, *gravidus* - pregnant, heavy with young (Latin).

PRIMIPARA (pry-MIP-ah-rah)

n. A woman who is birthing offspring for the first time or has only given birth once.

adj. *Primiparous.* Of giving birth for the first time.

"*Maternal mortality rates are not highest in primipara but rather in women over 40.*"

e. *Prīmipara* (Latin) that has given birth for the first time. (Sounds like 'primary' as in first).

PRIVIGN (PRIV-in)

n. An old term for step-son.

"*Because she had married a much older man, many mistook her privign for her husband.*"

e. *Prīvignus* (Latin) stepson, first born.

PROLIGEROUS (pro-LIJ-uh-russ)

adj. Inclined to bearing offspring. That inspires germination, growth.

n. *Proles.* Children, descendants, followers.

"*They were a proligerous couple with already five children and another on the way.*"

e. *Prōlēs* (Latin) *offspring* + *-gerous* - implying 'having'.

PROGENY (PROJ-uh-nee)

n. One's descendants, children, extended family. Also spiritual followers, members of your tribe or clan, disciples, successors.

"*The consequence of him fathering children to so many baby mamas was a numerous progeny.*"

e. *Progenie* (French) offspring; *prōgeniēs* (Latin) descendants.

PRURIENT (PROO-ree-uhnt)

adj. Characterised by overt curiosity in sexual matters. An inappropriate desire.

"After years of friendship it became apparent that their prurient banter was something they should share only amongst themselves as others quickly tired of it."
e. *Prurire* (Latin) an itching, a longing, being wanton.

PUDENDUM (pyoo-DEN-dum)
n. A posh word for the female external genitalia. The vulva. The pussy.
"It really takes some backwards belief systems to declare a woman's pudendum as a shameful thing. Are those people ashamed to be alive and of their mothers? How do they think they came into being?"
e. *Pudendum* literally meant "of which one should be ashamed"; *pudēre* to cause shame (Latin).

PUDIBUND (PYOO-duh-bund)
adj. Of a nature that is easily shocked or offended by matters relating to nudity or sexual intercourse. Easily embarrassed by immodesty and nakedness. Excessively concerned with 'moralistic' behaviour. Prudish.
"After working as an entertainer for several decades and birthing two children, she could easily forget that some people were pudibund when she had no problem stripping off in front of whoever."
e. *Pudibundusi* (Latin) easily ashamed, bashful, modest.

PUDICITY (pyoo-DISS-eh-tee)
n. When one has a sense of what brings shame upon themselves. Chastity, modesty, decency.
v. *Pudify*. To cause a person to be ashamed.
"With so many thirst traps on social media, accounts dedicated purely to the pursuit of gaining likes and followers seemingly at any cost, has for many blurred the lines of pudicity."
e. *Pudicité* (French) modesty, chastity, behaviour which shows a sense of shame; *pudīcitia* (Latin) sexual purity, chastity.

PUERPERAL (pyoo-ER-peh-rull)
adj. That occurs after giving birth; post-birth.

n. *Puerperium.* The time immediately following the birthing of a child; the time following delivery to when the uterus resumes its original size.

"She descended into a momentary puerperal madness because she was isolated and alone with a screaming baby and no family or friends to support her."

e. *Puerpera* (Latin) woman who has given birth; after childbirth.

PULCHRITUDE (POLL-kruh-tyood)

n. When a person is in possession of a beautiful quality or their entire being radiates with an *attirance* that you can't resist. Something or someone that you find stunning possesses pulchritude, attractiveness, beauty.

adj. *Pulchritudinous.* Possessing beauty. Of a beautiful nature or quality.

"The poor man was speechless after being taken aback by her pulchritude which hadn't gone unnoticed by the rest of those in attendance."

e. *Pulcritude* (French), *pulchritūdō* (Latin) - beauty, attractiveness.

PULCHROUS (POLL-kruhss)

adj. Beautiful, fair.

"He had a pulchrous face, all angles and intense deep set eyes that matched his mysterious and masculine personality."

e. *Pulchr/ Pulcer/ Pulcher* (Latin) - beautiful.

PUNALUA (poo-nah-LOO-ah)

n. A type of group marriage arrangement where the wife's sisters (clan A) and husband's brothers (clan B) are also considered married to one another.

"The punalua arrangement poses many problems around a person's autonomy just as arranged marriages do."

e. A direct borrowing, *punalua* (Hawaiian) the spouse of a sibling. (Interestingly when you put *punalua* into Google translate, it says that it means 'doubt').

PUTANISM (PYOO-tah-niz-um)

n. Harlotry, whoredom, prostitution.

"She openly admitted that her twenties was a phase of putanism and debauchery!"

e. *Putanisme* - prostitution, *une pute* - slut, whore (French).

PYRIFORM (PEER-ee-form)

adj. Shaped like a pear; pear-shaped.

"She had a gorgeous pyriform body, toned with small boobs combined with a set of hips that could kill."

e. *Pyriformis* - a deep pear-shaped muscle located in the area of the buttocks; *pirum* - pear (Latin).

PYROLAGNIA (pie-roh-LAG-nee-ah)

n. Sexual stimulation from watching fires. The state of being aroused by fire or things that are burning. Turned on by the flame.

"Nothing like an open fireplace in a cottage in the woods with rain falling outside to bring out the pyrolagnia in a pluviophile."

e. *Pyr* πυρ - fire, *lagnía* λαγνία - lust (Greek).

Q.

QUAEDAM (KWEE-dam)

n. A derogatory term for a 'loose' woman; an impudent or cocky woman who disrupts the peace. A woman who does not conform to normal societal expectations. Also a prostitute.

"*She longed for a quietly feminine, soft and peaceful woman, not the quaedams who lived for fast-paced clubbing life.*"

e. *Quaedam* - a certain woman; *quīdam* - something, an unknown person (Latin).

QUADRIGAMIST (kwuh-DRIG-ah-mist)

n. Someone who has married 4 times or who has four spouses at once.

"*There's a good reason quadrigamists are rare, that's a game for the super wealthy, the emotionally immature or the delusional.*"

e. *Quadrigamus* (Latin) married four times, the root *quattuor* - implying *four* such as in *quatre* (French), *cuatro* (Spanish), *quattro* (Italian). *Gamus* (Latin) game.

QUAINTRELLE (kwan-TREL)

n. A woman who expresses her passion for life through personal style, fashion and pastimes. A superbly-dressed woman.

"*An eye for a quietly eclectic yet elegant style, the quaintrelle woman seeks a well dressed mate to enjoy being seen with.*"

e. *Cointerelle* from *cointerel* (French) vain, assimilated with *quaint* - attractively unusual and *elle* - she, her, the female.

QUANDONG (KWON-dong)

n. Old Australian slang for a woman who maintains that she has high moral standards whilst simultaneously sleeping around a lot. Also of anyone who is a trickster, deceitful and imposing.

"She made an attempted claim of remaining chaste, but her reputation for being more of a quandong preceded her."

e. Guwandhaaŋ (Wiradjuri) named after a particular variety of fruit tree, perhaps for its bittersweet taste, with an edible kernel in the centre of the stone.

QUARION (KWOR-ee-on)

n. An archaic term for a candle, particularly in a large square shape. Also a *quarrier*.

"He had decorated the bathroom with quarions and rose petals, a perfect sensuous atmosphere for a loving soak with his man."

e. Of unknown origin but could be related to *quarré* now *carré* (French) square, from which *quarrier* could be implying something square-shaped.

QUATRIDUAL (KWHA-tree-dyoo-ul)

adj. Of the duration of four days.

"They met abroad for a passionate quatridual séjour, a four-day weekend of beach and bed-hopping."

e. *Quadrīduum* - a period of four days; *quattuor* - four; *diēs* - days (Latin).

QUEENITE (KWEE-night)

n. One who upholds a queen. A supporter or partisan of a specific queen. A queen worshipper. Also known as a *queenist*.

"Should not every husband think of his wife as a queen and himself a queenite, just as she thinks of him as her king and herself a kingite?"

e. Formed within English from *queen* - a female ruler or one who behaves as such, *-ite* - of the class of the first element.

QUERENCIA (Kuh-REN-see-ah)

n. A person's favourite place to occupy, their home ground, favourite haunt, homing instinct, a place of refuge.

"One of their greatest achievements was to have made a loving home together, a querencia for themselves and their children to nurture and evolve."

e. From the Spanish name for the place where a bull takes its stand in the bullfighting arena. *Querencia* has roots in the verb *querer* 'to desire, seek' so could be thought of as 'a place that one seeks'.

QUERIMONIOUS (kwair-ee-MOAN-ee-us)

adj. Prone to frequent protestations. Full of complaints. Making a habit of being whingy; whiny; lamentful; querulous.

n. *Querimony*. An expression of lament; a complaint.

"He had come to understand that when his wife was in a querimonious mood, it was usually linked to how overwhelmed she felt and therefore he would get about doing chores instead of getting into an argument."

e. *Quérimonie* (French); *querimōnia* (Latin) expression of grievance.

QUIDITATIVE (QWID-it-at-iv)

adj. Relating to the distinctive essence of someone or something. Quirky; eccentric; unique. Also *quidative*.

n. *Quiddity*. Something intangible, the unique essence of a person or thing. Eccentricity.

"How difficult it is to define chemistry with another person; is it not simply the quiditative nature of their being that inexplicably sets off sparks in your personal stratosphere?"

e. *Quidditatif* (French); *quidditativus* (Latin) in respect to the essence of something or someone.

QUIM (kwim)

n. An old slang term for a vagina, the female genitals, the vulva, the pussy. In later use it referred to sex with a woman or one considered a means for sexual gratification such as a whore.

"She arched her back in anticipation as her lover placed delicate kisses on her inner thighs before working up to her quim."

e. *Queemness* (Old English) pleasure, satisfaction.

QUIXOTIC (kwik-ZOT-ick)

adj. Displaying exaggerated actions of chivalry or over-the-top romanticism. Whimsical, capricious and naive demonstrations of affection. Enthusiastically and idealistically romantic.

n. A person who is foolishly impractical, known for unrealistic schemes.

"What a shame that quixotic displays of fondness have been largely associated with the love-bombing tactics of narcissists, leaving many suspicious of such displays of affection."

e. Attributed to the actions of the 17th century Spanish literary character Don Quixote, the story of a delusional knight that makes it his life mission to restore chivalry.

QUIXOTRY (KWIK-zoh-tree)

n. The act of pursuing a lover that is out of your league; an unrealistic, foolish or impractical courtship, goal or scheme. Also known as *quixotism*.

"Rather than display futile quixotry, is it not wiser to quietly go about becoming a desirable prospect oneself?"

e. An eponymous derivation of *Don Quixote*.

QUOB (kwob)

v. To throb, to quiver, to palpitate. Also *quab*.

"His sexual arousal only became apparent when he came closer for a hug, he could feel his member quabbing beneath his jeans."

e. *Quop* - to tremble, pulsate, writhe. *Quappen* (Low German) the sound made by fat slapping, *quabbelen* (Middle Dutch) to quiver, wobble.

QUODAMMODOTATIVE (quod-um-MOE-doe-tah-tiv)

adj. That operates or exists in a particular way.

n. A thing that exists in a certain manner.

"Their relationship was quodammodotative, something for them to understand and not for others."

e. *Quōdam modō* (Latin) in a special way.

QUONIAM (KWO-nee-am)

n. The female genitalia. The lady parts.

"Her bestie couldn't stop laughing after telling her that her new squeeze kept emphasizing she had the best quoniam he had ever seen!"

e. Directly taken from q*uoniam* (French and Latin).

QUOTANNAL (kwo-TAN-all)

adj. That happens annually, yearly. Later *quotennial*.

"Rather than have only a quotannal celebration of their nuptials, they decided to have a monthly outing on the date they tied the knot."

e. *Quotannīs* (Latin) every year.

QUOZ (kwoz)

n. A vaguely insulting expression to describe something or someone perceived as ridiculous, strange, absurd.

"When one is first falling in love do they not often behave like a bit of a *quoz!*"

e. A colloquial term of unknown origin, recorded as early as 1780.

R.

RAFFISH (RAFF-ish)

adj. Of a sleazy character; disreputable; vulgar. That has an unconventional behaviour or style.

"*Comments of sexual innuendo may be considered funny and cute from a specific person but more often come across as raffish.*"

e. *Raff* from *riff-raff* - implying of a lower callibre + *-ish* - of the quality of the first element.

RAGMATICAL (rag-MAT-ik-uhl)

adj. Out of control; wild; naughty.

"*His ragmatical behaviour was a turn on before she realised that he was more crazy than eccentric.*"

e. *Rag* - to tease or torment + - *matical* from *pragmatical* - energetic, active, methodical.

RAMAGIOUS (RAM-uh-juss)

adj. Of a nature that is wild, ferocious, frenzied, excited, unruly. Out of control.

"*She was consistently attending parties and being whisked away on dates which assisted in fueling her ramagious appetite for male consumption.*"

e. *Ramage* (French) untrained, untamed.

RAMFEEZLED (ram-FEE-zuld)

adj. To be rendered into a state of disorder. To be worn out, exhausted, tired, kaput, frazzled, muddled, confused, topsy-turvy.

"*Find yourself one who is stable and consistent with communication, that leaves no guesswork, rather than feeling ramfeezled by innumerable mixed messages.*"

e. Of uncertain origins but suggested as *ram-* (Scottish) a prefix that intensifies, *feeze* - a twisting or turning action such as when screwing.

RAMMISH (RAM-ish)

adj. Portraying characteristics of a ram. A powerful physique and sometimes aggressive behaviour. Lustful and horny, forceful, disagreeable but also pungent.

"Some women may steer clear of rammish men, all muscular and domineering, whilst others are turned on by their masculinity."

e. Formed within English *ram* - a male sheep, *-ish* - forming adjectives from nouns, of the quality of the first element.

RAMPASTURE (RAM-pass-cha)

n. A communal dormitory room in a lodging or boarding house for unmarried men. A bunkhouse for men.

"They gathered at the rampasture after a long day of work, where they shared stories, laughter and some their beds whilst settling in for the night."

e. A Canadian term formed within English *ram* - male sheep, *pasture* - land used for grazing animals, indicating an area for males to roam or rest.

RANTIPOLE (RANT-ip-ole)

v. To gallivant; to run a riot; to act wild (as a rantipole).

n. A rogue man or woman. A wild and raucous type. Also *rantipoler*.

adj. Disorderly; untameable; crazy; wild; eccentric.

"What others considered rantipoling or sexually deviant was just a regular Friday night for her."

e. A fanciful formation formed within English most likely from *rant* - to claim extravagantly + *poll* - the head particularly in reference to the state of the hair or its colour; a 'rant head'.

RAREESHOW (RAIR-ee-shoh)

n. A spectacle regarded as vulgar, lurid, garish, unusual or dazzling. An amazing, spectacular or cheap street show. A peep show.

"*Amsterdam is well known for its bike riding culture, canals, cannabis cafes and rareeshows.*"

e. Derived from *rare* - representing a pronunciation by non-native speakers, + *show*. Rareeshows were originally pictures or puppets exhibited in a box and performed on the street, implying a 'rarity box'. These peep shows were associated with the 17th century outlaws and desperadoes attributed to the Savoy precinct of London, known as 'Savoyards'.

REBARBATIVE (reh-BAR-but-iv)

adj. Extremely unattractive; repellent; irritating; repulsive.

"*Contrary to what he believed of himself, she found his sleazy compliments rebarbative.*"

e. *Rébarbatif* - off-putting, disagreeable; *rebarber* - to oppose (French).

RECADENCY (ruh-KAY-dun-see)

n. To fall back into an undesirable situation. A relapse.

"*Getting back together with a toxic ex-lover was a momentary recadency that took months to pull herself out of.*"

e. *Recadere* to fall back; *cadere* - to fall (Latin).

RECTOPATHIC (rek-toe-PATH-ick)

adj. Easily hurt emotionally. One who is "straight feeling", meaning for which every comment or action is directly connected to a strong emotion. Unable to control their emotional sensitivity.

"*It is important for the rectopathic personality to practice emotional resilience, perhaps best assisted by being supported with a loving and understanding foundation of communication.*"

e. A neologism said to be derivative of *rectus* (Latin) straight or right and *páthos* πάθος (Greek) suffering, passion or feeling.

RECTRIX (RECK-tricks)

n. A female leader or ruler. The head of an institution or governing body. A woman who commands attention. A boss lady. (Also the tail feather of a bird that controls direction during flight).

"She was the retrix of his world, the queen for his heart and fellow ruler of the kingdom they were building together."

e. *Rectrīx* - female ruler and controller, *regere* - to rule (Latin). Similar to *rectoress* - the female rector of a parish. The suffix -*trix* used to form feminines.

REDAMANCY (RED-ah-man-see)

n. To be fully loved in return by the one that you love. A mutual loving or to love again. A requited love. Also known sometimes as *redamation*.

"Many discussions arise around the question of redamancy, most interestingly around the possibility of being as equally loved in return, of unconditional mutual love."

e. *Redamāre* - to love in return, *amare* - to love (Latin), -*ancy* denotes a state, condition or quality.

REDOLENT (RED-eh-luhnt)

adj. Of a scent that is desirable. That smells good, sweet, pleasant.

"One way of picking a suitable partner is when one finds their natural body odour redolent, this determines a compatibility in pheromones."

e. *Redolent* (French) fragrant; *redolēre* (Latin) to give off a smell.

REFOCILLATE (ree-FOSS-uh-late)

v. To revive the senses; to energize; to invigorate; to comfort.

"Nothing quite like a romp in the hay to refocillate the soul."

e. *Refocillare* (Latin) to revive, to reanimate.

REMEANT (REEM-ee-uhnt)

adj. That is coming back; returning.

"It takes an exceptional amount of emotional work and maturity for a love to be remeant after infidelity, but the trust bond is forever damaged."
e. *Remeāre* (Latin) to go or come back; *remettre* (French) to put back.

RENIFLEUR (reh-niff-LER)
n. A person who derives a sense of sexual gratification from the scent of another's body. One who experiences pleasure from bodily smells. A 'sniffer'.

"She understood him to be a renifleur because he was very vocal about how good she smelt every time they saw each other."
e. *Renifleur* - one who is in the habit of sniffing, *renifler* - to sniff (French).

RESARCIATE (rez-ARS-ee-ate)
v. To attempt to mend; to compensate for; to make amends.

"After 30 years together, sometimes it felt almost impossible to resarciate the lack of passion in their relationship."
e. *Resarcīre* (Latin) to make amends. (Sounds like resuscitate).

RESIPISCENT (ress-ee-PISS-uhnt)
adj. To be restored to sanity. To recover a soundness of mind. To learn from one's experiences. To acknowledge one's misgivings. To finally come to one's senses. To see clearly once more.

"He was unavoidably resipiscent when he realised the error of assuming she reciprocated his feelings when he saw her happily dining with her husband."
e. *Resipīscere* (Latin) to regain consciousness, to see reason, reciprocate, *sapere* (Italian) to be wise.

RETINENCY (RET-uh-nen-see)
n. To continue to be under the power or possession of another. To be held in the service of another. To have the ability to retain.

"The way she resisted his charms and offers of exciting adventures despite being single and jobless, demonstrated a strength of character and highlighted the fact she was no longer under his retinency."

e. *Retinentia* - capacity to retain, *re* - again, against, anew, *teneō* - hold, have, grasp (Latin).

RETROMORPHOSIS (ret-roh-MORF-uh-siss)

n. A change for the worse.

"Gone are the days of romanticising marriage, many people would consider coupling up to be a retromorphosis; the challenges of maintaining a long term relationship often outweigh the chances of getting together with someone you can actually last the distance with!"

e. *Retrō* - backwards + *morphosis* - the act of forming (Latin).

RETROUVAILLES (re-troo-VAI)

n. A happy reunion after a long separation. The happiness of rediscovering someone after a long period of absence. A concept applied to the reconnection of long-distance lovers. Separated people re-finding each other. The joy of meeting again.

"After years apart, their joyful retrouvailles was filled with laughter, tears and shared memories."

e. *Retrouvailles* - reunion, *retrouver* - to find again (French).

REVIRESCENT (ree-vee-RESS-unt)

adj. The ability to come alive again; to grow new or strong again; to flourish once more.

"They had been a couple for a fleeting few months when they were in their twenties but seeing each other again after so many years proved their attraction to be revirescent."

e. *Revirēscere* (Latin) to become green again, to return.

RIBALD (RIB-old)

n. One who obscenely refers to sexual matters in a manner that is impermissible in polite society. One who inappropriately connotes everything to sex. A villainous and vulgar foul 'mouth'. Also, a promiscuous woman lacking in supposed morals.

adj. *Ribald* or *ribaldous*. Being vulgar, wicked, lewd or blasphemous in description, language or behaviour.

"*It was presumed because they worked in the pornography industry that they were all ribaldous but many banned vulgar talk on set and in the office.*"

e. *Ribaud* - wretch, rogue, rascal, a debauched person, *riber* - to succumb to pleasures (French).

RIDENT (RIGH-dunt)

adj. Of a nature that is radiantly cheerful. Beaming with happiness. Smiling brilliantly. A "happy chappy".

"*It's always easy to tell when somebody has "got some" the night before because they wake up extremely rident.*"

e. *Rīdēre* (Latin) to laugh.

RIDIBUND (RID-ee-bund)

adj. Prone to laughter or smiling broadly. Characterised by liveliness. One that is happy and cheerful.

"*It's an endearing and attractive quality when someone is ridibund, I'd rather be around someone who chooses happiness over self pity.*"

e. *Rīdibundus* (Latin) in a state of laughter.

RIGIDULOUS (ree-JID-yoo-luss)

adj. Having a degree of rigidity. Partially hard. Somewhat stiff.

"*Too many drinks causes most men to be rigidulous when it comes to bedroom antics.*"

e. *Rigidulus* from *rigidus* - rigid + *-ulus* implying diminutive of the first element (Latin).

RILKEAN HEART (RIL-kee-uhn-hart)

p. The lingering pain of a lost love. A state of reflection on the permanence of heartbreak. A heart full of sorrow.

"They say it takes half the amount of time you are with a person to properly get over them which explained why he was still nursing a Rilkean heart many years after becoming a widow."

e. An eponymous neologism of Austrian writer and poet Rainer Maria Rilke, known for exploring mysticism and life's suffering. Primarily a song by Scottish rock band *The Cocteau Twins* who were said to have written it as an ode to Jeff Buckley, a lover of Rilke's work.

ROBLET (ROB-let)

v. To lead someone astray. To be misleading. To hoodwink, deceive, fool.

"The notorious strippers had robletted the men of Wall street with their bodies and beauty, conning them into parting with thousands whilst intoxicated."

e. From a *roblet* - a goblin that leads people astray in the dark derived from *Robin Goodfellow*, the name of a sprite believed to haunt the countryside according to Elizabethan folklore.

ROBORANT (ROB-uh-runt)

adj. That which is restorative of one's strength. Invigorating.

n. A tonic that strengthens. An invigorating medicine.

"The effect of a love that is honest, compassionate, mature and kind is truly roborant on one's confidence and self-esteem."

e. *Roborantia* (Latin) strengthening medicines; strength.

ROUÉ (ROO-aye)

n. A man who is seduced from virtue who conducts himself without morality or principles. One who has given up to sensual pleasures and demonstrates a level of depravity. A lost or loose man. A playboy.

"Morally bankrupt is the man without discipline, empathy or emotional maturity, a roué of the modern era who succumbs to self-infatuation and overly frequent sexual gratification."

e. Roué originally 'a person who has been broken on the wheel', *rouer* - to be broken on the wheel, *roue* - wheel (French).

RUBEFACIENT (roo-buh-FAY-shunt)
adj. That causes a redness of the skin. Also *rubificative*.
n. *Rubefaction*. A reddening.
v. *Rubify*. To make red; to redden.
"Just a slight touch of his hand or the little curl in his lip when he looked at her had a rubefacient effect on her cheeks, something that made her all the more intriguing to him."
e. *Rubifier* (French) to redden. Chiefly a medicinal term in reference to plants and remedies with this property.

RUBESCENT (roo-BESS-ent)
adj. That which is reddish or has a tendency to redden. Prone to blushing.
"There is simply nothing more embarrassing than being rubescent in the face of a person one dislikes immensely."
e. *Rubēscēns* (Latin) inclining to red.

RUBSTER (RUB-stah)
n. A woman who engages in sexual contact with another woman. A lesbian.
"Being givers and receivers, rubsters were best placed to inform heterosexual men of how exactly to perform on the clitoris for their female partners' enjoyment."
e. Formed within English from *rub* - to apply friction to something + *-ster* (Old English) was used to form feminine nouns.

RUNCIBLE WOMAN (RUN-si-bull-WOO-man)
p. A slang term for a woman shaped like a spoon. A woman with a pear shaped physique, wider at the hips, thin in the waist and with a small chest.
"Jennifer Lopez is a super sexy runcible woman."
e. A nonsense word used in the writings of English artist Edward Lear of which derived 'runcible cat', 'runcible hat', and 'runcible spoon' the name of a particular spoon with three prongs and a knife's edge.

S.

SAPROSTOMOUS (SAP-russ-tom-us)
adj. Having a foul smelling breath.
"There really is not much of a greater turn-off than being saprostomous."
e. Sapros σαπρος - putrid + stomos στομος - mouth (Greek).

SARDANAPALIAN (sar-dah-nah-PAY-lee-an)
adj. Typically a man who is sensually effeminate, sexually luxurious or self indulgent, not in a traditionally masculine manner.
"His lavish lifestyle and obsession with clothing and beauty regimes could only be described as Sardanapalian."
e. Attributed to Sardanpalus Σαρδανάπᾰλος the name given by Greek historians to the last king of Nineveh/ Assyria who emulated women in dress, voice, and mannerisms, passing his days spinning and making clothing.

SARMASSATION (SAR-mass-ay-shun)
n. An erotic kneading, squeezing and fondling of female body parts. A medical term that refers to the erotic touching of female organs and tissue. A sexy massage as part of foreplay.
"Clever is the one who understands that emotional foreplay is the perfect prerequisite to sarmassation, stimulate their mind to get in touch with their body."
e. Sarx - flesh, massō μάσσω - to knead (Greek), masser - to massage (French).

SARMASSOPHOBE (sar-MASS-oh-fobe)
n. One who dislikes being fondled or touched, or who has a fear of romantic relationships. A fear of dating.

"Who wouldn't become a sarmassophobe after 10 years of failed dating and sexual horror stories?"

e. *Sarx* σαρξ - flesh, *massō* μάσσω - to knead, *phobos* φόβος - fear (Greek).

SATYRIASIST (sat-uh-RYE-uh-sist)

n. A man with an excessive appetite and eagerness for sex. Also a man who is obsessed with having an erection or experiences prolonged and painful erections. A horny devil.

"*One wonders whether satyriasists and nymphomaniacs are obsessed with sexual gratification because of a need to feel desired that stems from unresolved trauma of being unloved or unwanted.*"

e. *Satyriasis* (Latin) permanent erection of the penis, a form of leprosy or elephantiasis, *satyríasi* σατυρίασις (Greek) - swelling of the glands.

SATYRISM (SAT-uh-riz-uhm)

n. Excessive or prolonged sexual cravings in males. Immoderate or abnormal sexual desire in men. (Today known as *satyriasis*).

"*He displayed a concerning level of satyrism, pursuing sexual encounters at every opportunity.*"

e. *Satyriasis* (Latin) permanent erection of the penis, *satyríasi* σατυρίασις (Greek).

SAUDADE (sa-oh-DAH-jee)

n. A profound longing and nostalgia for something or someone beloved. A persistent desire for something that most likely does not or cannot exist. A wistful replaying of memories that creates a mysterious melancholy. A haunting feeling of lost love.

"*In the twilight's embrace, each wave crashes gently against the shore carrying a whisper of saudade, a memory that lingers like a shadow on my heart.*"

e. A Portuguese term derivative of *solitātem* (Latin) solitude.

SAWDER (SOR-dah)
v. To 'butter-up'; to flatter.
n. Flattery; excessive complimenting.
"In a room full of sensual and sexy people, there was a lot of sawdering going on as a precursor to hooking up for the evening."
e. From *soft sawder*; soft solder - ingratiating behaviour.

SCHWÄRMEREI (SHVAIR-meh-rye)
n. An erotic fantasy or attraction to someone; a crush. Fanatical zeal or religious dedication to a person or cause. Wild devotion; sentimental enthusiasm.
"It was illogical and irrational but she couldn't let go of her schwärmerei attachment to this unattainable and taboo man."
e. *Schwärmerei* (German) crush.

SCOPOPHILIA (skop-oh-FIL-ee-ah)
n. Intense desire attained from voyeurism. Arousal from viewing sexually stimulating scenes. A wanting of viewing fornication without necessarily participating.
n. *Scopophiliac.* One who is addicted to pornography or watching sex.
"You'll find those inclined to scopohilia at the peep shows in the red light district of Amsterdam."
e. *Skopía* σκοπία - observation, scope, *filía* φιλία - lover of, friendship (Greek).

SCORTATION (SKOR-tay-shuhn)
n. The consensual act of sexual intercourse between an unmarried man and woman. Engaging in sexual acts for money. Fornication. 'Getting it on.'
"A network of scortation had been operating in high class hotels for decades, their campaign was aimed at less discrimination against sex workers and a reduction in the shame attached to such a profession."
e. *Scortārī* (Latin) to associate with sexually promiscuous women.

SCORTATOR (SKOR-tay-tah)

n. One who is of the inclination to engage in sexual relations with courtesans. A person who frequently visits prostitutes. A hunter of harlots. A whoremonger.

"As his wealth grew, so did his addiction to no-strings-attached sex and the thrill of bedding numerous women, he was becoming an insatiable scortator."

e. *Scortum* (Latin) a sexually promiscuous woman, a prostitute.

SEJUGATE (SAID-joo-gate)

v. To remove from one another; to pull apart; to separate.

"A job abroad was the reason they had to sejugate."

e. *Sējugāre* - to dis-yoke; *jugāre* to yoke, join (Latin).

SEMOVEDLY (suh-MOO-vud-lee)

adv. Alone; separately.

"They travelled semovedly for the remainder of their trip having discovered their incompatibility after spending weeks living in each other's pockets."

e. *Sēmovēre* (Latin) to separate, move.

SEMPITERNAL (sem-pee-TER-nul)

adj. To be everlasting, perpetual, constant, eternal, enduring. That lasts forever.

"What a blessing it is to achieve 50 years of marriage, the closest one might get to a sempiternal love."

e. *Sempiternel* (French), *sempiternus* (Latin) eternal.

SENSUALIST (SEN-shoo-ah-list)

n. One who revels in sensual luxuriousness, dedicated to physical pleasure. A person solely interested in sensual or material things. Who enjoys everything that provides gratification of the senses. 'A pleasure puss.'

"She was most aroused when enjoying the fineries of life: soft cashmere, delicious food, massages and time in the hot tub, a true sensualist."

e. *Sensualiste* from *sensuel* (French) physically enjoyable or pleasurable.

SEPTIMANAL (sep-TIM-an-uhl)

adj. That occurs weekly; every 7 days. Also *septimane*.

"Seeing as their hookups were septimanal already, they decided to move in together to reduce costs."

e. *Septimānus* - falling on the seventh day; *septi* - seven (Latin).

SERAGLIO (seh-RAH-lee-oh)

n. The part of a palatial home where only women are allowed; a place reserved for wives or concubines; a harem.

"The Turkish prince was willing to exchange his entire seraglio for the daughter of the Viking jarl, never had he seen such an unusually exotic creature."

e. *Serraglio* (Italian) a menagerie; *serāre* (Latin) to lock up.

SERAPHIC (seh-RAFF-ick)

adj. That embodies the sublime, heavenly, angelic, blissful, serene.

"Their seraphic encounter now haunted her dreams, she continuously questioned whether their chance meeting was fated."

e. *Seraphim/n* (Latin); *serafím* σεραφίμ (Greek) the name of a flying, winged biblical creature.

SETIGEROUS (seh-TIJ-uh-russ)

adj. In possession of a hairy back or appendage; bristly, hairy.

"The setigerous man could empathise with women's societal pressure to remove all body hair, as he was familiar with getting a monthly back wax and understood the pain of it."

e. *Saetiger* (Latin) bristle-bearing, more mature.

SHUNAMITISM (shoo-NAM-it-iz-um)

n. The practice of an old man sleeping next to a young virginal woman, without sexual relations, in the hopes of becoming more youthful.

"While the young women sought out older men for financial gain and stability, for the old men it was a case of Shunamitism, an attempt at retaining their youth."

e. *Shūnammīth* (Hebrew). Based on the biblical story of King David and Abishag (known as a Shunammite), a native young woman of the town of *Shūnēm* north of Mt. Gilboa in ancient Palestine, who the king's servants sought out when he was old and could not stay warm. The belief was that by laying next to him, her heat and moisture would transfer to the old man and rejuvenate him. This practice was prescribed amongst scientific physicians of the 17th and 18th century.

SILLAGE (see-YASH)

n. The added depth and allure of a scent that makes it memorable. A lingering waft of fragrance left behind from a perfume. An unforgettable smell.

"Decades later he randomly reached out to her to say he still remembered her sillage from a secret rendezvous they once shared."

e. *Sillage* (French) wake, trail of something.

SIRENIZE (SIGH-run-eyes)

v. To enchant one into or out of a certain state. To use allure to persuade. To bewitch or to delight.

"It was easy to see how she intentionally or unintentionally would sirenize any man that came across her path, she was a goddess of a woman with long locks and green eyes, but also of a charming personality."

e. *Seirín* Σειρήν (Greek); *sīrēna* (Latin) - a mythical creature which in classical mythology is depicted as luring men to destruction.

SISYPHEAN (siss-uh-FEE-un)

adj. That which is a futile endeavour; endless, pointless, ineffective, laborious.

"His sisyphean attempts to win her over finally wore him out and he gave up on trying to gain her affections."

e. *Sisypheius* (Latin) relating *Sisyphus* who in Greek mythology was condemned by Hades to endlessly roll a boulder up a hill, only for it to roll back again and again.

SODOMITE (SOD-oh-might)

n. A person whose sex life is considered immoral or shameful. Chiefly used as a derogatory term for one who performs a sexual act that is stigmatized by particular cultural standards, historically anal and oral sex (intended to be offensive towards homosexuals). One who enjoys anal penetration. Another word for a gay man.

n. *Sodomitess* (*f*). A woman who participates in sexual acts considered immoral by specific groups of society. Another word for a lesbian.

adj. *Sodomitical*. Characterised by immoral or unnatural sexual activity.

"*Sexual acts considered 'immoral' today should hardly include gay and lesbian lovers, perhaps the definitions of sodomites and sodomitesses needs to be addressed. Rather they be simply synonyms for homosexuals rather than be pejorative terms.*"

e. *Sodomite* (French) person who performs a sexual act classed as sodomy. *Sodomitus* (Latin) inhabitant of the city of Sodom, which in the Abrahamic religions was destroyed along with the city of Gomorrah because of their wickedness relating to sexual acts and violence.

SOLECISM (SOL-uh-siz-um)

n. A violation of behaving or speaking correctly and appropriately. That which is combined in a way that is considered erroneous. A breach of good manners. Incorrect speech, grammatical errors.

"*As a sapiosexual, she couldn't get past the woman's constant solecisms, this unfortunately was a big red flag for her when it came to relationships.*"

e. *Solœcismus* (Latin), *sóloikos* σόλοικος (Greek) speaking incorrectly, ungrammatical.

SOOTHFAST (SOOTH-fast)

adj. Of a truthful nature. Honest; faithful; reliable; genuine.

"His soothfast confessions of love had everyone in tears at their wedding reception."

e. *Sóþfæst* (Old English) from *sooth sóð* - truth + *fast* (Germanic) - fixed in place.

SOUTENEUR (SOOT-uh-ner)

n. A man who makes a living from the earnings of a woman/women he keeps as a prostitute. A pimp.

"She tried to convince her friends that they were madly in love and he was the man of her dreams, but everyone knew he was her souteneur."

e. *Souteneur* - protector from *soutenir* - to sustain (French).

SPHALLOLALIA (sfal-oh-LAY-lee-uh)

n. Provocative talk that does not lead to amorous action. Flirtatious chatter that leads nowhere. A romantic situation where the desire is unequal between the two concerned parties. Flirty banter. An element of a flirtationship.

"They all enjoyed a bit of sphallolalia on vacation, harmless flirting with the other patrons of the hotel."

e. *Sfállo* σφάλλω - stumble, *laliá* λαλιά - talk, speech (Greek).

SPONSALIA (spon-SAY-lee-ah)

n. A formal promise or contract of one person intended to marry another. A betrothal, an engagement. A joining of two in matrimony. A spiritual acceptance of one another in ceremonial approval. The formal espousal of husband and wife. A betrothal, engagement or marriage. 'Getting hitched'.

adj. *Sponsal.* Relating to marriage, spouse or wedding. Wedded, married, spousal.

"It was with great satisfaction that they announced their sponsalia to both their families after 10 years of dating."

e. *Sponsālis* - spouse, belonging to betrothing; *spondēre* - to promise solemnly (Latin).

SPOUSEBREACH (SPOWSE-breech)

n. An act of infidelity. An adulterous misdemeanor. Cheating on one's partner. Or the one who commits a sexual act outside the agreements of their relationship, a cheat. One who gains the affections of a married person and is blamed for the dissolution of their marriage, a homewrecker.

"*A spousebreach was a clear line of no return for both of them, no second chances, no excuses. Respect, communication and loyalty were the biggest priority in their relationship.*"

e. *Spouse + breach* from *spouse-break, spousebriche; eaubruche* from **ǽw** - marriage + *bryce* - a breaking (Old English).

SPREZZATURA (spret-za-TOUR-ah)

n. When one makes things appear easy or effortless. An air of nonchalance. An ease of action or being. A studied carelessness.

"*He was a master of spezzatura, a confident and slightly cocky man that drove her to be completely infatuated.*"

e. *Sprezzatura* (Italian), first appearing in Renaissance author Baldassare Castiglione's 1528 *The Book of the Courtier*, describing a demeanour that makes one appear to do everything without effort or any thought to it.

STASIVALENCE (STA-zee-va-luhns)

n. To be in a state that only allows sexual intercourse whilst standing.

"*After bruising both his knees which disallowed the bending of them, bedroom activities were limited to stasivalence.*"

e. *Stasis* στάσις (Greek) - equilibrium, stability, *valentia* (Latin) - strength, capacity. Seemingly only attested to in Mrs Byrne's *Dictionary of Obscure Words*.

STEATOPYGIA (steeya-toh-PI-jee-ah)

n. An accumulation of fat cells on the buttocks, characteristic of particular peoples. Having a fat arse.

"*He wasn't a fan of steatopygia like his housemates were, but rather liked the waiflike supermodel types.*"

e. *Stéar* στέαρ - fat, tallow, *pȳgí* πῡγή - buttocks, rump (Greek).

STEGMONTH (STEG-month)
n. Referring to the period of time a woman takes to recuperate after birthing a child, whereby during that time the father of the child or husband pleads a sort of indulgence in gallantry. Meaning a time in which a partner tries to figure out what the hell to do while she recovers from giving birth. Medical practitioners used to claim that this period from parturition to 'perfect recovery' usually took one month.

"Her partner was an absolute gem during her stegmonth, doing the chores and making wholesome meals so that she could fully focus on recuperating and tending to the baby."

e. A *steg* is another term for a *gander* - male goose; a reference to the male goose wandering around aimlessly while the female sits on the nest.

STOCIOUS (STOH-shuss)
adj. Inebriated, intoxicated, drunk. Also *stotious*.

"Funny are the actions of those who are stocious in love, flitting about as though the world is a fair ground."

e. Anglo-Irish slang of unknown origin that appeared in literature from the 1930s.

STOLIDITY (stuh-LID-uh-tee)
n. Expressing little or no sensibility. An incapacity for emotion. Emotionless, impassiveness, restrained, reserved.

"She reacted to him breaking up with her with remarkable stolidity until she reached home, where she broke down in tears."

e. *Stolidus* (Latin) dull, stupid. Originally used to describe people who were considered stupid because of a lack of showing emotion, however after the 1800s it was not connoted to foolishness.

STUPRATE (styoo-PRATE)

v. To sexually violate or degrade a person. To defile their chastity. To rape.

n. *Stupre*. An act of sexual violation, particularly towards virgins. A rape.

"Did you know that a husband's right to stuprate his wife was only abolished in the UK in 1991? Prior to that time, the law upheld that it was not possible that a man could rape his wife as she was in permanent consent by way of their contract of marriage."

e. *Stuprāre* (Latin) to have illicit sex, to defile, to rape.

SUAVIATE (SWAAH-vee-ate)

v. To brush one's lips against another's. To plant a peck on another person. To kiss. To lock lips. To smooch.

n. Amorous smooching. Lovingly locking lips. Kissing.

"Rather than get any work done, they spent the afternoon suaviating on the sofa."

e. *Sāvium* - to kiss, *suāvis* - sweet (Latin).

SUBARRHATION (sub-eh-RAY-shun)

n. A solemn pledge given with the gift of a ring, traditionally from a man to a woman. The part of a wedding ceremony when a ring is exchanged. A type of betrothal, a vow of commitment.

"Modern day subarrhations are conducted with both parties giving a ring to one another as a symbol of their commitment to the longevity of their relationship."

e. *Subarrare* (Latin) to pledge.

SUBITANEOUS (sub-ee-TAY-nee-us)

adj. Created in haste. Suddenly, hastily, spontaneously.

adv. *Subito*. Quickly, immediately, rapidly.

"It was a mutual adoration for one another's creativity and mindset that led to their subitaneous coupling."

e. *Subitāneus* (Latin) suddenly; *subito* (Italian) quickly.

SUBRIDENT (suh-BRIDE-unt)

adj. That sports a smile from ear to ear. Wearing a smile. Grinning; smiling.

v. *Subride.* To smile

"It's a subrident joy that fills one with hope when one begins to fall in love."

e. *Subrīdēre* to smile; *sub* - under, close to + *rīdēre* - to laugh (Latin).

SUB ROSA (sub-ROE-zah)

adv. Conducted in secrecy. Privately done. In secret.

"Because they couldn't be together, he imagined her sub rosa; the gentle caress of her skin against his and a time where he could have her all to himself."

e. *Sub* - under + *rosā* - the flower (Latin); derivative of the phrase 'under the rose' seen in *onder de roose (Dutch)* and *under der rosen (German)*.

SUBSULTUS (sub-SOL-tuss)

n. A type of intermittent pulsation or twitching. A convulsive movement.

"She quivered in ecstasy as the subsultus from orgasm lingered for several minutes."

e. *Subsultus* pulsation; *subsilīre* jump up, spring up (Latin).

SUCCEDANEUM (suck-seh-DAY-nee-um)

n. Something or someone that acts as a substitute for another. A substitute.

adj. *Succedaneous* or *succedaneal.* In place of another.

"Her close gay pal acted as her succedaneum husband while they were on holiday in Spain."

e. *Succēdāneus* (Latin) killed in the place of another, a substitute.

SUCCUBUS (SUCK-yoo-buss)

n. A female demon that seduces and copulates with men whilst they are in a slumber. A she-devil that bonks you in your sleep.

"After years of little sex, he fantasised about his partner being a succubus, longed for her to jump his bones whilst he was sleeping.'

e. The female version of *incubus* - an evil spirit who seeks sexual intercourse with people while they are sleeping (particularly women), said to be the reason behind a heavy or groggy feeling from sleeping or nightmares (Christian demonology).

SUFFISANCE (sooff-ee-ZONSE)

n. A source of one's enjoyment or satisfaction. An abundance of contentment.

"What a gift to be in a relationship that is one's suffisance, a place of respite from the toils of the world."

e. *Suffisance* from *suffire* - to suffice (French); *sufficientia* (Latin) sufficiency.

SUMMOTION (sum-OH-shun)

n. Elimination, eradication, removal.

"They say it takes half the length of time you are with someone for the full summotion of your attachment to them to occur, but can one ever really remove the past?"

e. *Submovēre* (Latin) to remove.

SUNDER (SUN-dah)

v. To separate two people from one another. To part or become disconnected from a person or thing. The detachment of oneself from a specific emotional state. To break up.

adv. Asunder. Apart, separated.

"Though we are sundered in physical form, my heart and soul are with you until we see each other next."

e. *Asunder* (Old English) inherited from Germanic: *zonder* (Dutch) unusually, exceptionally, *sønder* (Danish) away, *suntar* (German) alone. Also *sanutar* (Sanskrit) apart.

SUPERFECUNDATION (soo-pah-feck-un-DAY-shun)

n. When two eggs are released in a menstrual cycle, fertilised by two separate acts of coitus, resulting in the conception of twins. (Making it possible for a woman to carry simultaneous babies from different sexual partners - sounds like 'super-fuck').

"Some suspected her of infidelity because superfecundation seemed to have occurred whereby one of her babies was brown and one white, but a paternity test revealed it was the fathers mixed race heritage that produced two different coloured offspring."

e. *Superfecundatio; super* - above, beyond + *fecundation* from *fēcundāre* - to fertilize (Latin).

SUPERFETATION (soo-per-fee-TAY-shun)

n. *Superfetation.* The presence of fetuses of different gestational ages within the womb. When a second egg is released and fertilised whilst already pregnant, resulting in a dual pregnancy.

v. *Superfetate.* To conceive again whilst already preggers.

adj. Also *Superfetant.* Overly fertile, capable of conceiving while pregnant.

"Superfetation, or a dual pregnancy is so rare that there are only 10 recorded instances of this happening in medical history."

e. *Superfētāre* (Latin) to conceive while pregnant. (Sounds like super-fetus).

SURGATION (ser-GAY-shun)

n. The rising of the instrument of copulation in a male. Erection of the penis.

"After spending the afternoon together, their chemistry was palpable and she could feel his surgation beneath his jeans when they hugged goodbye."

e. *Surgĕre* (Latin) to rise.

SWIVE (SWIGHV)

v. To enjoy conjugal intimacy with a female. To have sex with a woman. To bonk a chick.

"His favourite passtime was swiving into the early hours and then enjoying a late breakfast."

e. *Swifan* (Old English) to move; *schweiben* (Germanic) to sway; *svif* (Norse) to turn.

SYBARITE (SIB-ah-right)

n. A person devoted to pleasure and luxury. A sensualist.

adj. Sybaritic. Of a nature that is dedicated to luxuriating in sensuous pleasures.

"Likely to take a two hour long bath followed by a massage, the perfect date for a sybarite is a delicious meal followed by gifts and romping in freshly washed silk sheets."

e. *Sybarīticus* (Latin), *Syvarītikós* Συβαρῑτικός (Greek). An eponym for a citizen of the Ancient Greek city of Sybaris, traditionally noted for its luxuriousness and opulence.

SYMPHILISM (SIM-fuh-liz-um)

n. The state of being in a mutually beneficial situation. A symbiotic relationship. Living together for mutual benefit. Also *symphily*.

"Though marriage begins as a perceived romantic quest of love, in reality it's supposed to be a symphilism whereby both parties have the benefit of sharing the labours and costs of life."

e. *Symphilie* (German); *symfileín* συμφιλεῖν (Greek) to love mutually, to reconcile.

SYNALLACTIC (sin-ah-LACK-tik)

adj. That has the capacity to reconcile. Reconciliatory.

"A synallactic lunch date provided a starting point from which they could discuss their disagreements and mend their connection."

e. *Synallaktikós* συναλλακτικός (Greek) to reconcile, bring into intercourse, transactional. (Sounds like 'lacking sin').

SYNGENESIS (sin-JEN-eh-siss)

n. The act of both the male and female genes combining to make one embryo that has elements of both parents. Sexual reproduction. The making of a life.

"The connection between sex and reproduction was understood far earlier than syngenesis, whereby a child is created by and carries genetic traits from both parents."

e. *Syn* συν - together, plus + *génesis* γένεσις - origin of development (Greek).

SYRENIAN (sigh-REE-nee-uhn)

adj. That which is seductive and alluring, characteristic of a siren. In possession of a captivating 'air'. A place that possesses many attractive women.

"To many, the city was known for its beautiful architecture, but many tourists visited for its syrenian women."

e. Formed within English from *siren* - a mythical creature said to lure men to their deaths + *-ian* - of or belonging to.

T.

TACENDA (tah-SEND-ah)
n. Matters that should not be spoken of. Things to be kept in silence.
adj. Tacent. Silent.
"*A type of tacenda descended upon the household after the ending of their romance when he suddenly ended his life.*"
e. *Tacēre (Latin) to be silent.*

TACTION (TAK-shun)
n. The action of coming into contact. To experience touch from another. Touching.
"*The subtle taction of his knee against her thigh was enough to make her lose her train of thought and stumble on her words.*"
e. *Tangĕre (Latin) to touch.*

TÂTTONEMENT (TAT-on-mon)
n. An action that is preceded with caution. An experimentation. A process of trial and error.
"*Is not every relationship a kind of tâtonnement, a process of trial and test before one finds a person with whom they can remain compatible?*"
e. *Tâtonner (French) to feel one's way, proceed cautiously, to grope.*

TEKNONYMY (tek-NON-uh-mee)
n. The practice of naming a parent from the child, like when your child begins school and every parent is known as that child's mum or dad. For example, in West Africa the father of a boy named *Montie* would be *Baban Montie* and the mother *Maman Montie*.
"*And so began the task of remembering new names at a new school, though for now they would have to settle for a type of teknonymy whereby each adult would be referred to as 'so-and-so's mum or dad'.*"

e. *Téknon* τέκνον - child + *ónoma* ὄνομα - name (Greek).

TELARIAN (Teh-LAIR-ee-an)
adj. That spins a web.
n. A creature that spins a web.
"His telarian tendency to lie only landed him in hot water when he called his girlfriend the name of another lover."
e. *Tela* - web, loom, warp; derivative of *texere* - to weave, construct (Latin).

TEMERATE (TEM-uh-rate)
v. To break a promise. To violate a vow. To back out of a bond.
n. *Temerity*. To act with foolhardiness. Recklessness; cockiness.
"She wasn't going to sit around while he temerated his commitment to her, so instead she served him with divorce papers."
e. *Temerāre* (Latin) to be afraid; to act rashly; to treat without respect.

TEMPORANEOUS (tem-poh-RAY-nee-uss)
adj. That which is short-lived; temporary.
"It was a temporaneous love affair, fuelled only by the excitement of not being able to have each other."
e. *Temporāneus* (Latin) opportune, temporary, timely.

TENEBROUS (TEN-uh-bruss)
adj. Consumed by or appearing to be full of darkness. Gloomy, melancholy.
"Her tenebrous demeanour was explained by the discovery of her partner having a year long affair."
e. *Ténébreux* (French), *tenebrōsus* (Latin).

TENTIGINOUS (ten-TIJ-eh-nuss)
adj. That induces sexual excitement. Provocative of desire. Lust-provoking. That 'turns you on'.

n. *Tentigo.* An erection, priapism.

"Hypnotised by the way she moved to the music, her dancing was having a tentiginous effect on him."

e. *Tentīgo* (Latin) lust, tenseness.

THEOSEXUAL (thee-oh-SEK-shoo-al)

n. A person who has an erotic feeling towards a spiritual entity, a goddess or god.

"She created a sort of theosexual fantasy in her head as a way to reach arousal while masturbating."

e. *Theós* θεός - god (Greek) + *sexual* - relating to sex.

THEROID (THEER-oid)

adj. To describe one who is of an animalistic, brutish and bestial character or nature. An idiotic brute of a person.

"The bar was filled with theroid idiots, drunkenly sleazing over anyone who walked in the door, so we promptly left."

e. *Thero* - from theropod, a class of dinosaur, and *oid* - having the form of the first element.

THRASONIC (thrah-SO-nik)

adj. Boastful; bragging. Also *Thrasonical*.

"When he realised that she was in the room next door, he greatly regretted his thrasonic accounts of imagined sexual conquests."

e. An eponymous derivation of *Thrasōn/Thrasos* who in Greek mythology personified boldness.

THRENODY (THREN-uh-dee)

n. A chanson of lamentation. A song of grief or sorrow. A song for the dead, what is gone.

"The threnody of a broken heart is one of the most powerful lamentations of the human condition."

e. *Thrinodía* θρηνῳδία - dirge, mourning, *thrínos* θρῆνος - lament (Greek).

TIGERISM (tie-gah-RIZ-um)

n. A vain and unnecessary display of confidence in order to attract attention. Ostentation. Swagger.

"The humorous displays of tigerism were abounding when the young women entered the hall full of twenty year old men."

e. Tiger - a powerful feline quadruped + -ism - expressing the action or conduct of a person with the quality of the first element.

TOKOPHOBIA (tok-oh-FOE-bee-yah)

n. An intense and irrational fear of childbirth.

"Working as a mid-wife only increased her sense of tokophobia and she vowed she would never give birth."

e. Tókos τόκος - the act of bringing forth, breeding (usually in a financial context but used more generally here) + phobos φοβος - fear (Greek).

TORSCHLUSSPANIK (TORSH-looss-pla-nik)

n. A sense of inner panic as middle age approaches that one finds oneself alone or in a hapless relationship whilst the urge to rediscover a sexual promiscuity is awakened. A sneaking suspicion that some opportunities may have passed. A longing to rediscover the passions and eagerness of youth. A fear of being 'left on the shelf'. A mid-life crisis.

"She was haunted by torschlusspanik even though she was happily married, a growing sense of regret seemed to be looming. She contemplated starting a new passion project to take her mind off things in the hopes that diverting the energy would fill the sense of longing."

e. Tórschlusspanik (German) final panic or "shut gate panic". Tórschluss - closing of the gate, pánik - panic.

TORTIOUS (TOR-shuss)

adj. The committing of a wrongful deed. Hurtful, illegal.

"If there is to be any reconciliation after infidelity, one first has to admit that their actions were tortious!"

e. Torcious (French) shameful; 'avoir tort' to be wrong.

TRABOCCANT (TRAB-eh-kunt)
adj. Overly abundant or dominant. Excessive.
"Their traboccant displays of sexiness came across as slimy and lacking class."
e. *Traboccare* (Italian) to overflow.

TRIBADISM (TRIB-ah-diz-um)
n. Sexual activity between two women. Lesbianism.
"Out of fear of judgement and not wanting to jump on any trends, she kept it to herself that she went through a period of tribadism when she was a teen."
e. *Tribade* (French) homosexual woman.

TRINOCTIAL (try-NOCK-shull)
adj. That has the duration of three nights.
"It was a trinoctial sex-fest whenever her boyfriend came to stay for a long weekend."
e. *Tría* τρία - three + *nýchta* νύχτα - night (Greek).

TROILISM (TROY-liz-um)
n. Sexual activities that simultaneously involve three people. A threesome.
"Troilism was appealing as a fantasy, but they soon discovered the reality was quite different."
e. *Trois* (French) three + *-ism* - expressing an action of the first element.

TUMESCENCE (TYOO-mess-unss)
n. Demonstrating a readiness for sexual activity by the swelling of the genitals. Swelling that occurs during sexual arousal.
adj. *Tumescent*. Visibly swollen. Also *tumid*.
e. *Tumēscĕre* (Latin) to swell.

U.

UBERMENSCH (OO-buh-mench)

n. A man in possession of superpowers. Another word for a superman.

"*A modern day übermensch is one who actively strives for better, who protects women and children and seeks to better himself.*"

e. Übermensch (German) superman.

UKIYO (OO-key-yoh)

n. The fleeting beauty of day to day life. A transient lifestyle of living in the moment and appreciating life's pleasures. Detached from life's burdens. 'The floating world'.

"*Oh, to live in a state of ukiyo when one is consumed with the initial infatuation of love.*"

e. 浮世 (Japanese) world. 憂き世 - 'sad world' originally referred to the Buddhist notion of life's transitory nature. During the Edo period 'transitory' came to mean 'to float', implying a joy of living, *ukiyo* describing the pleasure-seeking aspects of urban Edo period Japan.

ULOID (YOO-loid)

adj. Having the appearance of a cicatrix. To be scarlike.

n. A scar, a permanent mark on the skin.

"*Drawn to her natural beauty and fun loving nature, she made a deep impression on him, a uloid on his heart forever more.*"

e. Oulí ουλή (Greek) scar.

ULTION (UHL-tee-on)

n. An avengement. Retribution, revenge, retaliation.

"*He considered an ultion after he discovered his closest friend had stolen the affections of his girlfriend but soon realised the greatest revenge was to let him have her.*"

e. Ulciscī (Latin) to avenge.

ULTRONEOUSLY (ul-TROH-nee-uss-lee)

adv. To do voluntarily; spontaneously.

adj. *Ultroneous.* Of a voluntary will. Of one's own volition.

"*She led him to the bedroom ultroneously, it wasn't like anyone would have denied that gorgeous man-god!*"

e. *Ultrōneus* of *ultrō* - voluntarily (Latin).

UMBRAGIOUS (um-BRAY-juss)

adj. That which is jealous, shaded, suspicious, overshadowed or obscure. That makes shade, creates shadows. 'Shady'.

"*Susceptible to high passion in love and friendships, she was umbrageous of newcomers who borrowed attention away from her.*"

e. *Ombrageux* (French) shady, *umbra* (Latin) shadow.

UNCTUOUS (UNK-tyoo-wuhss)

adj. Offensively suave. One of a superficial or self-satisfied nature. Literally meaning slimy or greasy like an ointment.

"*There's a certain class of unctuous man that belonged to a generation of sleaze bag types, those ones who patted your behind and stroked your hair inappropriately.*"

e. *Unctuōsus, unctum* (Latin) ointment.

UNDIGHT (un-DIGHT)

v. To divest one's garments. To take one's clothes off. To remove adornments. To strip off.

adj. Without adornments or clothing.

"*He requested she slowly undight her clothing while he watched in awe as her naked form revealed itself.*"

e. *Un* - in this sense expressing removal + *dight* - to deal with, to appoint from *dictāre* (Latin) to dictate.

UNDINISM (UN-dee-niz-uhm)

n. The arousal experienced when watching someone pee or play with water. Association of water with erotic thoughts, now more commonly known as *urolagnia*. A peeing or water fetish. (Sounds like *undies*).

"The escort revealed in an interview that she was frequently asked to perform acts of undinism on the rich and powerful."

e. *Undine* from *Undina*, a female supernatural being, a nymph that inhabited water. From *A Book on Nymphs, Sylphs, Pygmies, and Salamanders, and on the Other Spirits* by Paracelsus, a 16th century Swiss theologian and philosopher.

UNFELLOWED (un-FELL-owed)

adj. One who has never been in a relationship. Having no companion, being alone. unmatched, peerless or uncoupled.

"It seems that many modern day populations believe it is better to be unfellowed than submit to meaningless relationships."

e. *Un* - denoting a negative or opposite, *fellowed* - joined in a pair, coupled.

UNIPARA (yoo-nee-PA-rah)

n. Of a woman who has only birthed one child.

"She was unipara because her birthing experience had been so risky that they weren't prepared to go through that again."

e. *Uni* - one + *parare* - to produce, prepare (Latin).

UNIVOCAL (yoo-nee-VOH-kul)

adj. Having only one possible meaning. Denoting a singular significance. Unequivocal; unmistakable.

"He made no attempt to hide his infatuation, his words and actions were univocal in demonstrating his desire for them to be together."

e. *Ūnivocus,* (Latin) having one meaning.

UNPREVARICATE (un-pruh-VAIR-ee-cut)

adj. That is not perverse. That does not deviate from its intended disposition. That doesn't go astray.

"She sought a mature, unprevaricate man who had his shit together and knew that he wanted to make space for a good woman in his life."

e. *Un* - indicating an opposite + *praevāricārī* (Latin) treacherous; "untreacherous".

UNSINEW (un-SIN-yoo)

v. To render more feeble than before. To take the strength away from. To disconnect; weaken.

"His love had the capacity to unsinew the walls of insecurity and past relationship trauma of his partner."

e. *Un* - indicating the reversal of a process + *sionwe* (Germanic) sinew, a strong cord that connects a muscle to a bone.

UNTIMEOUS (un-TIME-uss)

adj. That happens at the wrong or inappropriate time. Untimely; inopportune; unseasonable.

"Their intense chemistry and attraction was untimeous as they were both in relationships."

e. *Untíma* (Norse) unsuitable, improper, untimely.

URANISM (YOO-rah-niz-um)

n. Expressing sexual desire between two males. Male homosexuality. A *Uranian* being a gay man.

"A smart man he was, to move to an area where uranism was prevalent was to cut out half the competition for heterosexual men!"

e. *Ūrania* (Latin); *Oúranía* Οὐρανία (Greek) heavens. Initially *Uranian* referred to a celestial love between men associated with the goddess Urania before being adapted to mean male homosexuality by German theorist Karl Heinrich Ulrichs.

USANCE (YOO-zunts)

n. A repeating practice or use of something. A habit or custom.

"She was tired of love's usance on her weary heart and soul, wondering if she had the strength to go through another relationship."

e. *Usance* (French) custom; *usantia* (Latin) using.

USTULATION (uss-tyoo-LAY-shun)

n. A smouldering carnal desire. A sexual inclination. A burning need for sex. Literally something which is on fire, the act of burning.

"Their ustulation was evident in the way they touched each other constantly."
e. Ūstulāre (Latin) to set ablaze, burn.

UTINAM (YOO-tin-um)
n. A fervent hope for something. An earnest wish.
"His utinam was that she would realise they were meant to be together."
e. Utinam (Latin) I wish.

UVID (YOO-vid)
adj. That has the quality of being moist; wet.
"She was uvid at the thought of him sliding his hands between her thighs."
e. Ūvidus (Latin) damp.

UXORIAL (ux-OR-ee-uhl)
adj. Relating to a wife. Wifely.
"She had many qualities that he considered uxorial and could see in the future mother of his children."
e. Ūxōrius (Latin) wife + al - with a sense of the first element.

UXORIOUS (uck-ZOR-ee-uhss)
adj. When one is viewed as overly submissive towards their wife. Devotedly attached to one's missus. Excessive affection towards your woman. Immoderately doting on your wife.
"Only insecure macho men called him uxorious, he was getting the best sex of his life and a home full of love because he actually saw his wife's needs as a priority and not a burden."
e. Ūxōrius, ūxor (Latin) wife.

V.

VACATUR (vay-KAY-tah)
n. The declaration of something being invalid. An annulment.
"*In their sober state they came to their senses and realised their drunken spontaneous engagement required a vacatur.*"
e. *Vacāre* (Latin) to be vacant; made null and void.

VACIVE (VASS-iv)
adj. Devoid of substance. Empty.
n. Vacuity. A complete emptiness.
"*The resolve that comes with putting an end to months of torment and heartbreak leaves one with a vacive heart, no room for future loves but only space to fill with healing.*"
e. *Vacīvus* (Latin) empty.

VADELECT (VAD-uh-lekt)
n. A man who is in a disposition to serve. A male servant.
"*The men who came to see the dominatrix had a desire to be vadelects, to submit and to serve.*"
e. *Vadlectus* (Latin); *vaslet, varlet* (French) a man acting as a male attendant.

VAFROUS (VAFF-russ)
adj. Displaying keen insight or ability to apply knowledge or resources. Cunning; sly.
"*Her friends watched in disbelief as she got every man to bend to her will, exclaiming it was her experience as a barmaid and hearing the drunken confessions of men that made her so vafrous!*"
e. *Vafer* (Latin) industrious.

VAGARISH (VAY-guh-rish)

adj. A person who tends to have a wandering eye. Prone to wandering.

n. *Vagarian.* A whimsical or wandering person.

v. *Vagulate.* To wander vaguely.

"Even at his wedding, those who gave speeches made remarks about the groom's vagarish eye and how all he needed to do was to remain faithful."

e. *Vagary* - a devious journey; *vagārī* (Latin) to wander.

VAHINE (VAH-ee-nay)

n. A wife of Tahitian nationality. A woman from Tahiti.

"No matter what excuses he used to try to justify his actions, nobody sympathised with the way he brazenly cheated on his faithful wife with a vahine half his age."

e. *Vahine* (Tahitian) woman.

VAINGLORIOUSLY (vain-GLOR-ee-uss-lee)

adv. To do in a manner that is vain and boastful.

adj. *Vainglorious.* That which is boastful; vain; conceited; full of themselves.

n. *Vainglory.* Boastfulness; vanity; braggadocio; cockiness.

"The irony of those who vaingloriously declare their attraction to far younger mates whilst simultaneously evidencing their lack of emotional maturity is indicative of societal dysfunction and disillusion."

e. *Vāna glōria* (Latin) vain - that lacks substance or honesty + glory - praise and honour by many; *vaine gloire* (French).

VANILOQUENCE (va-NIL-oh-kwenss)

n. Chatter that is of a vain or empty nature. Boring or self serving chit chat. Idle talk. Foolish flabbergastering.

adj. *Vaniloquent.* To have the characteristic of boring or vain self talk.

"Though he had plenty of charisma which he used well to woo many, she felt his attempts to chat her up were vaniloquent."

e. *Vāniloquentia* (Latin) idle talk, vanity, *vanus* - idle, empty, vain - *loqui* - to speak.

VANITARIANISM (van-it-AIR-ee-ah-niz-um)

n. The pursuance of vain things; consumed with vanity.

"So consumed with self-love, righteousness and vanitarianism are the ones who miss the opportunity to connect with an authentic, unselfish type of love."

e. *Vanity* - the quality of being vain + *arian* - actioning the first element + *ism* - forming a noun of an action.

VARIETIST (va-RYE-ah-tist)

n. One who craves variety in life and particularly in sexual activities. Someone who practices unorthodox sex.

"Varietists claimed sexual liberation from engaging in plural sexual relations, kinks and role play but for her it felt more satisfying to focus on connecting deeply to one person."

e. *Variety* - the fact of being varied.

VAUNTINESS (VORN-tee-nuss)

n. Utterances that are of a boastful nature. Bragging; showiness; cockiness. Also *vauntage*.

adj. *Vaunty.* Vain, proud.

"Those who are dating out of their league seem to be susceptible to a special type of vauntiness; their super attractive partner gives them a skewed sense of their own attractiveness."

e. *Vaunt* - an arrogant or vainglorious utterance; *vanāre* (Latin) to lie; *avanter* (French) to advance which also sounds similar to *inventer* - to invent.

VECORDY (VECK-or-dee)

n. The state of being consumed with a folie of the mind; a type of madness; a foolishness.

"The vecordy of romantic infatuation has the power to consume the senses, occupy the mind with a constant longing, a distraction from everyday functioning."
e. Vēcordia from vēcors (Latin) foolish, senseless.

VEGETE (veh-JEET)
adj. Describing a person who is glowing with health and fitness. One who is full of life. Flourishing; healthy.
"She was most attracted to vegete types; those who cared for their bodies and minds who had a healthy glow about them."
e. Vegēre (Latin) to invigorate; energise; to make vigorous; to grow.

VELLEITY (vuh-LEE-uh-tee)
n. Desiring something through wistful thinking rather than activity towards seeking it. An effort deprived longing. An ambition without realization. A slight or faint desire. A mere wish or dream.
"Emotion versus action determines the difference between a lustful velleity and a partner who is truly emotionally mature and prepared to make a relationship work."
e. Velleitās, velle - to wish, will (Latin). Velléité (French), veleidad (Spanish) fickleness, velleità (Italian) ambition.

VENEROUS (VEN-eh-russ)
adj. Prone to lustfulness, sensual pursuits. Chasing sexual pleasure.
n. Venery. The pursuit of sexual gratification. The practice of sensual pleasure; sex. The hunting of game.
"It was mostly in their teens and twenties that they were consumed with venerous activities, by 30, they focused on career and mental growth."
e. Vener (Latin) from Venus - goddess of beauty and love.

VENUST (VEE-nust)
adj. Of a person that carries themselves with grace and elegance, that is attractive, handsome, beautiful, comely, or elegant. Of a Venus like quality.

n. *Venustity, venustness.* Beauty, beautifulness.

"Her striking features and graceful movements were considered venust by all who watched her on stage."

e. *Venustus* from *Venus* (Latin) a beautiful or attractive woman, the Ancient Roman goddess of love and beauty.

VENUSTATION (vee-nuss-TAY-shun)

n. The practice of making more beautiful. The act of becoming more handsome. A glow-up.

v. *Venustate.* To render beautiful, to charm.

"They say that if your ex goes through a venustation after your breakup, that it was you who was the problem."

e. *Venustāre* (Latin) to be charming.

VENUSTRAPHOBIA (vee-NUSS-tra-foh-bee-yah)

n. An anxious fear towards engaging with beautiful women. A fear of sexy women.

"His venustraphobia was the result of having been mocked and bullied by the hottest girl in high school."

e. *Venus* - goddess of love and beauty + *phobos* φόβος - fear (Greek).

VERECUND (VEH-ruh-kund)

adj. Having a strong sense of modesty. To be of a coy, bashful, demure or shy nature. To not show one's feelings easily.

"It was challenging to get to know him on a personal level because he was so verecund, he never revealed much about himself."

e. *Verēcundus* (Latin), *verērī* - to fear, show reverence, *-cundus* indicates an inclination towards or a capacity for.

VERIDICAL (vuh-RID-uh-kuhl)

adj. Relating to or representing the truth. Speaking truthfully. Being real, honest, veracious. Also *veridicous*.

"A *veridical* love, of a reliable and consistent nature was what she longed for in a romance."
e. *Vērum* - truth, *dīcĕre* - to speak (Latin). *La vérité* (French), *la verdad* (Spanish) - the truth.

VERILOQUENT (vuh-RIL-oh-kwent)
adj. To speak with honesty and sincerity. Speaking in a truthful manner.
"The way he recounted the story of how he won their mum's love in such a *veriloquent* manner, meant the children grew up with a sense of pride and belief in loving someone fully and honestly."
e. A neologism suggested in the *Collins Dictionary* (2013) derived from *vērum* - truth and *loquens* - speaking (Latin).

VERNALAGNIA (ver-nah-LAG-nee-ah)
n. A romantic and lustful feeling one experiences during the time of year where flowers abound, the sun is warm and shade abundant. A libidinous sensation that occurs only during the Spring time. "Spring fever."
"The park was full of teenagers and couples overcome with *vernalagnia* romping amongst the trees and bushes."
e. *Vernus* (Latin) Spring, *lagneía* λαγνεία (Greek) lust.

VERTIGINOUS (ver-TIJ-uh-nuhs)
adj. That causes one to feel giddy or faint. Overcome with a feeling of dizziness. Unsettled of mind, unstable or inconsistent.
"That signature perfume and her exotic scent had a *vertiginous* effect on all who came near to her."
e. *Vertīginōsus* -one experiencing giddiness, *vertīgin* -vertigo (Latin).

VESPERTINE (VESS-puh-TEEN)
adj. That occurs as the sky turns to darker shades of indigo. That takes place, comes or appears only in the evening.
n. One who is active or only visible in the evening.

"*Of a vespertine nature, he came alive in the evenings as though a flick was switched and suddenly the city became a playground for fraternising.*"
e. *Vespertīnus* (Latin) the evening.

VIBRATIUNCLE (vigh-bray-shee-UNK-ull)
adj. Capable of minimal vibration.
"*Her vibrator ranged from perfectly vibratiuncle settings to more intense pulsations.*"
e. *Vibratiuncula* from *vibrātio* (Latin) vibration.

VIDUAGE (VID-yoo-ij)
n. The state of being a widow; widowhood; a collective of widows. Also *viduity*.
adj. *Viduifical*. That renders one a widow. Widow-making.
"*The viduage of such young women was the consequence of war.*"
e. *Viduitās* (Latin) widows; *viduite* (French) widow.

VINCTURE (VINK-cha)
n. Something that binds or is binding; a tying together.
"*Their shared experiences of travel, heartbreak, triumph and family was the vincture of their relationship.*"
e. *Vincīre* (Latin) to bind; to win.

VINDICTIVOLENCE (vin-dik-TIV-uh-luhnss)
n. A desire to take revenge; vengefulness. Vengeance.
"*It wasn't the act of cheating itself that caused her vindictivolence, it was his lack of accountability, a complete disregard for her as a person that she wanted revenge for.*"
e. *Vindicta* (Latin) vengeance + -ence - of a quality of the first element.

VIPARIOUS (vuh-PAIR-ee-us)
adj. That is in possession of a noticeable "joie de vivre". Has a tenacity for life, is life-renewing, vivacious, lively, animated.

"Ever the charismatic man, his viparious nature was a magnet for all those who came into contact with him."
e. A variant or alteration of "vivacious" (apparently a mistake in print).

VIRAGINITY (vee-rah-JEE-nah-tee)
n. Characteristics, behaviour or appearance in a woman that are considered stereotypically masculine. Of a woman who is considered overbearing, violent or bad-tempered. The quality of a 'tomboy', a 'she-man'.
"A manifestation of viraginity, they described her as an obdurate male soul in female flesh and form, due to the huge muscles she possessed."
e. *Virāgō* (Latin) a heroic woman, a warrior, a woman with male traits. *Viro* (Sanskrit) hero.

VIRGUNCULE (ver-GUNK-yool)
n. A young virginal maiden. A virgin girl. A young woman.
"The concert was filled with virguncules screaming in adoration at the young man fronting the band."
e. *Virguncula* (Latin) young girl, young virgin.

VIRILESCENCE (veer-uh-LESS-uhnss)
n. Acquiring the characteristics of a male as one ages. The development of male characteristics in a woman, such as dominance, chin whiskers or large muscles. The state of becoming virile or a 'she-man'.
"Social media would have you be fearful of the virilescence of women and the emasculation of men, but these are not new concepts, rather they now simply have platforms. Why should it affect you how a man or a woman presents themselves? Let people be whatever version of the sex they are, it's their body not yours."
e. Formed within English from *virile* - characteristic of a man, *-escent* - assuming a state of the first element.

VIRILIA (veh-RIL-ee-yah)
n. The male appendage. The penis.

"There was a collective gasp in the cinema when the actor exited the surf completely naked, exposing his bold virilia."

e. *Virīlia* (Latin) penis.

VIRIPOTENCE (vee-ree-POH-tuhnss)

n. When one possesses the qualities desired by one who seeks a spouse, typically displaying strength, energy and sexual energy: 'Marriageableness.'

"Full of energy and allure, they had a type of sensual confidence that exuded viripotence."

e. Formed within English from *viripotent* - virile + *ence* - of the quality of the first element.

VIRIPOTENT (vee-ree-POH-tuhnt)

adj. Full of life and sexual energy. Refers to a man or woman's sexual maturation or sexual capabilities. One's ability to procreate or sire children. Literally means "having the power of man." In possession of an energetic and powerful nature. In prime shape.

"Their sexual potency was evident during the most viripotent stage of their lives between 16 - 35 years."

e. *Vir* - man, *potens* - powerful/ "fit for" (Latin).

VISCEROTONIC (viss-uh-roe-TOH-nik)

adj. A type of personality that enjoys creature comforts, is laid back and sociable.

"He was more of a viscerotonic man who enjoyed lazing around the house rather than going out raging, but his laid back nature was not evident when it came to matters of the bedroom."

e. Formed within English from *viscero/visceral* - inner organs/deep inward feelings + *tonic* - producing tension/remedy.

VITIATE (VISH-ee-ate)

v. To decrease the quality of; to spoil; to render less appealing; to make incomplete.

adj. Depraved; spoiled; ruined.
"Nothing will vitiate one's relationship faster than infidelity, disloyalty, selfishness and lying."
e. Vitiātus, vitiāre (Latin) to spoil.

VITUPERATION (vuh-tyoo-puh-RAY-shun)
n. The action of abusing, rejecting, blaming. Abuse.
v. *Vituperate.* To blame; to abuse. To find fault in. To speak ill of.
adj. *Vituperative.* Using violently abusive language. Conveying extreme depreciation.
"They awakened to the fact they were a victim of vituperation after their child was born and found the strength to finally leave."
e. Vituperaciun (French); vituperātio (Latin) blaming.

VIVENCY (VIGH-ven-see)
n. The active and vital force of something or someone. Vitality. Life force.
"Her vivency and passionate approach to work and her interests were a huge draw card for the self made entrepreneur."
e. Vīvĕre (Latin) to live; vivre (French); vivir (Spanish); vivere (Italian).

VOLUPTUARY (vuh-LUP-chuh-ree)
n. One who is immoderately ruled by sensual and sexual pleasures. A sensualist, a Sybarite.
adj. Pertaining to a sybaritic indulgence of the senses. Characterised by sensuous and luxurious gratification.
"Abrubtly brought back into reality, she was dismayed that her alarm clock rudely interrupted her voluptuary dreams of lovers and travelling."
e. Volupty - pleasure, delight; Voluptuārius/ Voluptas (Latin) pleasure.

VULNERARY (VULL-nuh-ruh-ree)

n. That which is capable of healing. A person, potion, medicine or herbal mixture that heals wounds. (Has also been used in the opposite sense).

"Does not the loyalty and compassion of a healthy and emotionally mature love have a vulnerary effect on those bruised by heartbreak?"

e. *Vulnerārius* (Latin) vulnerable; *vulnus* - wound.

VULNEROSE (VUL-nuh-rohss)

adj. That is wounded. Full of wounds.

v. *Vulnerate.* To wound; to hurt.

"He was incapable of piecing together his vulnerose heart for many years after his divorce."

e. *Vulnus* (Latin) a wound.

VULNIFIC (vul-NIFF-ick)

adj. That causes wounds. Wounding. Also *vulnerative*.

"His vulnific words stayed with her long after they had split up, causing her to attiend months of therapy to rebuild her confidence."

e. *Vulnificus* (Latin) wounding; *vulnifique* (French) hurtful.

VULVIFORM (VUL-vee-form)

adj. Shaped like a vulva. That looks like a woman's bits. Pussy-shaped.

"Once she saw that the pattern on her duvet was rather vulviform, she couldn't unsee it."

e. *Vulviformis* from *vulva* - womb, female external genitalia, uterus + *formis* - form (Latin), *forme* (French).

Lexicon of Limerence

W.

WAGTAIL (WAG-tail)

n. A disdainful term for a man or woman considered lewd or desiring to know many things beyond measure. A prostitute.

"*She hung about like an impertinent little wagtail, hoping to find an opportunity to manipulate someone into her web of lies.*"

e. Referring to a breed of bird from the genus *Motacilla* that has a long and mobile tail. From *wag* + *tail*, similar to wagstart *wakstert* (German) grow up.

WANHOPE (WON-hop)

n. A vain, delusional or faint hope, like wistfully awaiting a change of heart from a previous paramour that once rejected you but understanding that it will most likely never happen. To be in a state of despair or hopelessess.

"*Waste not your time with wanhopes of previous loves, but rather look to the prospects of future adventures.*"

e. *Wan* - expressing negation, *hope* - expectation of something desired, "without hope". *Vanhop* (Swedish) - despair.

WAKAMEZAKE (WAH-ka-may-ssah-kay)

n. An ancient sexual practice of drinking alcohol from a woman's crotch originating in Japan. Also known as *wakame sake* and *seaweed sake*, the woman "host" closes her thighs tight to form a triangular valley in the pubic area proceeded by pouring sake from between her breasts into the "cup" for her guest to drink.

"*Though with only vodka on hand, she offered her lover a wakamezake as an aperitif.*"

e. The name is inspired by the idea that the woman's pubic hair resembles soft seaweed floating in the ocean beneath the sake. Originating during the Edo period (1603-1868) in Japan in legal red light districts known as *yūkaku* where brothels and prostitutes operated.

WAYMENTATION (way-men-TAY-shun)
n. Mourning, a lamentation, a grieving such as when a marriage comes to an end, a miscarriage or when a loved one dies.
"He was filled with waymentation after submitting the last of his divorce papers."
e. Variant of *waiment* (French) and *weyment* (Anglo-Norman).

WEDBED (WED-bed)
n. The rectangular resting place designated to husband and wife. The marital bed, a bed for a married couple.
"Due to his postings overseas, they had not laid together in their wedbed for some time."
e. Wed - a nuptial pledge or promise, bed - a structure for sleeping.

WEEMOED (VAY-mood)
n. A quiet nostalgia for something that was. A melancholy.
"She was consumed with a weemoed, a longing to go back in time and change what had happened."
e. A direct borrowing, *weemoed* (Dutch) melancholy; *weemoedich* - melancholic.

WEGOTISM (WEE-goh-tiz-uhm)
n. The excessive use of the editorial "we" such as when a couple speak of everything they experience as if they only exist as one rather than two separate beings with differing interests, desires and goals.
"Their friends were tired of hearing their wegotisms: 'we like ice cream.. we love holidays in Mauritius... we love the Top Gun films... we like French wines... we'd like to hike Machu Pichu...' they wondered if they had any separate interests?!".
e. We - plural pronoun for 'I', egotism - the vice of being overly absorbed in one's self.

WELTER (WEL-tuh)
n. A surge of turmoil and upheaval. A state of mass confusion. Chaos.

"She was taken aback in a welter of emotion after learning of her girlfriend's numerous infidelities."

e. From the verb *welter* – to roll to and fro.

WHANGDOODLE (wang-DOO-dil)
n. A mythical bird that grieves continuously and therefore slang for someone who can't get over their ex. Also slang for a penis, of which other slang "wanger" and "doodle" perhaps derived.

"I was getting tired of them wallowing in their post-breakup blues for the last six months and just wanted to scream at them to stop being such a whangdoodle."

e. An arbitrary formation most likely influenced by *whang* – slang for penis and the sound of a blow, and *doodle* – an aimless scrawl while the mind is otherwise occupied. Perhaps implying one who is just slapping about without purpose.

WHIRLYGIGS (WER-lee-gigs)
n. Slang for testicles (1800s).

n. *Whirlygig*. A plaything. A flighty, fickly or giddy person. Something that repeats or continuously moves. A repetition of an event or time.

"He was beginning to feel the physical repercussions of having a celibate period after much promiscuity, his whirlygigs were swollen and aching."

e. *Whirl* – implying something that spins, *gig* – a person whose appearance is eccentric, foolish or peculiar.

WHISKERANDO (wiss-kuh-RAN-doh)
n. A man in possession of an exceptional beard, a heavily whiskered man.

"She loved a tattooed and bearded man so she moved to North Fitzroy in Melbourne where many whiskerandos congregate."

e. An eponym of the character *Don Ferolo Whiskerandos*, a character in Anglo-Irish playwright Richard Brinsley Sheridan's play *The Critic* (1779), that mimics the suffix of Spanish words with *-ando*.

WHOREPIPE (HOR-pipe)
n. The phallic appendage between a man's legs. The penis.

"As they kissed behind the cloak room, she could feel his whorepipe rubbing up against her."

e. Attested to in writing since the late 1600s, a combination of *whore* + *pipe*.

WIFE IN WATER COLOURS
p. Implying a woman that is of less importance than the wife. A mistress. One whose engagements are easily erased from thought or replaced. A concubine. A side piece.

"Better to remain single and free from drama than accept a married man and be his wife in water colours."

e. Appearing in *Dictionary of the Vulgar Tongue* by Francis Grose (1811).

WIGHT (wight)
adj. That demonstrates strength, courage and robustness. Of a supernatural presence. Marked by valiant determination and bravery.

"Many were in awe of him as he possessed a wight ambition that was evident in how he achieved success in work, family and love."

e. *Vigt* - in self defence, *vigr* - of fighting age (Old Norse).

WILDER (WILL-duh)
v. To cause a disorientation of one's purpose or direction. To drive one to get lost. To lead astray. To end up in a type of wilderness, 'to wild'.

"He had wildered her heart and destroyed all common sense, resulting in an unbridled passion and thirst for each other."

e. Uncertain origins but most likely derivative of *wilderness* and related to *bewilder*.

WILDLING (WYLED-ling)

n. An unorthodox and untameable person, a wild creature or plant.

"There is no taming the wildest of women for they need to let their spirits run free with the wolves, only their fellow wildlings may match their zest for the unthinkable."

e. *Wild* - living in a state of nature, untame, *-ling* - denotes a person or thing belonging to the first element.

WIMPLE (WIM-pull)

v. To veil or cover something; to wrap up or enfold, to wear a veil or perhaps blindfold.

"You cannot wimple falsehoods with truths when it comes to matters of the heart, for feelings speak without words."

e. *Wimple* - a garment of silk or cloth worn to enfold the head.

WINSOME (WIN-sum)

adj. Of a pleasantness that is charming and attractive; delightful; agreeable; handsome; well-mannered.

"His winsome demeanour was so genuinely alluring that all the women fawned over him at every gathering."

e. *Wyn* (Old English) joy, delight, pleasure + *some* - of a quality of the first element.

WITTOL (WIT-ol)

n. A complaisant husband who is aware of and tolerates his wife's infidelity, 'a contented cuckold'. A foolish person who has little sense.

"Though many criticised his acceptance of his wife's unfaithful nature, his declaration of punching far above his weight explained his satisfaction with being a wittol."

e. Formed within English from *wit* - to have knowledge of + *cuckold* - a man with an unfaithful partner.

WOMANTHROPE (WOOM-un-thrope)

n. One who despises women. An alternative word for a misogynist, a woman hater.

"Lets not focus on the opinions of womanthropes and misandrists but rather look at dysfunctional behaviours and toxic demands in any sex and address that rather than play the blame game."

e. A blend of *woman* + *misanthrope* (hater of human kind), appearing circa 1863.

WOOER-BAB (woo-uh-BAB)

n. A garter or piece of cloth tied in a love knot below the knees as a lover's keep sake, worn by a suitor as a proposal of marriage. To woo your love.

"She kept her wooer-bab beneath her dress and led his hand to it beneath the table once seated."

e. Old Scottish dialect, *wooer* - one who gives another a lot of attention in the hopes of persuading them to love or marry them, *bab* being an affectionate term for love, dear. 'To woo your love'.

WOOFITS (WOOF-its)

n. Being mentally on edge with a sense of fragility. A queasy feeling from over-indulging the night before. Feeling ill, moody or depressed.

"He had a great time partying with her until the wee hours, she could easily drink him under the table so now he was suffering from a serious case of the woofits."

e. Of unknown origin but appearing in text from the early 20th century. I would imagine that it could be related to *whoof* - the bark of a dog, implying that one is feeling *doggish* - feeling rubbish.

WOOPIE (WOO-pee)

n. An older person who is financially well-off. A retiree with cash. A silver fox with a stash.

"Hollywood loves to normalise huge age gaps amongst couples, as though it's normal for twenty somethings to shack up with woopies."

e. North American slang particularly in advertising (1980s).

WYRD (weerd)

n. The power that governs one's fate or fortune. A magical power that determines your destiny. An enchantment or fortune teller.

"He couldn't help but feel it was not a coincidence but rather some kind of wyrd, a predetermined fate that they crossed paths in three different countries without pre-arrangement."

e. Old English inherited from Germanic. In mythology, *wyrd* takes the form of three goddesses – *The Fates*, who determine the fate of humankind.

X.

XANTIPPE (zan-TIP-ee)

n. A woman who is easily annoyed or angered. A lady who scolds her husband constantly. An angry bitch.

"It was with great sadness that she conceded her son would marry that Xantippe of a woman, she couldn't understand it but she resigned herself to his wishes."

e. An eponym of Ancient Greek philosopher Socrates' wife Xantippe Ξανθίππη, who was known for being one of the hardest women to get along with.

XANTHOCROID (ZAN-thuh-kroid)

n. A person with pale skin, blue or green eyes and fair hair. 'Blue-eyed blondes'.

adj. *Xanthous, xanthocomic, xanthotrichous.* Yellow or orange-haired.

"Contrary to popular belief that most people desire a mate with tanned skin, there are some that are most attracted to xanthocroids."

e. From biologist Thomas Huxley's categorisation of races in 1870 (no longer in use today), derived from *xanthos* ξανθός (Greek) blonde, yellow and from *ochrós* ὠχρός (Greek) pale.

XANTHODONTOUS (zan-tho-DON-tuss)

adj. That is in possession of yellow teeth. Has yellow chompers.

n. *Xanthodont.* A person with yellow teeth.

"In the modern day, many people are concerned with being xanthodontous because it can really improve your whole face and sexual appeal if you have lovely pearly whites."

e. *Xanthos* ξανθός - yellow, *dóntia* δόντια - teeth (Greek).

XASSAFRASSED (ZASS-uh-frasst)

adj. One who is endowed with a child. Pregnant; with child.

"She was really over being xassafrassed and ready for that baby to come out!"

e. Only attested to in Mrs Byrne's *Dictionary of Obscure Words*.

XENODOCHEINOLOGY (zen-uh-doh-KAY-uh-noh-luh-jee)

n. A love of hotels. The study of hotels, the lore of places to lodge.

"He was a wealthy man familiar with the xenodocheionology of the city, convenient for all his visiting mistresses."

e. Xenodochía ξενοδοχία (Greek) hotel + *ology* - field of knowledge.

XENODOCHIAL (zen-oh-DOUGH-kee-uhl)

adj. Inclined to receive strangers with pleasure. Hospitable, welcoming.

"His xenodochial nature made for a very welcoming atmosphere at his place."

e. Xenodochía ξενοδοχία (Greek) hotel, xénos ξένος - stranger, foreign, déchesthai Δέχεσθαι - accept, receive (Greek).

XENOEPIST (zen-oh-EP-ist)

n. A person who converses with intonations of a different country. Someone who speaks with a foreign accent.

"She hadn't considered herself a xenoepist having moved from one English speaking country to another, but her accent was apparently sexy to Londoners."

e. A neologism likely derived from *xénos* ξένος - foreign, *omilitís* ομιλητής - speaker, *epistími* επιστήμη - knowledge, science (Greek).

XENOGENESIS (zen-oh-JEN-uh-siss)

n. The production of offspring with characteristics completely different to those of the parents.

"The birth of a white skinned, ginger haired baby to dark skinned parents aroused suspicion about the mothers' fidelity, however was quickly proven to be the result of xenogenesis."

e. Formed within English from *xeno* ξένος (Greek) stranger, foreign, strange and *genesis* – the origin of something.

XENOPHILE (ZEN-oh-file)

n. One who is attracted to people from a foreign land or culture.

"They never dated anyone from their own country as they were much more attracted to people who looked and sounded different, like a true xenophile."

e. *Xenos* ξένος (Greek) strange, foreign and *-phile* denoting a lover of the thing stated in the first element.

XERIC (ZEER-ick)

adj. Lacking in moistness. Characterised by a minute amount of wetness.

"Though she was incredibly aroused, she was self consciously xeric and needed the help of some lubricant."

e. *Xirós* ξηρός – dry + *ikós* ικός – in the manner of (Greek).

XERONISUS (zuh-RON-eh-suss)

n. A little-used term for the inability to reach orgasm despite sexual or intimate stimulation, more commonly known as anorgasmia.

"Being physically active became a solution to the sexual tension and frustration he experienced from xeronisus."

e. Of unknown origin, it's likely that the term comes from the Greek word *xirós* ξηρός, *xeronisis* + *nisus* – effort, endeavour: 'a dry effort' implying a useless cause or an effort that leads to nothing.

XEROSTOMIA (zeer-oh-STOW-mee-ah)

n. An excessive dryness of the mouth. 'Desert mouth'. A medical term for a lack of saliva production leading to dryness of the mouth.

"He was overcome with nerves any time they were alone together, experiencing mild xerostomia which inhibited being able to speak properly."

e. *Xirós* ξηρός – dry, *stóma* στόμα – mouth (Greek).

XEROTRIPSIS (zeer-oh-TRIP-siss)

n. Sustained dry friction or rubbing. Figuratively a 'dry hump'. A medical term for wearing something down or scraping it away.

"Wanting to stick to her rule of no sex on the first five dates, they engaged in a lot of fully clothed xerotripsis."

e. Xirós ξηρός - dry, tripsis τριψις - rubbing (Greek).

XIPHOIDAL (zi-FOI-dul)

adj. Something anatomically shaped like a sword. Sword-like.

"He sported a pair of very snug fitting trousers from which they couldn't help but notice the xiphoidal shape protruding."

e. Xiphoidēs (Latin), xífos ξίφος (Greek) sword.

Y.

YA'ABURNEE (YA-ha-BOOR-nee)
p. An expression of devotion that conveys a hope that a loved one will live longer than oneself. A way of expressing the intense love you feel for someone but implying that life would not be worth living without them and therefore you hope to die first.
"*I wouldn't want to live without you, ya'aburnee!*"
e. Directly translates as "you bury me" ينربقي (Arabic).

YAPNESS (YAP-nuhss)
n. A sensation of being starved of something. Hunger, ravenousness, famishment.
"*She was experiencing a yapness for love, sex and intimacy after giving up on dating for a year.*"
e. Of unclear origin but most likely derivative of *yap* in the sense of slang for *mouth* - 'shut your yap', and therefore related to the mouth.

YARELY (yeah-lee)
adv. Implying doing something with readiness or eagerness. Acting promptly, quickly or briskly. Conducting an action in a diligent manner. Doing it quickly.
"*They yarely began undressing each other as soon as they stepped in the door.*"
e. Derivative of *gearolice* (Germanic), *garoliko* (Old Saxon), *earu* (Old English) ready.

YARLING (YAH-ling)
adj. An utterance of a discordant noise. A shrieking sound; hollering, howling, wailing.

"It was hard to tell if the yarling coming from their bedroom was pleasurable or painful."
e. Old English dialect *yarl* - to make a loud sound.

YAULD (yawld)
adj. Sprightly, vigorous, strong, wide eyed and bushy tailed. Being nimble, active and enthusiastic.
"They reminisced fondly of each other when they seemed to draw on an endless fountain of excitement, as yauld lovers in their youth."
e. Scottish and northern dialect of unknown origin.

YCLAD (ee-KLAD)
adj. Clothed, dressed, covered, clad literally or figuratively.
"She lounged around drinking coffee yclad in his old band t-shirt."
e. (Middle English) The prefix -y denoting something passed, *clad* - covered with clothes or armour.

YEN (yen)
n. An intense craving for someone. A yearning; an unignorable longing. An addiction to something.
"Cursing to himself for not grabbing her number, he now had a burning yen for her after they connected so intimately at the party."
e. Most probably a borrowing from yǎn 眼 (Cantonese) eye, craving, 'have an eye for someone'.

YENTA (YEN-tah)
n. One who relishes in prying into people's private lives and sharing rumours. A nosy, interfering, vulgar and gossipy woman, a busybody. One who gossips.
"With nothing better to do, all the yentas gathered to eavesdrop and probe the women on their relationship status."
e. Yiddish from a 1920s-30s Jewish newspaper comic strip by B. Kovner.

YENTZ (yents)

v. To fornicate, to have sexual intercourse, to cheat, to deceive, to swindle.

"*She knew he was yentzing that little tart before his wife found out.*"

e. U.S slang from *yentzen* (Yiddish) - to copulate.

YESTREEN (yes-TREEN)

adv. Last night, pertaining to the evening of yesterday; yesterday.

"*The neighbours kept me awake because they were at it all yestreen.*"

e. Variant of Scottish *yester-even* (yesterday - evening) chiefly poetic.

YEVEROUS (YEH-vuh-russ)

adj. Acting without thought, done rapidly or with force, overly eager or greedy, impetuous.

"*One should never be yeverous when it comes to love making.*"

e. Formed within English from *yever* - desirous, yearning, covetous, greedy.

YHTE (ort)

n. A valuable or highly prized possession, that which one claims as one's own.

"*Woman of his dreams, she was yhte to him.*"

e. Variant of *aucht* (Old English) inherited from *ēht* (Germanic) - property.

YOKEMATE (YOHK-mayt)

n. A person closely connected or associated with another person in some way such as a partner, spouse, close friend or business partner. Also 'yokefellow'.

"*Living and working together for a long time, they were important to each other before becoming yokemates.*"

e. Formed within English *yolk* - a device fitted to a pair of animals to pull a plow or cart, *mate* - companion, comrade, friend.

YONDERLY (YON-duh-lee)

adj. To be of an emotionally distant demeanour. Mentally far away. Melancholic, sullen or gloomy.

"*It's true a yonderly demeanour seems to create a touch of mystique around a person but it quickly wears thin when one becomes romantically involved with such a person.*"

e. Formed within English from *yonder* - over there, in the distance.

YOUNKER (YUNG-kah)

n. A lively or fashionable young gentleman. A boy. A youngling, before 'youngster'. Used as a title like *sir* or *duke*, 'younker Johan'.

"She wasn't interested in younkers, she wanted a man similar in age to her who had lived, travelled and grown emotionally."

e. *Joncker* (Dutch), *junchērre* (German), *junkhärra* (Swedish) - young lord.

YUANFEN (YAN-fen)

n. A concept that describes serendipitous meetings or inexplicable connections. A binding force that links two people together in any relationship. A type of fate that draws two people towards an encounter. A fateful encounter or coincidence. (Similar to Karma in Buddhism).

"*The way they kept bumping into each other in different parts of the city didn't feel simply random, it felt like yuanfen!*"

e. *Yuánfèn* 缘分 (Chinese) fate.

Z.

ZAFTIG (ZAFF-tig)

adj. Describing a woman who is buxom and curvy in figure. A pleasingly plump lady.

"*He was a fan of the zaftig woman, all those curves to hold onto and get lost in.*"

e. *Zaftik* (Yiddish) juicy, *Zaffic* (German) juicy.

ZAPATA (zuh-PAH-tah)

n. A type of moustache that hangs down towards the chin on either side of the mouth. A 'handlebar mo', a 'pornstar mustache'.

"*Zapata moustaches were big in the 1970s, synonymous with porn stars, hipsters, outlaws and today, Movember.*"

e. Eponym of Mexican revolutionary *Emiliio Zapata*, portrayed by Marlon Brando in the film *Viva Zapata* (1952). Also *zapato* (Spanish) means shoe.

ZATCH (zach)

n. The female genitalia. A woman's buttocks or vagina. Lady part. Also an act of copulating, a fucking.

"*The bunch of women were giggling like school girls after their friend whispered under her breath after the sexy waiter left, that he was so fine she wanted him to snatch her zatch.*"

e. Unclear origins but is suggested to be derivative of *satchel* - a bag closed by a flap (women's labia are also referred to as *flaps*).

ZELOPHOBIA (zee-low-FO-bee-yah)

n. When one is overwhelmed with an intense fear of feeling strong emotions or a fear of feeling jealous. Such as when one has experienced numerous failed relationships, repeatedly mending a broken heart and being hurt too many times.

"*The prospect of being involved in a relationship again filled her with a sense of zelophobia.*"

e. Zílos ζῆλος - zeal, phobos φόβος - fear (Greek).

ZELOTYPIA (zee-low-TI-pee-yah)

n. Extreme, excessive or obsessive jealousy. At times portrayed as an illness, a morbid jealousy.

"*The philandering ways of his wife drove the man to zelotypia.*"

e. Zēlotypia (Latin), Zilotypía ζηλοτυπία (Greek) - jealousy, rivalry, envy.

ZENANA (zuh-NAH-nah)

n. Women's quarters where men are forbidden from entering. Part of a house or building used to seclude women, to segregate them from the men.

"*He fantasised about the women of the zenana, being surrounded by softness, sweet scents and beauty.*"

e. Zanāna ज़नाना (Hindi), zan (Persia) woman. From Hindu or Muslim dwellings in South Asia that reserve parts of the house for the use of females only.

ZITELLA (zi-TEL-ah)

n. An unmarried, young or virginal woman. Often of a woman considered past a 'marriageable age' or her prime, who resigns herself to the fact she will be single for good. A spinster. A maiden. A virgin. A single lady.

"*It's interesting how threatening women with 'being alone forever' is mistakenly viewed by some men as something to fear, ignorant of the fact that the majority of women would happily remain zitellas rather than suffer an intolerable man-boy.*"

e. Zitella, citella - young unmarried girl, cita - betrothed girl, bride (Italian).

ZOETIC (ZOH-et-ick)

adj. Of a nature that is full of life. Living life to its fullest. Lively, vital, relating to life. (Interesting how it sounds like 'poetic').

"*Her zoetic energy was a fountain from all to drink from but for only a few to taste.*"

e. Zōē (Latin) life, -etic - of the nature of.

ZOILISM (ZOY-li-zum)

n. Nagging, disparaging or reproachful criticism such as when a relationship deteriorates and both parties are focused on diminishing the other.

"*Everyone close to them could see it was time for the two to part ways due to all their interactions being that of zoilism.*"

e. Eponym of Greek literary critic, grammarian and philosopher Zoilus, famous for his severe criticism of Greek poet Homer.

ZONDEK (ZON-dek)

n. Slang for a pregnancy test. The A-Z test was used to detect whether a woman was pregnant by injecting her urine into immature mice and noting the effect it had on the mice's ovaries, developed by German gynaecologists Selmar Aschheim and Bernhard Zondek in 1927. With a 98.9% success rate, it became obsolete in 1960 with the introduction of immunoassays.

"*She said she had to go grab a couple of zondeks because her period was very late.*"

e. Eponym of Bernarhd Zondek.

ZYGOTE (ZIGH-goat)

n. The union of a male and female cell to create a fertilised cell. Could perhaps be used figuratively to describe the coming together of two people.

"*We are all a miracle in some sense, a chance meeting, a zygote of magic that predetermined what we will look like and who we will be.*"

e. Zygotós ζυγωτός (Greek) - yolked, yolked together.

PORTMANTEAUS/ NEOLOGISMS

(n.) Portmanteau: a word combining the syllables of two different words.

e. *Porter* - to carry, *manteau* - coat, mantle, cape or cloak (French). Originally of a court official who carried a prince's cloak, to a travelling bag that had two compartments.

(n.) Neologism: a word that is recently in circulation and not necessarily classified in the dictionary.

e. *Néologisme* (French) the coining of new words.

ALKITUDE – *Alcohol + attitude*

(n.) An attitude that one develops whilst under the influence of alcohol. A drunken bad mood.

ANTISTALKING – *Anti + stalking*

(v.) Studying the intricacies of an ex paramour's daily trajectory in order to circumvent an unprecedented interaction. Learning a person's routine in order to avoid running into them. Purposefully avoiding someone.

AUTOEROTICISM – *Auto + eroticism*

(n.) The practice of sexually arousing and stimulating oneself. Masturbation.

AUTOSEXUAL – *Auto + sexual*

(adj.) Pertaining to sex with yourself. Sexually arousing yourself.

BANGOVER – *Bang + hangover*

(n.) A sense of dread felt the day after bedding someone you have little recollection of or didn't really want to copulate with; regretting the "bangin'" buddy of the night before. (Also used for having a sore head the day after 'head-banging' at a concert).

BEDGASM – *Bed + orgasm*

(n.) The immense feeling of euphoria one sustains upon committing oneself to the bedchamber; a feeling of ecstasy from getting into bed (particularly with freshly washed sheets).

BEDSWERVER – *Bed + swerver*

(n.) A partner who is unfaithful. One who avoids their marital bed.

BOREGASM – *Boredom + orgasm*

(n.) A sense of dismay felt when one's date is exceptionally boring or speaks only of themselves; the feeling experienced when the sex is uninspiring.

BRAGASM – *Bra + orgasm*

(n.) The euphoric feeling of removing one's bra at the end of the day; a sense of relief when a woman finally gets to pull off her bra.

BREASTAURANT – *Breast + restaurant*

(n.) A restaurant in which the waiters are scantily clad from the waist up; an establishment that has topless staff.

BRIDEZILLA – *Bride + Godzilla*

(n.) A bride-to-be that behaves like a monster.

BROLETTE – *Bro + bralette*

(n.) A bra worn by a man. Also a female 'bro'.

BROMANCE – *Brother + romance*

(n.) The unbreakable bond of friendship beseeched upon two gentlemen; a close friendship between two guys.

BUNT – *Boy + cunt*

(n.) Male orifice that is considered a sexual cavity. Also known as a *bussy*.

BYESEXUAL – *Bye+sexual*

(n.) Being single for so long that you don't remember what it's like to have romantic or sexual desires; being overcome with a sense of being desireless. A sense that you have said 'goodbye' to your own sexuality.

CANADIAN BALLET

(p.) A slang term for strip clubs.

CHESTICLES – *Chest + testicles*

(n.) A slang term for a set of breasts. A set of tits on a man.

CHEMSEX – *Chemical + sex*

(n.) Sexual activity experienced under the influence of chemical compounds. Having sex high on drugs.

CONDOMPLATE – *Condom + contemplate*

(v.) Contemplating whether to place a condom on the phallic component of your fornicularium; deciding on a condom or not.

CRIME SCENE SEX

(p.) Sex with a woman who is on her period.

CYBERSEX – *Cyberspace + sex*

(n.) Sexual interactions conducted over the internet. 'Sex on the net'.

DEMISEXUAL – *Demi + sexual*

(n.) Those who experience a sexual attraction only after forging an emotional connection strong enough to invoke arousal. Halfway on the spectrum between allosexual and asexual.

DICTIM – *Dick + victim*

(n.) A person who 'acts like a dick', then plays the victim.

DO-ME-QUEEN

(n.) A rather lazy and submissive sexual partner (especially in male homosexual relationships).

DUDEVORCE – *Dude + divorce*

(n.) When two male friends or lovers have a falling out; two males realising they are no longer friends.

EVE-TEASING – *Eve + teasing*

(p.) The sexual harassment of women (primarily in Indian English); in other countries it may be interpreted more as playful flirtation.

FAGHAG/FAGSTAG – *Fag + hag/stag*

(n.) A woman or man who enjoys hanging out mostly with gay men.

FEMMITUDE – *Femme + attitude*

(n.) The attitude of a self-assured, power babe woman. Of a woman who has a full-on attitude.

FLAMBIANCÉ – *Flamboyant + fiancé*

(n.) A fiancé that is flamboyant.

FLING CLEANING – *Fling + Spring cleaning*

(n.) Scurryfunging the bedchamber in anticipation of fornicating thus; deep cleaning and tidying one's room to get laid.

FLIRTASHIONSHIP – *Flirt + relationship*

(n.) A flirty relationship that leads nowhere.

FUCKET LIST – *Fuck + bucket list*

(n.) An enumeration of prospective love interests that one may potentially enjoy fornicating with; a list of people you hope to fuck before you die.

GENDERQUAKE – *Gender + earthquake*

(n.) Experiencing being sexually attracted to both sexes.

GLORYHOLE – *Glory + hole*
(n.) A hole in a wall used for anonymous sexual activity usually found in adult entertainment venues. The 'hole' from which one derives pleasure from.

GRIEFCASE – *Grief + briefcase*
(n.) A metaphorical place where one stores all their emotional baggage.

GROANTONE – *Groan + ringtone*
(n.) A really sexy sounding ringtone. Also *moantone*.

HARASSHOLE – *Harass + arsehole*
(n.) A person who incessantly pesters another, to go on a date with them for example.

HETEROFLEXIBLE – *Heterosexual + flexible*
(adj.) One who is primarily interested in sexual and romantic encounters with the opposite sex but is open to new same-sex experiences.

HIBERDATING – *Hibernate + dating*
(v.) Ignoring one's friends in favor of seeing a secret lover; dating indoors or in seclusion in winter.

HIMBO – *Him + bimbo*
(n.) A man who acts like a bit of an airhead.

HOBOSEXUAL – *Hobo + sexual*
(n.) Someone who dates because they are in need of a place to stay.

HOOKERHAG/HOOKERSTAG – *Hooker + hag/stag*
(n.) A person that only hangs out with prostitutes.

JACKINTOSH – *Jack + Macintosh*
(n.) One who spends an inordinate amount of time masturbating while watching pornography. "Jacking off to their Macintosh".

JUSTIFACTORY – *Just + satisfactory*
(adj.) Describing something that didn't live up to expectations.

KADOODLE – *Canoodle + doodle*
(v.) To 'cuddle' another with your private parts; implying a special 'hug' with one's penis.

LIPTEASE – *Lip + tease*
(n.) When someone is in possession of an incredibly seductive set of lips and every time they speak it begins a type of seducing.

LOLICOM – *Lolita + complex*
(n.) The lusting after much younger women by older men.

LOVERNESIA – *Lover + amnesia*
(n.) The inability to remember how many people one has bedded in their life.

MASTURDATING – *Masturbate + dating*
(v.) Taking oneself on a 'date' to enjoy some sensual and restorative chillout time that usually involves masturbating.

MASTURWAITING – *Maturbate + waiting*
(v.) Patiently practising restraint from masturbating.

MENTERTAINMENT – *Men + entertainment*
(n.) A bunch of men together enjoying some entertainment. When the way a group of men is behaving is unknowingly a source of entertainment for some spectators.

MONOSEXUAL – *Mono + sexual*
(n.) Attracted to one gender only.

MUSSY – *Male + pussy*
(n.) Male anus viewed as a sex cavity. Also known as *munt*.

NAPSTURBATION – *Nap + masturbation*
(n.) Lying down for a nap then deciding to masturbate.

NOSTALGASM – *Nostalgia + orgasm*
(n.) Fantasising about an ex-lover to reach climax.

PALIMONY – *Pal + alimony*
(n.) Spousal support paid to your ex lover who was once a pal.

PANROMANTIC – *Pan + romantic*
(adj./n.) Romantically attracted to people of all genders.

PORNOCCHIO – *Porn + pinocchio*
(n.) One who lies about how much pornography they actually watch.

PORNOTOPIA – *Porn + utopia*
(n.) A destination or setting that is ideal for the antics of pornography. The perfect location for sex.

PREGRET – *Pre + regret*
(n.) Regretting something before it has happened, such as accepting an invitation to go on a date when you'd really rather stay home.

PRICKTATOR – *Prick + dictator*
(n.) A man who bosses everyone around. A dude that is totally ruled by his dick.

PRUDINATI – *Prude + illuminati*

(n.) A group of people who are embarrassed or ill at ease with nudity, sex or sensual topics; a bunch of prudish people.

QUEERPLATONIC – *Queer + platonic*

(adj.) Describing a relationship that challenges traditional notions of intimacy, a close and committed emotional connection that provides support beyond that of friendship but that is not romantic or sexual in nature.

SAPIOSEXUAL – *Sapiens + sexual*

(n.) Attracted to those who demonstrate a high level of emotional, analytical and logical intelligence. Sexually aroused by smart people.

SATISDICKTION – *Satisfaction + dick*

(n.) When you have satisfied that burning desire for some phallicle pleasure. When you got some good dick.

SCREWVENIR – *Screw + souvenir*

(n.) An item pinched from a lover's room or house to keep as a souvenir of your hook up.

SEXCAPADE – *Sex + escapade*

(n.) An adventure or activity that involves sex.

SEXILE – *Sex + exile*

(n.) To send your housemates off on their merry way so that one can copulate loudly. To have been banished from one's house so that your housemate can have sex with their lover.

SEXORCISM – *Sex + exorcism*

(n.) Sleeping with someone new to get over an ex; becoming a temporary lothario in the hopes of forgetting your feelings for a past love interest.

SEXOSOPHY – *Sex + philosophy*

(n.) A body of knowledge that consists of principles and knowledge that people have about their own experiences of eroticism and sexuality.

SEXSOMNIA – *Sex + insomnia*

(n.) When sex is the reason you are losing sleep. Engaging in sexual activities while in a slumber.

SEXTING – *Sex + texting*

(v.) The action of sending text messages with the intention to arouse the receiver. Sending dirty texts.

SEXUOEROTIC – *Sex + erotic*

(adj.) That which encompasses both physiological and psychological desire and arousal. Tending to arouse sexual love and desire.

SITUATIONSHIP – *Situation + relationship*

(n.) A relationship that only exists in certain situations such as when you are out partying at the same event, or when you are both alone late at night on a Saturday evening with nothing else better to do.

SMEXY – *Smart + sexy*

(adj.) A way to describe those that attract a person with sapiosexual tendencies, ones who are both intelligent and ooze sex appeal.

SNIFFERITED – *Sniff + excited*

(adj.) Aroused by the smell of one's crush or their particular parts.

TESTERICAL – *Testosterone + hysterical*

(adj.) When a man is acting overly sensitive, intense and angry about something futile.

TEXTPECTATION – *Text + expectation*

(n.) Anticipating a text from someone you have the hots for or are really wanting to hear from.

THE RIPPERS

(p.) The strip club.

WHOJA-VU – *Who + déjavu*

(n.) That eerie feeling one gets when you feel as though you've hooked up before.

Etoile's Neologisms

It is my hope to one day create a dictionary of my own made up words, much as John Koenig has done with *The Dictionary of Obscure Sorrows* (2021). Below are some examples of words I have imagined for my own and hopefully your entertainment. I invite you to make up some of your own words and see what you come up with!

CHALOKORIS (ka-loh-KO-riss)

adj. Of a person that is difficult to seduce or capture their attention. Unable to catch, not easy to woo.

"*Rather than be dissuaded by her chalokoris demeanour, he enjoyed the challenge of earning her affections.*"

e. *Chalosis* χάλωσης - breakdown, captured, taken by storm + *choris* χωρίς - without (Greek).

CONTUMATIC (kon-tyoo-MA-tick)

adj. When a person is stubborn to the point of being unable to see that their attitude is the root of the problem.

"*Her narcissism gave her a deluded sense of righteousness which he found far too contumatic to tolerate.*"

e. *Contumacy* - disobedience, resistance, stubbornness + *problematic* - that causes problems.

EPHELIDIST (eh-FEEL-uh-dist)

n. One who is infatuated with people who are in possession of a lot of freckles. A fan of freckles. A frecklehead.

"*He hated his dark freckles as a child and it was only thanks to social media that he discovered that there is a whole community out there who are ephelidists.*"

e. *Ephelides/ephelis* - freckle + *-ist* - implying an expert or admirer of the first element. From which I would also suggest *ephelidism* - a fetish for freckles.

EVACULOUS (eh-VAK-yoo-luhss)
adj. Incapable of pulling oneself out of a state of hopelessness. Dead inside.
"*After a terrible breakup and the utter betrayal of her spouse, she couldn't shake her evaculous state.*"
e. *Evacuate* - to empty + *-ulous* being slightly or in a very minimal way.

EVAMITICAL (EVE-ah-mit-ik-ul)
adj. Of a woman who is in a state of nakedness; describing a naked lady.
"*Exhausted from travelling through the snow at altitude to reach the small village, they were in seventh heaven when they stumbled upon a bath house full of evamitical women.*"
n. Based on *Adamitical* which is derived from the biblical *Adam*, therefore *Eve* for specifically a female in her 'natural' or primary state.

GYNOTIKOLOMASSOPHILE (guy-no-tik-oh-loh-MASS-oh-file)
n. Someone who has a specific sexual interest in female genitalia. One who loves a woman's vagina and arse.
"*The dedicated gynotikolomassophile endeavours to be the king or queen of cunnilingus.*"
e. *Gynotikó* γυνοτικό - genital + *kolomass* κωλομασς - ass, vagina + *fílos* φίλος - friend, (Greek). (Different to Gynotiko<u>lobo</u>massophile - one who enjoys ear nibbling).

INSECURABLE (in-suh-CURE-ah-bull)
adj. Unable to be cured of one's own insecurities and therefore destroying all potentially good relationships.
"*The greatest repellant to anyone who is emotionally mature is an insecurable display of accusations.*"

e. *Insecure* - wanting assurance, unsure, unsafe + *incurable* - incapable of being remedied or fixed.

LICKOPHILE (LIK-oh-file)

n. One who is aroused by the act of being licked or who enjoys licking others.

"He was not only aroused by her going down on him but really the fact she seemed to be a total lickopile."

e. *Lick* - to moisten or lap up with the tongue + *-phile* - a lover of the first element.

PRUDINATI (prood-uh-NAH-tee)

n. Those who maintain overly strict views on sexual liberation. Prudish people who think themselves above those inclined to sexual promiscuity. Sex snobs, nudey naysayers.

"The prudinati try to demonise sex and therefore ironically create more temptation around it."

e. *Prude* - excessively modest in regards to sexual matters + *illuminati* - a special group of people said to possess secret knowledge.

QUATTORVIMULLIER (KWAT-or-vee-MOOL-ee-air)

n. A posh sounding word for a sexual foursome.

"They had fantasised about a quattorvimullier with another couple but when it came to the reality of sharing their spouses, it wasn't such a turn on."

e. *Quattuor* - four + *virī*- men + *mullier* - woman (Latin).

SCUGGISHLY (SKUH-gish-lee)

adj. In a manner that is shifty or deceitful.

"The ease at which some people scuggishly orchestrate numerous infidelities is testament to their own lack of dignity and ability to find fulfillment."

e. *Scuggery* - a Northern English dialectical term for concealment or trickery + - *ish* - of a nature of the first element; *scug* - a rascal.

SEXUAL CRAPULENCE (SEK-shoo-uhl-CRAP-yoo-lunts)

p. Excessive drunken sex. When one is having sexual intercourse too frequently whilst overly intoxicated.

"*The city lifestyle and weekend benders was leading to too much sexual crapulence.*"

e. *Sexual* - that involves sex + *crapulence* - being sick from drinking too much, a gross lack of control, intemperance.

THEOLYKIST (thee-OL-uh-kissed)

n. A person who only dates women who resemble mythical goddesses. Those who are obsessed with godly-looking women.

"*It was obvious from the types of women he dated that he was an utter theolykist.*"

e. *Theós* θεός - god + *thilykós* θηλυκός - female + -*ist* -indicating an enthusiast of the first element.

XENOGAMIST (zuh-NOG-am-isst)

n. A man who likes to spread his seed around, a serial casanova.

"*A serial xenogamist, he had fathered numerous children with different women.*"

e. *Xenogamy* - the transferral of one plant's pollen to another to cross-pollenate + -*ist* - indicating an expert in the field of the first element.

XEROPHILIST (zuh-ROFF-uh-lisst)

(n.) One who intentionally abstains from sex and has adapted to it as a lifestyle, another word for one who is celebate. Someone good at 'dry spells'.

"*A period of being a xerophilist is useful to gain clarity on what one truly desires and needs from a partner and what that should look like without the distraction of lust.*"

e. In botany, *xerophilous* - refers to plants adapted to a dry climate with little moisture + *-ist* - implying a person with a particular mindset.

XEROSISM (zuh-ROW-siz-um)

(n.) a period of abstinence, a "dry spell" of no sex.

"I'm going through an unintentional xerosism period because I'm not meeting anyone that I'm attracted to physically and emotionally."

e. Based on the medical condition of abnormal dryness *Xerosis* - a drying, a dryness + *-ism* - referring to an attitude or behaviour.

ZELOTYPATH (zee-loh-TIP-uth)

n. Someone who experiences jealousy frequently.

"It was impossible to move forward with a partner who was such a zelotypath, she was a free spirit that needed space to lead her own life alongside the 'couple life'."

e. *Zelotypia* - jealousy + *-path* -denoting a person with a particular tendency or disorder.

INDEX

Admiration/Affection/Attraction
- Ambosexual 18
- Attrahent 22
- Cafuné 30
- Cloying 35
- Duende 56
- Empressement 61
- Engouement 61
- Enigma 62
- Epigamic 63
- Fulgent 72
- Genderquake 237
- Kinsey Scale 107
- Megascopic 123
- Monosexual 240
- Optasia 142
- Panromantic 240
- Queenite 165
- Queerplatonic 241
- Quiditative 166
- Quixotry 167
- Sapiosexual 241
- Schwärmerei 180
- Sexuoerotic 242
- Theolykist 247
- Univocal 201
- Xenoepist 223
- Xenophile 224

- Yhte 228
- Yokemate 228

Aggression/Control/Frustration
- Adronitis 13
- Breedbate 28
- Encraty 61
- Eve-teasing 237
- Nudnik 134
- Querimonious 166
- Sisyphean 183
- Testerical 242
- Vitiate 212
- Vituperation 213
- Womanthrope 220
- Xantippe 222
- Yeverous 228

Appearance/Body
- Adamitical 12
- Adamitism 12
- Adamskostum 12
- Alopecoid 17
- Apodyopsis 22
- Auricomous 22
- Beblubbered 25
- Binately 27
- Breviped 28
- Bugaroch 29
- Callipygian 31
- Chaetophorous 33
- Cheiloproclitic 34
- Corpulant 40

- Coruscate 41
- Dealbation 49
- Eidetic 59
- Embonpoint 60
- Eonism 62
- Ephelidist 244
- Epicene 63
- Epigamic 63
- Erubescent 64
- Featous 68
- Gaminesque 73
- Gelasin 75
- Glabrous 76
- Goluptious 77
- Gracility 78
- Gynaecomazia 80
- Gynandroid 81
- Habiliment 83
- Hiplings 87
- Inguinal 95
- Junoesque 101
- Juvenescent 102
- Kraurosis 108
- Lentiginose 112
- Leucomelanous 112
- Leucos 113
- Macrotous 119
- Mammiferous 120
- Mammose 120
- Matroclinous 122
- Megaprosopous 122
- Micropodal 124

- Nucha 134
- Optasia 142
- Palpebrous 145
- Phoeniceous 156
- Rammish 170
- Rubefacient 177
- Rubescent 177
- Runcible Woman 177
- Subrident 189
- Tenebrous 195
- Viraginity 211
- Virilescence 211
- Woopie 220
- Xanthocroid 222
- Xanthodontous 222
- Zaftig 230

Beauty/Allure/Virtue
- Aesthete 14
- Bellibone 25
- Caligynephobia 31
- Callisteia 31
- Coruscate 41
- Cynosure 44
- Dapatical 48
- Duende 56
- Ephelidist 244
- Fulgent 72
- Goluptious 77
- Halo Effect 83
- Illecebrous 91
- Junoesque 101

- Kalokagathia ... 103
- Kalology ... 104
- Kalon ... 104
- Kalopsia ... 104
- Lautitious ... 111
- Lucency ... 116
- Mellifluous ... 123
- Optasia ... 142
- Orchidaceous ... 143
- Philocalist ... 155
- Prefulgent ... 158
- Pulchritude ... 162
- Pulchrous ... 162
- Smexy ... 242
- Syrenian ... 193
- Ukiyo ... 199
- Vegete ... 207
- Venust ... 207
- Venustation ... 208
- Venustraphobia ... 208
- Veridical ... 208
- Veriloquent ... 209
- Vivency ... 213
- Winsome ... 219

Bed/Sleep/Reclining
- Bedgasm ... 234
- Bedswerver ... 234
- Cubation ... 42
- Lectual ... 112
- Libken ... 114
- Napsturbation ... 240

- Sexsomnia 242
- Wedbed 216

Betrayal/Envy/Jealousy/Revenge
- Drygulch 55
- Famicide 67
- Infandous 95
- Irredivivous 96
- Ultion 199
- Umbrageous 200
- Vindictivolence 210
- Womanthrope 220
- Zelophobia 230
- Zelotypath 248
- Zelotypia 231

Bewilderment/Confusion/Manipulation
- Emberlucock 60
- Embrangle 60
- Fantod 68
- Gormless 78
- Lovernesia 239
- Pregret 240
- Ramfeezled 169
- Textpectation 243
- Vertiginous 209
- Wilder 218
- Yeverous 228

Bitterness/Heartlessness/Wickedness
- Amaritude 17
- Amarulent 17
- Dapocaginous 48

- Famicide 67
- Indurate 95
- Infandous 95
- Tortious 197

Buttocks/Breasts
- Breastaurant 235
- Bumbaste 29
- Callipygian 31
- Chesticles 236
- Dasypygal 48
- Mammiferous 120
- Mammose 120
- Nates 130
- Natiform 130
- Niplet 133
- Onolatry 142
- Steatopygia 186

Celibacy/Modesty/Virginity
- Daphnean 48
- Parthenology 150
- Parthenophobia 150
- Pudicity 161
- Semovedly 181
- Verecund 208
- Virguncule 211
- Xerophilist 247
- Xerosism 248
- Zitella 231

Clothing
- Bragasm 235

- Brolette 235
- Chones 35
- Habilable 83
- Habiliment 83
- Peignoir 151
- Undight 200
- Wooer-bab 220
- Yclad 227

Connection/Chemistry/Energy/Memory
- Benthic 26
- Engram 62
- Inhaust 95
- Mamihalpinatapai 119
- Megascopic 123
- Metagnostic 123
- Nostalgasm 240
- Quiditative 166
- Quodammodotative 167
- Univocal 201
- Untimeous 202
- Veridical 208
- Weemoed 216

Debauchery/Lewdness/Wildness
- Camsteary 32
- Dionysian 53
- Groantone 238
- Hornworks 88
- Impudicity 92
- Incicurable 94
- Inverecund 96
- Junketaceous 101

- Lascivious 111
- Libertinage 113
- Luxuria 118
- Lychnobite 118
- Molrowing 128
- Prurient 160
- Ragmatical 169
- Ramagious 169
- Rantipole 170
- Ustulation 202
- Varietist 206
- Wagtail 215
- Wilder 218
- Wildling 219
- Woofits 220

Deception/Secrecy/Superficiality
- Abditive 11
- Accismus 11
- Amatorculist 17
- Celation 33
- Cloakatively 36
- Dangleation 47
- Dangler 47
- Eccedentesiast 57
- Glozing 76
- Gnathonic 76
- Halo Effect 83
- Hiberdating 238
- Inveigle 96
- Jauk 98
- Jamphing 98

- Kalopsia 104
- Kenodoxy 105
- Lusorious 117
- Mantrap 121
- Meretricious 123
- Obreption 138
- Parlous 149
- Roblet 176
- Scuggishly 246
- Sub Rosa 189
- Tortious 197
- Wimple 219

Desire/Lust/Promiscuity
- Acolaust 11
- Agapet 15
- Allosexual 16
- Amorist 18
- Andromania 20
- Beguin 25
- Blissom 27
- Concupiscence 38
- Cyprian 45
- Cytheromania 46
- Desideratum 51
- Desirous 51
- Dionysian 53
- Donjuanist 55
- Ecdemolagnia 58
- Ecstasiate 58
- Elumbated 59
- Epithymetic 63

- Erotogenic 63
- Fleshling 70
- Frottage 71
- Gilliver 76
- Goliardy 77
- Harridan 84
- Hornworks 88
- Kerasine 106
- Lascivious 111
- Libidinist 114
- Lickerish 114
- Lolicom 239
- Lupanarian 117
- Luxuria 118
- Luxurist 118
- Nympholept 136
- Nympholepsy 136
- Nymphomaniac 136
- Obsolagnium 138
- Orectic 143
- Pangamy 147
- Paraphilia 148
- Peccaminous 151
- Ribauld 174
- Satyrism 179
- Scopophilia 180
- Sexuoerotic 242
- Sybarite 192
- Tentiginous 195
- Ustulation 202
- Vagarish 205
- Venerous 207

- Vernalagnia 209
- Xenogamist 247

Despair/Sadness/Illness
- Beblubbered 25
- Cagamosis 30
- Dealation 49
- Disconsolate 54
- Dolorifical 54
- Eccedentesiast 57
- Evaculous 245
- Griefcase 238
- Insecurable 245
- Lachrymose 109
- Lackadaisical 109
- Lectual 112
- Lugent 117
- Maudlin 122
- Retromorphosis 174
- Threnody 196
- Vulnerose 214
- Wanhope 215
- Waymentation 216
- Weemoed 216
- Welter 217
- Whangdoodle 217
- Woofits 220

Disillusion/Egoism/Fickleness
- Billynoodle 27
- Boregasm 235
- Bovarism 28
- Coeur d'artichaut 36

- Contumatic 244
- Coxcomb 41
- Dictim 236
- Erotomania 64
- Gormless 78
- Irrecusable 96
- Jactancy 98
- Kenodoxy 105
- Luxurist 118
- Meretricious 123
- Minestra Riscaldata 124
- Misacceptation 125
- Mistetch 126
- Oneirataxia 141
- Outrecuidance 144
- Panegoist 146
- Pervicacious 153
- Quixotic 167
- Recadency 171
- Resipiscent 173
- Retinency 173
- Situationship 242
- Thrasonic 196
- Tigerism 197
- Unctuous 200
- Vagarish 205
- Vaingloriously 205
- Vaniloquence 205
- Vanitarianism 206
- Vauntiness 206
- Vecordy 206
- Wanhope 215

- Yenta 227

Displeasure/Irritation/Unattractiveness
- Antistalking 234
- Cloying 35
- Fustilugs 72
- Harasshole 238
- Harridan 84
- Hindermate 87
- Hoyden 88
- Inappetent 93
- Incompossible 94
- Irrespectuous 97
- Jactancy 98
- Jejune 99
- Kenodoxy 105
- Lubricious 116
- Lurdan 117
- Misbeseem 125
- Misqueme 126
- Nudnik 134
- Querimonious 166
- Quoz 168
- Raffish 169
- Rebarbative 171
- Solecism 184
- Theroid 196
- Thrasonic 196
- Traboccant 198
- Unctuous 200
- Vitiate 212
- Wegotism 216

- Zoilism 232

Fate/Heaven/Destiny
- Ananke 19
- Elysian 60
- Isangelous 97
- Joss 100
- Kismet 107
- Koi No Yokan 108
- Minimfidian 125
- Mirificence 125
- Olamic Love 140
- Retrouvailles 174
- Seraphic 182
- Soothfast 184
- Untimeous 202
- Utinam 203
- Velleity 207
- Vincture 210
- Whojavu 243
- Wyrd 221
- Yuanfen 229

Feeling/Sense/Emotion/State
- Alkitude 234
- Bangover 234
- Calefacient 30
- Calescent 31
- Cordate 40
- Decathect 48
- Ebullition 57
- Ecstasiate 58
- Empressement 61

- Encraty 61
- Eucrasy 65
- Fantod 68
- Heteroflexible 238
- Ignoscency 91
- Ilunga 92
- Incalescent 93
- Irremiable 96
- Irroborate 97
- Ivresse 97
- Jism 99
- Jouissance 100
- Katzenjammer 105
- Lipothymy 115
- Lubency 116
- Madefy 119
- Mellifluous 123
- Mitescent 126
- Nectarean 131
- Parlous 149
- Piloerection 157
- Rectopathic 171
- Refocillate 172
- Rigidulous 175
- Saudade 179
- Sprezzatura 186
- Stocious 187
- Tacenda 194
- Telarian 195
- Tenebrous 195
- Tórschlusspanik 197
- Ukiyo 199

- Unprevaricate 201
- Unsinew 202
- Usance 202
- Uvid 203
- Verecund 208
- Viscerotonic 212
- Weemoed 216
- Wight 218
- Woopie 220
- Xenodochial 223
- Xeric 224

Female terms
- Bellibonne 25
- Bridezilla 235
- Coquette 39
- Cuckquean 43
- Cyprian 45
- Cytherean 45
- Daphnean 48
- Demimondaine 50
- Emmenology 61
- Evamitical 245
- Femmitude 237
- Flatcock 70
- Gilliver 76
- Grisette 79
- Gynaecomania 80
- Gynandroid 81
- Gyniolatry 81
- Gynophobia 81
- Harridan 84

- Hetaera 86
- Inamorata 93
- Jillet 99
- Kickie-Wickie 106
- Kraurosis 108
- Leman 112
- Leveret 113
- Lorette 115
- Mata Hari 122
- Motrix 128
- Muliebral 128
- Nymphomaniac 136
- Odalisque 139
- Oiran 140
- Parnel 149
- Philogyny 155
- Pudendum 161
- Quaedam 164
- Quaintrelle 164
- Quandong 164
- Quim 166
- Quoniam 168
- Rectrix 172
- Ribald 174
- Rubster 177
- Runcible Woman 177
- Seraglio 182
- Succubus 189
- Vahine 205
- Virguncule 211
- Xantippe 222
- Zatch 230

- Zitella 231

Flattery/Foolishness
- Adulation 13
- Baisemains 24
- Blandiloquent 27
- Fatuous 68
- Fulsome 72
- Glozing 76
- Gnathonic 76
- Jactancy 98
- Kenodoxy 105
- Periclitate 153
- Pervicacious 153
- Pickthank 157
- Quixotry 167
- Quoz 168
- Sawder 180
- Temerate 195
- Vaniloquence 205
- Vanitarianism 206
- Vecordy 206

Flirtation/Seduction/Cunning
- Agacerie 14
- Amourette 19
- Amorist 18
- Canadian Ballet 236
- Casanova 32
- Coquette 39
- Dangleation 47
- Dicacious 52
- Ecdysiast 58

- Eve teasing...237
- Flirtationship..237
- Grisette..79
- Inveigle..96
- Jillet...99
- Liptease..239
- Mata Hari..122
- Minauderie..124
- Odalisque..139
- Oeillade...139
- Sexting..242
- Sirenize...183
- Sphalolalia..185
- Syrenian..193
- The Rippers..243
- Vafrous..204

Happiness/Liveliness/Playfulness
- Beatified..25
- Delirifacient...50
- Eudaemony...65
- Felicific..69
- Gelastic...75
- Hyperhedonia..90
- Jism..99
- Junketaceous..101
- Laetificate..110
- Lubency...116
- Ludibund...116
- Macarism..119
- Oblectation..138
- Revirescent...174

- Rident 175
- Ridibund 175
- Subrident 189
- Suffisance 190
- Vegete 207
- Viparious 210
- Viripotence 211
- Viripotent 211
- Vivency 213
- Wight 218
- Xenodochial 223
- Yauld 227
- Zoetic 232

Hair

- Auricomous 22
- Chaetophorous 33
- Crockinole 42
- Cymotrichous 44
- Dasypygal 48
- Elflock 59
- Glabrous 76
- Hirsute 87
- Hoary 87
- Hypertrichologist 90
- Jubate 100
- Leiotrichous 112
- Palpebrous 145
- Pelurious 151
- Setigerous 182
- Whiskerando 217
- Zapata 230

Heartache
- Amaritude ... 17
- Anagapesis ... 19
- Chagrin d'amour ... 34
- Cordolium ... 40
- Decathect ... 49
- Dolorifical ... 54
- Eccedentesiast ... 57
- Frangible ... 71
- Irredivivous ... 96
- La Douleur Exquise ... 110
- Lovelorn ... 115
- Rilkean Heart ... 175
- Waymentation ... 216

Homosexuality/Bisexuality
- Bunt ... 235
- Demisexual ... 236
- Domequeen ... 236
- Faghag ... 237
- Flambiancé ... 237
- Flatcock ... 70
- Fricatrice ... 71
- Mussy ... 240
- Queerplatonic ... 241
- Rubster ... 177
- Sodomite ... 184
- Swive ... 191
- Tribadism ... 198
- Uranism ... 202

Indifference/Withdrawal/Laziness
- Accismus ... 11

- Anhedonia 20
- Anorgasmia 21
- Autarkeia 23
- Chalokoris 244
- Decathect 49
- Desamor 51
- Diriment 53
- Domequeen 236
- Fainéant 67
- Gallionic 73
- Indurate 95
- Jauk 98
- Jejune 99
- Justifactory 239
- Minimfidian 125
- Passiuncle 150
- Stolidity 187
- Vacatur 204
- Vacive 204
- Yonderly 229

Infatuation/Longing/Reconciliation
- Cathexis 33
- Egestuous 59
- Erotomania 64
- Fantasticate 68
- Limerence 114
- Phrenesis 156
- Saudade 179
- Schwärmerei 180
- Synallactic 192
- Taˆtonnement 194

- Yen 227

Infidelity/Divorce/Separation/Substitution
- Briarean 28
- Cuckold 43
- Cuckquean 43
- Diffareation 52
- Dudevorce 237
- Hornworks 88
- Houghmagandy 88
- Internuncio 95
- Irredivivous 96
- Irremiable 96
- Jamphing 98
- Lairwite 110
- Palimony 240
- Periclitate 153
- Sejugate 181
- Semovedly 181
- Sexorcism 241
- Spousebreach 186
- Succedaneum 189
- Summotion 190
- Sunder 190
- Viduage 210
- Whangdoodle 217
- Wife In Water Colours 218
- Wittol 219
- Yentz 228

Intimacy
- Cafuné 30
- Demisexual 236

- Lapling 111
- Queerplatonic 241
- Resarciate 173
- Soothfast 184
- Vincture 210

Kinks/Obsession
- Algolagnia 16
- Anilingus 21
- Bumbaste 29
- Cyesolagnia 44
- Erotopathy 64
- Gallomaniac 73
- Gamomania 74
- Gynaecomania 80
- Gynotikolomassophile 82
- Kinbaku 106
- Lickophile 246
- Nantaimori 130
- Nyotaimori 137
- Oculolinctus 139
- Paraphilia 148
- Parlous 149
- Pegging 151
- Pyrolagnia 163
- Undinism 200
- Wakamezake 215

Kissing/Lips/Mouth/Taste
- Adosculation 13
- Baisemains 24
- Basiation 24
- Basorexia 24

- Buss 29
- Cataglottism 33
- Cheiloproclitic 34
- Delibate 49
- Deosculate 51
- Exosculate 66
- Glutition 76
- Gynotikolobomassophile 82
- Labrose 109
- Lambition 111
- Lickerish 114
- Lickophile 246
- Liptease 239
- Mordaciously 127
- Morsure 128
- Nucha 134
- Osculant 143
- Oscular 143
- Osculum 144
- Paizogany 145
- Philematology 154
- Suaviate 188
- Subrident 189
- Xanthodontous 222
- Xerostomia 224
- Yapness 226

Love/Devotion/Promise

- Agape 15
- Amatory 18
- Anacampserote 19
- Benthic 26

- Coeur d'artichaut 36
- Dilection 53
- Forelsket 70
- Gyniolatry 81
- Ignoscency 91
- Inamorate 93
- Jurament 101
- Koi No Yokan 108
- Labascate 109
- Leman 112
- Limerence 114
- Nuncupate 135
- Objuration 138
- Olamic Love 140
- Pandemian 146
- Pefervid 152
- Penelopize 152
- Pollicitation 157
- Redamancy 172
- Resarciate 173
- Schwärmerei 180
- Sponsalia 185
- Subarrhation 188
- Temerate 195
- Unprevaricate 201
- Ya'aburnee 226

Male terms

- Agapet 15
- Benedict 26
- Billynoodle 27
- Bromance 235

- Bunt 235
- Casanova 32
- Catamite 32
- Cicisbeo 35
- Coxcomb 41
- Cuckold 43
- Damoiseau 47
- Dangler 47
- Donjuanist 55
- Dudevorce 237
- Garçonnière 75
- Gynaecomazia 80
- Heautontimorumenos 85
- Himbo 238
- Mentertainment 239
- Penectomy 152
- Philanderer 154
- Phimosis 156
- Pricktator 240
- Rampasture 170
- Roué 176
- Sardanapalian 178
- Satyriasist 179
- Satyrism 179
- Sodomite 184
- Testerical 242
- Übermensch 199
- Uranism 202
- Vadelect 204
- Xenogamist 247
- Younker 229

Marriage/Coupling/Wedding

- Adelphogamy 13
- Affine 14
- Agamist 15
- Anuptophobia 21
- Benedict 26
- Binately 27
- Bridezilla 235
- Cagamosis 30
- Charivari 34
- Coherentific 36
- Concomitant 38
- Concubitant 38
- Confarreation 38
- Connubialize 39
- Creeling 42
- Deuterogamy 52
- Diriment 53
- Drachenfutter 55
- Exogamy 65
- Fiduciary 69
- Flambiancé 237
- Gamidolatry 73
- Gamomania 74
- Hetaerism 86
- Hindermate 87
- Hymeneal 89
- Hypergamy 89
- Incompossible 94
- Indiscerptible 94
- Internuncio 95
- Jointure 100

- Jugate 100
- Jurament 101
- Ketubah 106
- Kirking 107
- Levirate 113
- Mantrap 121
- Mariturient 121
- Misyoke 126
- Monandry 127
- Morganatic 128
- Neogamist 131
- Neolocal 131
- Nexal 132
- Nidificate 132
- Nuncupate 135
- Nuptiality 135
- Nupturient 135
- Opsigamy 142
- Paranymph 148
- Pari Passu 149
- Penelopize 152
- Pentagamist 152
- Petheraphobia 153
- Privign 160
- Punalua 162
- Quadrigamist 164
- Sejugate 181
- Situationship 242
- Sponsalia 185
- Subarrhation 188
- Symphilism 192
- Uxorial 203

- Uxorious 203
- Vacatur 204
- Vahine 205
- Viripotence 212
- Wegotism 216
- Wittol 219
- Yokemate 228
- Zygote 232

Movement/Outburst
- Absquatulate 11
- Apodyopsis 22
- Cafuné 30
- Cubation 42
- Deliquesce 50
- Diffibulate 53
- Disbosom 54
- Ebullition 57
- Fling Cleaning 237
- Gumfiate 79
- Habilable 83
- Huggery 89
- Ignescent 91
- Illaqueate 91
- Inchoate 93
- Jactitation 98
- Labascate 109
- Palpebration 145
- Primifluous 159
- Quob 167
- Recadency 171
- Remeant 172

- Subitaneous..188
- Subsultus...189
- Ultroneously..200
- Vibratiuncle...210
- Vulnific..214
- Welter..217
- Xerotripsis..225
- Yarely..226
- Yarling...226

Nudity
- Adamitical..12
- Adamitism..12
- Adamskostum..12
- Apodyopsis..22
- Evamitical..245
- Gymnophobia...80
- Gymnosophy...80
- Kouros..108
- Nakedize...130
- Naturism...131
- Nantaimori..130
- Nyotaimoiri...137
- Undight...200

Pain/Suffering
- Dyspareunia..56
- Dolorous...55
- Dystocia..56
- Heautontimorumenos..85
- La Douleur Exquise...110
- Lovelorn..115
- Viduage...210

- Vulnerose 214
- Vulnific 214

Parenthood/Pregnancy/Family/Genetics
- Agenocratia 15
- Antiperlargy 21
- Atavism 22
- Ballottement 24
- Bersatrix 26
- Celation 33
- Coitus interruptus 37
- Couvade 41
- Cyesis 44
- Cyesolagnia 44
- Dystocia 56
- Ecbolic 57
- Fecundate 69
- Gamogensis 74
- Gravida 79
- Kelder 105
- Kinchin 107
- Mamzer 121
- Matroclinous 122
- Multipara 129
- Neanic 131
- Neonate 132
- Nidificate 132
- Niyoga 133
- Nulligravida 134
- Nullipara 134
- Oikonisus 140
- Paedotrophy 144

- Panmixia ... 147
- Parturition ... 150
- Philoprogenitive ... 156
- Primigravida ... 159
- Primipara ... 160
- Proligerous ... 160
- Progeny ... 160
- Puerperal ... 161
- Stegmonth ... 187
- Superfecundation ... 191
- Superfetation ... 191
- Syngenesis ... 193
- Teknonymy ... 194
- Tokophobia ... 197
- Unipara ... 201
- Xassafrassed ... 223
- Xenogenesis ... 223
- Zondek ... 232

Penis
- Condomplate
- Dodrantal ... 54
- Godemiche ... 77
- Gumfiate ... 79
- Jism ... 99
- Phallephoric ... 154
- Phimosis ... 156
- Priapism ... 158
- Priapus ... 159
- Satisdicktion ... 241
- Surgation ... 191
- Tentiginous ... 195

- Virilia 211
- Whirlygigs 217
- Whorepipe 218

Philosophy/ Vision
- Autarkeia 23
- Cyrenaic 45
- Eidetic 59
- Engram 62
- Gymnosophy 80
- Hamartiology 83
- Hetaerocracy 86
- Imago 92
- Kalology 104
- Kenodoxy 105
- Naturism 131
- Òsunality 144
- Paneroticism 146
- Pantagamy 147
- Philogyny 154
- Sexosophy 242
- Shunamitism 183
- Theosexual 196
- Yuanfen 229

Phobias
- Aichmophobia 16
- Anuptophobia 21
- Caligynephobia 31
- Coitophobia 37
- Erotophobia 64
- Erythrophobia 65
- Genophobia 75

- Gymnophobia 80
- Gynophobia 81
- Hamartophobia 84
- Haphephobia 84
- Hedenophobia 85
- Kainotophobia 103
- Parthenophobia 150
- Petheraphobia 153
- Philematophobe 154
- Philophobia 155
- Sarmassophobe 178
- Tokophobia 197
- Venustraphobia 208
- Zelophobia 230

Pleasure/Fantasy
- Aggrate 16
- Algolagnia 16
- Anhedonia 20
- Flaneur 70
- Hedonics 85
- Hyperhedonia 90
- Jouissance 100
- Kinbaku 106
- Oblectation 138
- Ophelimity 142
- Parlous 149
- Sarmassation 178
- Sensualist 181
- Succubus 189
- Sybarite 192
- Theosexual 196

- Voluptuary 213

Polyamory
- Briarean 28
- Cuckold 43
- Cuckquean 43
- Monothelious 127
- Pangamy 147
- Pantagamy 147
- Pentagamist 152

Pornography/Literature/Art
- Curiosa 43
- Erotology 64
- Facetiae 67
- Fescennine 69
- Grapholagnia 78
- Graustark 79
- Jackintosh 239
- Kouros 108
- Pornerastic 158
- Pornocchio 240
- Pornotopia 240
- Rareeshow 171
- Scopophilia 180

Potions/Gifts/ Remedies
- Amatory 18
- Anacampserote 19
- Drachenfutter 55
- Nepenthe 132
- Panpharmacon 147
- Philter 156
- Quarion 165

- Roborant 176
- Screwvenir 241
- Vulnerary 214

Prostitution/ Sex work
- Cytherean 45
- Grisette 79
- Hetaera 86
- Hetaerocracy 86
- Hookerhag 238
- Lorette 115
- Lupanarian 117
- Oiran 140
- Parnel 149
- Philopornist 155
- Pornerastic 158
- Putanism 163
- Quaedam 164
- Scortation 180
- Scortator 181
- Seraglio 182
- Souteneur 185
- Wagtail 215

Prudishness/ Chastity
- Comstockery 37
- Pudicity 161
- Prudinati 241
- Pudibund 161

Scent
- Bromopnea 29
- Hircismus 87
- Kakidrosis 103

- Olfactoeroticism 140
- Redolent 172
- Renifleur 173
- Saprostomous 178
- Sillage 183
- Snifferited 242

Sex/Genitalia/Masturbation/Maturation
- Agenocratia 15
- Ambisextrous 18
- Ambosexual 18
- Andromania 20
- Anilingus 21
- Anorgasmia 21
- Autoeroticism 234
- Autosexual 234
- Bangover 234
- Catamite 32
- Chemsex 236
- Coitophobia 37
- Coitus interruptus 37
- Condomplate 236
- Creemaster 42
- Crime Scene Sex 236
- Cybersex 236
- Cytheromania 46
- Dyspareunia 56
- Elumbated 59
- Epicene 63
- Erotology 64
- Erotopathy 64
- Flatcock 70

- Fucket List 237
- Gamomorphism 74
- Genophobia 75
- Gloryhole 238
- Jackintosh 239
- Jouissance 100
- Karezza 104
- Kinsey Scale 107
- Manustupration 121
- Masturdating 239
- Masturwaiting 239
- Neoteny 132
- Nyphomaniac 136
- Obsolagnium 138
- Olisbos 141
- Onanism 141
- Orgiophant 143
- Paracoita 148
- Pareunia 149
- Priapize 159
- Priapus 159
- Pudendum 161
- Quattorvimullier 246
- Quim 166
- Quoniam 168
- Sarmassation 178
- Satisdicktion 241
- Scortation 180
- Sexcapade 241
- Sexile 241
- Sexorcism 241
- Sexual Crapulence 247

- Stasivalence 186
- Stuprate 188
- Succubus 189
- Swive 191
- Troilism 198
- Tumescence 198
- Viripotent 212
- Xeronisus 224
- Yentz 228
- Zatch 230

Shape/Size
- Cordiform 40
- Cucumiform 43
- Dodrantal 54
- Godemiche 77
- Mammiform 120
- Mammilliform 120
- Micropodal 124
- Natiform 130
- Papilliform 148
- Phallephoric 154
- Pyriform 163
- Uloid 199
- Vulviform 214
- Xiphoidal 225

Singledom
- Agamist 15
- Anaebil 20
- Anuptophobia 21
- Byesexual 235
- Jamphing 98

- Sejugate 181
- Semovedly 181
- Unfellowed 201
- Zitella 231

Time/Duration/Place
- Biduous 26
- Canadian Ballet 236
- Ephemera 62
- Fugacious 72
- Hesternopothia 86
- Hobosexual 238
- Incipient 94
- Jauk 98
- Jentacular 99
- Murklins 129
- Noctidiurnal 133
- Nychthemeron 136
- Pernoctation 153
- Plurennial 157
- Postconnubial 158
- Puerperal 161
- Quatridual 165
- Querencia 165
- Quotannal 168
- Rampasture 170
- Sempiternal 181
- Septimanal 182
- Seraglio 182
- Subitaneous 188
- Temporaneous 195
- Trinoctial 198

- Untimeous 202
- Usance 202
- Vespertine 209
- Xenodocheionology 223
- Yestreen 228
- Zenana 231

Touch/ Embracing
- Attingent 22
- Bumbaste 29
- Chirapsia 34
- Cingulomania 35
- Confrication 39
- Effleurage 58
- Flatcock 70
- Frottage 71
- Frotteurism 71
- Grabble 78
- Haphephobia 84
- Haptics 84
- Huggery 89
- Hyperaphia 89
- Illaqueate 91
- Illinition 92
- Kadoodle 239
- Lapling 111
- Lubricious 116
- Mollitious 126
- Noli Me Tangere 133
- Sarmassation 178
- Sarmassophobe 178
- Taction 194

THANKYOUS

Special thanks to the people who helped make this book come to fruition:

I feel compelled to mention the lovely communities that have grown on my Instagram and TikTok accounts @etoilemarley over the last few years, where I have been sharing my findings in a daily video of an obscure word. To the lovely people who leave interesting and thought provoking comments, who engage with the questions I ask of you, who have reached out, out of the blue to say how much they enjoy the words, please know that your kindness and humour have spurred me on to write this book and to keep creating 'word' content. The power of having your support is immeasurable!

To my mum. The best a girl could have, I love you with all my heart and am so lucky to have you to bounce ideas off, to offer insight and to have deep conversations about life!

To the raddest girl pals who have cheered me on, offered feedback, sent me hilarious raising teenagers memes, and who just always asked "how is the book going?" Jo and Mel, you are my British family!

To my husband and children, I am so lucky to be one of an awesome foursome, I love you to the moon and back and round again and again!

REFERENCES

Ayto, J. (2011) *Dictionary of word origins*. New York: Arcade Pub.

Bird, C.S. (no date) *Grandiloquent Dictionary third edition*. Available at: https://www.islandnet.com/~egbird/dict/words.pdf

Chrisomalis, S. (1996) *The Phrontistery, Free online dictionary of unusual and weird words: International house of logorrhea*. Available at: https://phrontistery.info/ihlstart.html

Collins online dictionary | definitions, thesaurus and translations. Available at: https://www.collinsdictionary.com/

Dent, S. (2023) *An emotional dictionary: Real words for how you feel, from angst to zwodder*. John Murray Publishers.

Edoro, A. (2013) *Untranslatable African words: Collins online dictionary | definitions, thesaurus and translations*. Available at: https://www.collinsdictionary.com/ (Accessed: 13 June 2025).

Foyle, C. (2008) *Foyle's Philavery: A Treasury of Unusual Words*. Larousse Kingfisher Chambers.

Foyle, C. (2008) *Foyle's further philavery: A cornucopia of Lexical delights*. Edinburgh: Chambers.

Funk, C.E. (1993) *2107 curious word origins, sayings and expressions: From White Elephant to song and dance*. New York: Galahad Books.

Grose, F. (2004) *Dictionary of the vulgar tongue: 1811 edition*. San Diego, CA: ICON Group International, Inc.

Haag, P. (2021) *10 relationship words that aren't translatable into English*, Big Think. Available at: https://bigthink.com/the-present/the-top-10-relationship-words-that-arent-translatable-into-english/

Heifetz, J. (2012) *The indispensable dictionary of unusual words: Over 6,000 obscure America's most trusted dictionary (no date) Merriam-Webster*. Available at: https://www.merriam-webster.com/ (Accessed: 13 June 2025).

Jones, P.A. (2020) *The cabinet of linguistic curiosities: A yearbook of forgotten words.* Chicago: University of Chicago Press.

Koenig, J. (2021) *The dictionary of obscure sorrows.* New York, NY: Simon & Schuster Audio.

Larousse, É. *Encyclopédie et dictionnaires gratuits en Ligne, Larousse.fr : encyclopÃ©die et dictionnaires gratuits en ligne.* Available at: https://www.larousse.fr/

Merriam-Webster. Available at: https://www.merriam-webster.com/

Oxford English Dictionary. Available at: https://www.oed.com/

Schur, N.W. (1990) *1000 most obscure words.* New York: Facts on File.

Skeat, W.W. (2007) *The concise dictionary of english etymology.* Ware: Wordsworth.

Urban dictionary (no date) *Urban Dictionary.* Available at: https://www.urbandictionary.com/ (Accessed: 13 June 2025).

Webster's encyclopedic unabridged dictionary of the English language (1996). New York, Avenel, N.J: Gramercy Books ; Distributed by Outlet Book Co.

www.ingramcontent.com/pod-product-compliance
Lightning Source LLC
Chambersburg PA
CBHW071151070526
44584CB00019B/2748